Sail Ho!

My Early Years at Sea

By
Sir James Bisset
The 1ˢᵗ Book of the Sail Ho! Trilogy

K.B., C.B.E., R.D., R.N.R., LL.D. (Cantab.)

Commander of the Legion of Merit (U.S.A.) Commodore (retd) of the Cunard White Star Line Wartime Captain of Queen Mary and Queen Elizabeth

Updated 2ⁿᵈ Edition by
Kyle Vernon

Other books by Kyle Vernon

Digby the Church Mouse: Saving Home

A Davis Mountain Ghost Story

Edited by Kyle Vernon

Tramps and Ladies 2nd Edition

Commodore 2nd Edition

Some stories are just too good to be allowed to fade away. This is one of those stories.

In 1995 I was recommended this book, *"Sail Ho!"* written by Sir James Bisset along with *"Two Years Before the Mast"* by the American author Richard Henry Dana Jr., by a friend of mine that was serving in the US Navy Reserve. He knew of my penchant for travel and touring books and encouraged me to expand my horizons through these historical milestones. He had discovered them separately in two different ship's libraries over his 40-year-long military service in both the Navy and commercial ships.

The book penned by Dana was both enthralling and easy to find, my local library had no less than three copies since it has never been out of print since its telling. Not so for the other. I was only able to locate a copy of "Sail Ho!" on interlibrary loan from a small midwestern college, and it arrived about a month after my request was made. It was in December of 1995 that I read this heady blend of travel, adventure, romanticism; and it was wrapped up in the era of sailing wind power was giving way to coal and other more modern forms of ship propulsion. Indeed, the well over two thousand yearlong era of sail dies in this trilogy.

I enjoyed the book so much I made it a point to reread it each December since then, but I also vowed to acquire my own copy because the librarian was on to me – remembering me the third time I showed up at her desk to request it. In those days the Internet was only beginning to get going and I shied away from using it as anything more than research at my job of teaching US Army soldiers.

With the transfer of my wife to England came opportunity. When possible, I set out to search for this title on my days off with trips to used bookstores scattered about the area where I lived. I was finally able to locate a copy in a used bookstore in Lincoln, England in 2001 after visiting nearly 40 used books stores spread across Lincolnshire, Nottinghamshire, and Cambridgeshire; and its finding remains one of my happiest memories of my three years abroad, especially since my five year old daughter, playing with a toy three aisles over, "discovered" a copy of Sail Ho! completely by accident as the shop owner was informing me the book did not exist in his collection!

This trilogy makes for an interesting observation illuminated by the passage of time. While Sir James Bisset was almost entirely in the right spot at the right time throughout his lengthy career, when it came to post-WW2 publishing it appears his luck ran out. His trilogy was released in the late

1950s, which was about the worst possible time for a three volume memoir such as his to be published.

His problem, by which I mean the book's problem, was that the 1950s was all about the future. The world was still recovering from the horrors of the previous decade and that world-war-induced trauma helped to act as a barrier into looking back, but the same war also caused the marketplace to fill with countless war memoirs, action novels, and spy thrillers. Readers of all ages would quickly pass over memoirs from the real world of sail in favour of all things bright, violent, or futuristically shiny. The stories of sail that did sell often revolved around swashbuckling tales of piracy, islands of treasure, and lusty adventure.

So, his trilogy was printed in disappointingly small numbers only to promptly fade after its release. Without anyone understanding what a treasure it was, it had no champions save for Bisset himself, who appeared at over 1800 events in his retirement to boost sales and lessen the impact of a diminishing pension measured against the inflation of the period. Bisset lived through one of the largest technological changes in the history of mankind full stop. He wasn't an industrial mover or shaker. Like most people he simply wanted to live life to the fullest. He went to sea on a sailing ship with all of the risks and threats that go with it (e.g. storms, groundings, doldrums, and starving) and his young mind was quick to record the realities, some of them uncomfortable or unsettling, of the trade. His was the last generation to sail the world with only a compass, a crude map, and a "bet your life" hunch that skills, observation, and experience would even the odds – the hallmarks of great endeavour.

By the beginning of his second book "Tramps and Ladies" Bisset makes the jump to the coal burning cargo and passenger liners and the readers are rewarded with the telling of the sinking of the Titanic from the safety of the ship *RMS Carpathia*, on which he was the first officer. Again, without Bisset's arrival on the Carpathia, many of the gaps and almost all the survivors from the Titanic saga might have been lost forever.

In his third book Bisset deals with both the routine of shipboard life and the impact of two World Wars on the British mercantile fleet. Having worked up to being the commanding officer of both the *RMS Queen Mary* and the *RMS Queen Elizabeth* – the only man to have commanded both.

Bisset would captain both *Queen Mary* and *Queen Elizabeth* on a total of sixty-six wartime voyages during WW2. In his war service Bisset steamed 424,563 nautical miles (683,267 km) and delivered 447,777 troops from 1939 to 1946. On 16 October 1946, he captained the *Queen Elizabeth* on her maiden voyage in commercial service to New York. On 10 January 1947, Bisset formally handed over command of the *Queen Elizabeth* and retired from the Cunard Line having attained the age of 63, the compulsory retirement age from the Cunard service.   **KV JUNE 2025**

ABOUT THE COVER

Cover art for all three volumes of the Second Edition of the Sail Ho! trilogy was generated using AI. In this art a three masted barque is "rolling home" with fair skies and a following breeze. Sea green was selected as the background colour representing Bisset's first ocean going experience. The white border found only on this book in the series represents sailing.

James Gordon Partridge Bisset

(15 July 1883 – 28 March 1967)

HONORS AND AWARDS

- Decoration for Officers of the Royal Naval Reserve(RD) – 28 March 1923
- Commander of the Order of the British Empire (CBE) –1942 Birthday Honours
- **Knight Bachelor, 10 July 1945**
- Honorary Doctor of Laws (LL.D.)(Cambridge), 1946
- British War Medal, 1914-1918
- Mercantile Marine Medal, 1914-1918
- Victory Medal, 1914-1919 (U.K.)
- 1939-1945 Star
- Pacific Star
- Atlantic Star
- War Medal, 1939-1945
- Legion of Merit, Commander (U.S.A.)

British Knight Bachelor

The Knight Bachelor is an award given to men by the monarch of the United Kingdom. It is the oldest form of knighthood in the British honours system.

Editor Notes about this Updated Second Edition.

Because of their rarity, it took me nearly a decade to find and collect all three of the books in the series. A quick check of the Internet reveals that original copies of the trilogy are available, but mostly at collectors and rare book prices. Since I feel the message is more important that the value, I decided to redo the trilogy in hopes others may enjoy it as much as I have. I also sincerely hope that I can do the series a favour through enhancing it.

I must acknowledge that others have reprinted the series, but the attempts I have seen seem to be unprofessional and lacking. With AI and access to Public Domain materials I feel the works of Bisset can be improved much more than when they originally went to press in the last century.

Even though the AI pictures may be lacking in detail it is my goal to give the reader something visual to ponder over – by filling in those missing details the reader can be transported back to THAT scene and imagine the world Bisset experienced. I hope you enjoy my edition, but I hope you enjoy Bisset's personal story more.

Kyle Vernon
Summer 2025

About the Editor

Originally from Midland, Texas and now living in Lubbock, Texas, Kyle Vernon has taught assorted topics since 1990 across four nations spanning two continents, including working in a combat zone as a civilian contract instructor for Central Texas College and the US Army.

As a senior in High School in 1983, he created a boardgame about his hometown. Called "Midland Millions," it went on to break state and national sales records. Vernon graduated from Midland College in 1986 and Texas Tech University in 1990.

Married since 1988 to Teri, Kyle was able to move overseas due to her service in the US Army that transported their young family to England 1999-2003. This allowed allowed Kyle to collect Books 1 and 3 of the Sail Ho! trilogy. Book 2 was purchased via an eBay auction after returning to the USA.

Vernon presently teaches Astronomy to students at Frenship High School in Wolfforth, Texas.

This updated second edition of this trilogy is dedicated to my wife Teri.

TABLE OF CONTENTS

The First Atlantic Leviathan — I Remember the "Great Eastern," —
My Childhood on Merseyside — School Days — A Happy Home —
The Busy Port of Liverpool — Sail and Steam — Roaming the Quays
— Lure of a Sailor's Life

WHEN I was five years of age, in the year 1888, I saw the *S.S. Great Eastern* lying at her moorings in the Mersey. I remember scarcely anything of her, except that my uncle, a master mariner in sail and steam who smelled strongly of rum and cigars, hoisted me to his shoulder at the dockside and said, "Look, Jimmy! The biggest ship ever built, and too big to handle!"

Vaguely I remembered going in a rowing boat, with my parents, my uncle, my seven year-old brother, and other sightseers, across a stretch of dirty Mersey water to visit the giant ship. I was carried up her gangway and set down to toddle along her deck, holding tight to my uncle's hand. Then, in the last year of her life, the *Great Eastern* was already condemned to the shipbreakers and was earning some final revenues for her owners as a floating exhibition. In 1889, this "wonder of the waves" was broken up for scrap; but she was not quickly forgotten. In my boyhood, I often saw her picture on parlour walls or postcards and listened to arguments among nautical wiseacres who contended, on the one hand, that she was "too big" and, on the other, that she was a triumph of British shipbuilding genius, but "before her time."

I heard her spoken of as "the Great Iron Ship" or as "The Leviathan Ship" and sometimes as "the Great White Elephant" or "the Great Freak"; but no matter how much she was disparaged; she was a mighty legend. Like many another pioneering effort, she failed for the benefit of her successors. She was the first mammoth iron ship, made with a hull of riveted plates: a revolutionary idea in shipbuilding design. True, she was "ahead of her time" — by nearly fifty years — but she was an inspiration to ships' architects in her sheer magnitude and audacity of conceptions which would be proved, in course of time, with some slight modifications, to be basically correct. In my wildest boyhood dreams I could never have envisioned that a time would come when I would command vessels which would make that old time Leviathan seem a midget.

Beginning this narrative of my seagoing experiences, I salute the memory

Post Card of S.S. Great Eastern (Public Domain)

of that predecessor of the sea giants of today. Launched sideways on the Thames in 1858, the *Great Eastern* cost one million pounds to build and employed the labour of 2,000 workmen for four years. She was a combined steamship and sailing vessel. She had six masts, — two square rigged and four fore and aft rigged — and five funnels between the masts. She had four paddle engines and four screw engines and was 695 feet (212m) in length and 83 feet (25m) beam, with a width across the paddle boxes of 120 feet. (37m)

Of 12,000 tons register, she could carry 22,500 tons of coal and cargo, besides 4,000 passengers and a crew of 400. Her designer, Isambard Kingdom Brunel, was an inventor who could not only "think big" but also carry his ideas to fruition. His basic problem was to create a steamship that could voyage from Britain to India via the Cape of Good Hope and return, without refuelling, a distance of 22,000 miles (35,405 km). The *Great Eastern* had bunkers for 12,000 tons of coal.

She was flat bottomed and had double hulls, three feet (1m) apart, divided by bulkheads into watertight compartments which made her, as Brunel claimed, "unsinkable." Instead of being used for the purpose for which she was designed, she was put on the Atlantic run. On her maiden trans-Atlantic crossing, in June 1860, she made a record with a crossing time of eleven days. An amusing incident occurred when one of the milking cows, carried on the upper deck, got loose and fell, through a skylight into the dining saloon — beefsteaks on the hoof!

For various reasons of mismanagement, but also because of the outbreak of the American Civil War, the *Great Eastern* failed to be profitable as a passenger liner on the Atlantic run. In 1861 she was chartered by the British War Office as a troopship, and on one voyage to Granada carried 8,000 troops. Next, she made a mighty contribution to human progress as a cable layer. She was the only vessel that could carry the immense weight — 14,000 tons of cable — and in addition the vast amount of bunker coal and ballast required to cross the western ocean from Ireland to Newfoundland, paying out the cable over her stern all the way, to link electrically the old world and the new. The laying of this and other transoceanic submarine cables, with their immeasurable benefits to worldwide commerce and news transmission, was the ultimate justification of the *Great Eastern's* existence. She served a purpose for which she was not designed; but if such a vessel had not been available the cable companies would have had to build one like her, to solve their practical problem. So the effort that was made to create her was not in vain.

The legend she left behind her remains with me. When, as a schoolboy, I wandered around the Mersey docksides, I saw many ships more beautiful and more appealing to a boy's imagination than my vague memory of that great old freak; yet the fact that nearly seventy years ago I trod her decks has forged a link between my childish imaginings and the practical desires of a maritime nation to excel in mastering the transits of the oceans, in ships increasing size and speed, until the mammoths of today have been attained.

My love of the sea and of ships was acquired from my boyhood experiences on Merseyside and not from any inherited tendency. My parents viewed oceans with distrust and did everything they could to persuade me to keep my feet on solid ground. My seagoing uncle was a relative only by marriage. He joined with my parents in warning me never to go to sea.

My father, James Smith Bisset, was a Scot, from Blairgowrie in Perthshire. He was an accountant, employed by an engineering firm, J. R. Cooper & Sons of Liverpool, and earning a very moderate salary. His hobby was music. For over forty years he sang in the chorus of the Liverpool Philharmonic Society and Church.

My mother was English, from Bolton, Lancashire. Both of my parents were hard working, strong minded, religious people, who brought up their children to strict obedience and respectability, in accordance with the ideas of domestic discipline that prevailed throughout Britain in the closing years of Queen Victoria's reign. In consequence, we were an affectionate and united family with a happy home life.

I was born on 15th July 1883, in Liverpool, and given the Christian names of James Gordon Partridge. My brother David was two years older than I. In steady progression we acquired two more brothers and two sisters. As the family increased, we moved three times, to slightly bigger or better dwellings nearer to the city. My brothers and sisters and I attended St. Saviour's Infant School and later the Granby Street Board School, where the fee was one penny per week per child. This was the extent of my school education, and it ended when I was fourteen years of age. I have been learning, I hope, ever since.

My father's salary, even with the strictest economy, was barely sufficient to provide food, clothing, shelter, and elementary schooling for a family of six children. We had very few bought luxuries or entertainments. A penny to spend on sweets was a rare treat; yet we grew up healthy and happy and made our own fun. I liked swimming, diving, and football. At school I was of only average ability at my lessons. I learned the three Rs, and not much more. My father intended that I should become a clerk.

The Mersey River saved me from that fate. In the 1890s the Port of Liverpool was, even more than today, one of the world's greatest havens of ships. This was Britain's "front door to the western ocean," far better situated for that purpose than Glasgow or Bristol — or so the people of Liverpool were always prepared to proclaim. As a Merseysider, I could not fail to be aware that our port was the main sea gate of the industrial Midlands and the North of England. The Mersey, with its extension, the Manchester Ship Canal, and a network of railways spread inland, was the chief inlet of raw materials, especially cotton, brought from the world's ends. It was also the outlet of a great range of manufactured goods produced ln the thriving, grimy cities of Lancashire and the adjacent counties. We were at the portals of Ireland and America and all the world.

The Liverpool docks, extending for seven miles (11.2 km) along the northern shore of a well sheltered tidal basin one mile (1.6 km) wide, were thronged with sailing vessels and steamers. The dockside hummed with activity by day and by night, except on Sundays, when all work in the port came to a standstill. At any season of the year, there would be not less than a hundred overseas vessels at anchor or docked in the Mersey, discharging or taking in cargoes or awaiting charter. The idea of a "quick turnaround," especially for sailing touch in a terminal port, had not yet occurred to shipowners or stevedores. The windjammers could not arrive or depart on fixed schedules and usually remained in port for a month, or longer, between voyages.

Their crews, signed on for a voyage, were, with a few exceptions, paid off on arrival at this home port and promptly went ashore for a spree. A few weeks, or sometimes a few days, later, their hard earned money gone, they signed on again, in the same or another vessel, for a new voyage. Consequently, a "floating population" of some thousands of sailors enlivened the dockside districts with their carousals and brawls; and many others, including riggers, tradesmen, apprentices, and stevedores, were to be seen at work in the vessels along the quays, engaged in overhauling the rigging and running gear, chipping and painting overside, or taking in stores and loading or unloading cargo. The steamers, including some large passenger liners, had a quicker turnaround in port than sailing vessels.

Tugs and barges, colliers from Wales, herring smacks from the Irish Sea, and the ferries — running between Liverpool and Birkenhead and other towns on the Cheshire side — all contributed to the scenes of lively movement on the Mersey. The daily arrival and departure of the Dublin and Belfast packet steamers, and frequent departures of emigrant vessels, both sail and steam, for America or Australia, provided yet another element of excitement.

Being only 122 miles (196 km) from Dublin, Liverpool had a continual inflow of immigrants from Ireland, some seeking work in England and some awaiting an opportunity to tranship to America or "the Colonies." Many of these never got beyond Liverpool.

Some of the "Liverpool Irish" spent most of their lives on Merseyside and some were born there but remained Irish. They worked as longshoremen or draymen or went to sea from the Mersey as sailors, stokers or coal trimmers. They were a vivid and rowdy element in the city's life, fond of larking and banter, but scarcely more so than the Lancashire lads, who could sparkle in exchanges of wit as well as any Irishman, though with their own brand of irrepressible humour.

Saturday nights were the rowdiest. The warehouses, docks, and factories were closed but the shops, pubs, dance halls and music halls remained open until 11 p.m., the streets being thronged with crowds spending their week's wages. On Sundays all places of business and amusement were closed and there was nothing to do except to go to church. The streets were deserted and "Liverpool dead." A visitor (presumably from Hull) remarked he "had spent a whole year in Liverpool, one Sunday."

On the way home from school, especially in the summer evenings or on Saturdays, as I grew older, I, like many other Liverpool boys, had the habit of rambling along the quays, in quest of something interesting to see or do and there was always plenty. At times, enterprising boys could succeed in getting on board a ship at a wharf, to watch the sailmaker at work on deck, or seamen overhauling the gear, or even to climb into the rigging — until chased ashore by an irate officer with profuse profanity.

At other times a few of us for a lark would get into a dinghy or painters' punt, left unattended, and would go for a row in the dock, trailing our fingers overside in water that was covered with floating rubbish from ships and the city drains. The estuary, which the ancient Danish raiders had named "Liver Pool" (like Liffey Pool on the other side of the Irish Sea), had water of a dark brown colour, due to suspended particles of coal, peat, and silt brought down by the Mersey from the Peak of Derbyshire; but, with the drainage of several large industrial cities added to it, the mixture had become so murky that it gave an excuse for the Liverpool joke that never failed to raise a local laugh: "The quality of Mersey is not strained!"

In these surroundings of maritime movement, I gradually developed a desire to see for myself what lay on and beyond the wide ocean into which the Mersey forever poured its stream of traffic and rubbish on the ebb tide, to be carried far from the shore.

The vessels in port at Liverpool included about equal numbers of steam driven and wind driven craft. In the early 1890s, windjammers were not yet considered to be doomed to extinction by the competition of steamers. Many ship owners and thousands of seamen and landlubbers believed that steam would never oust sail from the world's waterways. They were accustomed to the idea that wind wafted craft, which had crossed the oceans for thousands of years using natural forces, were in harmony with nature, and therefore could never be superseded by mere mechanical contraptions. To conservatives such as these, who had also a vested interest in their beliefs — either financial or through their laboriously acquired skill at handling sail — steamers appeared to be a newfangled fad. So the windjammers lingered on, dying hard and slowly. Hundreds of beautiful full rigged ships and barques under the British flag still plied on the Atlantic routes to Canada, the U.S.A., and Central and South America; to India, Australia, and China via the Cape of Good Hope; and to the west coast of the Americas via Cape Horn. Despite the ever increasing size and speed of steamers, the men of the tall ships had the prestige of real sailoring, and they knew it; yet the fact was that steam had come to stay; and already, in the 1880s, had fifty years of experience to prove it.

The first vessel to cross the Atlantic wholly under steam power was the paddle wheeler *Royal William*, in 1834. Built of timber, in Quebec, she steamed from Pictou, in Nova Scotia, to the Thames, in twenty-five days. In 1840, Samuel Cunard's Britannia, also a paddle wheeler, crossed from Liverpool to Boston in fourteen days. Then began the prolonged tussle for the mythical "Blue Riband" of the Atlantic, between steamers of the Cunard, White Star, Collins and Inman lines. In 1885, when I was a two year-old nipper, the Cunarder *Etruria*, 12,000 tons, held the Blue Riband with a crossing of just over six days. In 1893, the *S.S. Campania* reduced the *Etruria's* record by eleven hours.

After this, only diehards could have believed that sail could endure in competition with steam. As a boy, I was one of the diehards. My fixed idea, from the age of twelve, was to go to sea under canvas. When I mentioned this to my father, he simply said, "A sailor's life is a dog's life. Keep your feet on the ground, Jamie!"

It was well meant advice, but I could not take it.

My Brief Career as an Office Boy — Marine Insurance — The Logbooks — A Ferry Story —A Black Eye for the Boss — An Attempt to Stow Away — Supperless to Bed — The Anglo-American Oil Company — Tough Sea Captains — Ambitions Discouraged — Persistence Rewarded — The Doctor's Decision.

WHEN I was fourteen years of age, having attained the Seventh Standard at school, my father considered that I was well enough equipped to begin earning my own living. He got me started in my first job, as an office boy at the Liverpool branch of the London and Provincial Marine Insurance Company.

My wages were four shillings a week. My working hours were from 9 a.m. to 6 p.m. daily and from 9 a.m. to 1 p.m. on Saturdays. It was a white collar and soft handed job, with great prospects, as my father pointed out, of advancement in a respectable clerical career. "You can learn to be an underwriter, Jamie," he encouraged me. "And you'll know all about shipwrecks and disasters and the like, without going to sea!"

This ingenious argument failed to quell my desire to sail the seven seas, but I began my office duties with due deference to parental authority.

The manager of the branch, Ambrose Ellis Cookson, was a shining example of the advantages of shore life. Each morning, he arrived at the office garbed resplendently, in a top hat, frock coat, fancy waistcoat, gold watch and chain, a high white collar and a large cravat with a diamond pin, striped trousers, spats, shiny boots, a polished walking stick, waxed moustaches, a gold signet ring and an eyeglass on a cord — the full rig of dignity, authority and prosperity.

My first duty of the day was to stand by with a feather duster as the boss unlocked his rolltop desk. I then had to adjust the windows for ventilation, dust the desk and tee that the inkwells on it were filled, and see that everything else was shipshape for his high-and-mightiness to begin his important labours. For the rest of the day, I had to stay in the offing, at his beck and call. When he wanted me to fetch something he rang a bell that was on his desk, and I would hurry in to await his commands. In the meantime, the four clerks in the outer office also had the right to haze me to their hearts' content with menial tasks of many kinds, chiefly fetching and carrying papers and ledgers from one to another, keeping their inkwells filled, and running errands. The clerks brought their lunches with them, as I did, but often I was sent out to the little shop nearby to buy a "Wet Nelly" for one of them. This was a Chester Cake, priced at a halfpenny, made of two thin slabs of pastry with currants in between. I was always instructed to ask for a Wet Nelly "from the bottom of the heap" — it had more sugary juice in it.

To keep out of mischief between tasks, I was permitted to begin learning the business of marine insurance by perusing the files of claims which steadily accumulated in the office. After being dealt with in orderly and leisured routine, these were pigeonholed for reference. These declarations, as my father had forewarned me, concerned disasters at sea, including wrecks, fires, dismastings, strandings, mutinies, collision, and damage to cargo — sad reading for the underwriters, but for me enthralling as chronicles of violent events.

The claims were supported by ships' logbooks, the first I had ever seen. Many of these were stacked away on our shelves, and it was my duty to keep them dusted. I read them from cover to cover, as eagerly as true adventure stories. It did not occur to me that logbook entries become most expansive when something unusual occurs, being especially eloquent when an insurance claim is likely to be lodged.

Skipping the routine entries, I pored over the detailed narratives of horny-handed Master Mariners describing their mishaps and other remarkable incidents; these made it appear to me that life at sea was a continuous series of exciting adventures. Absorbed in the logbooks, I had my head stuffed with only partly understood sea lore and nautical phrases, which glowed for me in the hues of high adventure. My father had miscalculated this effect. I considered that it would be far more interesting to be at sea in a ship on fire than on shore in an office assessing the damage.

Underwriters, I ascertained, were born cynics. They calculated only in pounds, shillings, and pence, and thought seldom or never in terms of flesh, blood, and spirit of the men who risked death to bring ships safely to port. I began to look on our immaculate manager and his pen pushing, seat polishing clerks as softies who had chosen a way of life in which no adventures could ever occur.

One afternoon our manager threw the whole staff into turmoil by bustling to get the day's work finished early so that he could leave for an important appointment. Frequently looking at his watch, he bellowed instructions right and left, banged his bell, cursed everyone in sight for incompetence, and finally departed like a whirlwind at 3.30 p.m., complete with his gaff topsail hat and flying jib coat, leaving his clerks so prostrated from the feverish excitement of their undue exertions that they would be almost incapable of further pen pushing for the rest of that day.

Typical dock scene in the late 1800s. (AI)

The boss took me with him, to carry his satchel of documents or simply to enhance his presence with the attendance of a menial. "Hurry, boy, hurry!" he urged, as he strode along the street toward the wharves, and I trotted in his wake. "I have to catch the ferry to Birkenhead for my appointment there at four o'clock. I can just make it!"

As we neared the landing stage, he snatched the satchel from my hands and began to run. A ferry was under way, churning the water about eight feet (2.4m) from the stage. With his stick in one hand and the satchel in the other, and his coat tails flying, my dignified employer vaulted the barrier and sprinted across the landing stage. With a magnificent leap he hurtled across the water, landed on the ferry's deck amidships, and sprawled flat on his back.

A deckhand helped him to his feet. "By heavens," gasped the boss, "I nearly missed it!"

"Nearly missed it?" echoed the deckhand. "Ye dom fool, we're just coming in!"

Next day the boss was at the office as usual, but my confidence in his invincibility had been shaken. A few days later he had a visit after lunch from the manager of another underwriting firm, of equal calibre to himself. I showed the visitor, who was slightly drunk, into the boss's sanctum and closed the door.

Presently I heard voices raised in anger, then sounds of a scuffle. The visitor opened the door and stormed out of the office, muttering curses as he made for the street. Mr. Cookson's bell rang, and I went in to find him seated on his chair in a fainting condition, nursing a bruised eye. "Fetch me a glass of water, boy," he moaned. "That rascal assaulted me. I'll have the law on him!"

This incident further destroyed my confidence in the respectability of the demigod, and I could see no attractive future for myself as a top hatted marine insurance underwriter.

I had now no desire to climb any higher in that profession than the lowest rung of the ladder on which I then stood.

I renewed my appeals to my parents, begging them to allow me to go to sea. My father remained obdurate. "What?" he said. "Go to sea after you've been reading of all the wrecks and disasters? Dinna be sae daft, laddie!" One day, in desperation, I decided to stow away in a windjammer. I was then about fourteen years and three months old, and small for my age. When the day's work at the office ended, I went down to the docks and reconnoitred in the twilight until I found a full rigged sailing ship with the Blue Peter whipping at her masthead.

Although I was appalled at the enormity of the crime I was about to commit against my loving parents, especially my dear mother, I succeeded in sneaking on board without being detected — or so I hoped — and hid in the rope locker.

There I crouched in darkness, listening to the sounds of strenuous activity and bawled orders on deck, as the mates hounded the crew to get everything ready for sea. Presently I began to feel hungry and thought longingly of the good meal waiting for me on the hob at home. The pangs of hunger, as well as the pangs of a guilty conscience, gave me a hollow feeling in my stomach.

Suddenly the door of the rope locker was flung open, and a burly bearded figure with a lantern — I suppose it was the Mate — looked at me with the interest of a scientist examining a beetle. "Huh?" he grunted. "Stow away, would ye? A wee bit of a thing like you will be no use on this ship. Wait until you're bigger, laddie, then take my advice, and don't go to sea at all!"

He extended a hairy hand and seized my ear between his finger and thumb. "Lay ashore quick and lively, before I throw you over the side," he growled. The pain in my ear, increased by the contemptuous words, made me utter a loud howl of dismay. Scampering across the deck and down the gangway to the wharf, I crept away to hide my sorrows in the darkness. Toward 11 p.m., hungry and very sorry for myself, I arrived home. "Where have you been?" asked my father severely. "Down to the docks," I mumbled. "What were you doing there?" "I — I — want to go to sea," I blubbed.

"Don't anger me," roared my father. With this he began laying into me with a strap, punctuating my howls with the remark that no boy has ever understood: "This hurts me mair than it hurts you, Jamie!" Then he laid the strap aside and said, "Up to your bed the noo, with no supper, and keep away from ships for the rest o' y'r life!"

Humiliated, sore, and hungry, I crept into my bed, determined to cause my parents no further anxiety; yet within a few days, the lesson was forgotten, and I was busy again with my daydreams of a life free of care on the wild, wide waters of the boundless blue oceans.

Soon after this, my father saw an opportunity of improving my status in the commercial world on shore. He obtained for me a new position as a junior clerk in the office of the Anglo-American Oil Company, at a salary of six shillings a week. My new employers were concerned principally with importing "case oil" — which included lighting kerosene and lubricating oil — from Texas, U.S.A.

Several sailing ships and steamers were engaged in this trade, on the run from Galveston, in the Gulf of Mexico, to Liverpool. Our work in the office consisted principally of selling and distributing the oil to consumers in Britain.

The duty of a junior clerk was to copy invoices and order forms and to address envelopes, without ever seeing the oil we sold. It happened that my handwriting was fairly good for a boy's. There were no typewriters or female clerks in our office; all the clerical work was done by hand, by male clerks. My task of copying lists of names and addresses and columns of figures made no appeal whatsoever to my adventurous imagination. Occasionally romance rolled into our drab office in the persons of swaggering captains of the oil ships, burly, bearded men, reeking of rum, some of them Yankees, who came to collect their pay. This was handed to them in golden sovereigns. Seated at a polished table, chewing cheroots, they counted the clinking golden coins in the presence of our manager, signed the receipts, and pocketed their wealth. To me, they were men of heroic stature. I could see for myself that seafaring was a profitable as well as a healthy profession. After some months I confided to the manager that it was my ambition to go to sea, and I asked if he could use his influence to get me apprenticed in an oil ship. I did not realize that my services in the office were fully worth the six bob a week I was paid and that the manager wanted me to stay on my stool.

He thought of a method of curing my sea desires. Unknown to me, he primed three captains, who happened to call at the office together one day, to knock the seagoing nonsense out of my head. I was summoned to the inner office, where the three shipmasters were seated with the manager in a reek of cigar smoke. "This is young Bisset, who wants to go to sea, said the manager. "Could any of you gentlemen take him as an apprentice?"

With mock seriousness the burly captains played the farce of pretending to appraise me. "You're not big enough, m'son, one of them said. "Why, you'd be lost overboard on your first voyage! Take my advice and stay at home."

Another of the captains continued the argument. "Yes, young fellow, my lad," he said, "going to sea is a hell of a life. Only fools go to sea, and there's no good career in it. Take my tip and stay ashore!"

They all agreed that I was unfitted for a sailor's life, and that I would never be any good at it. "There you are," said the manager, dismissing me. "I told you so! Stick to clerking, and you'll get on in the world."

Despite these discouragements, I continued to pester my parents to have me bound as an apprentice in a windjammer. Several months went by, as I plugged along at my office work, trying to think of new tactics. Then a bright idea struck me. In my lunch hours I began visiting shipping offices, to inquire if an apprentice was wanted.

At the first office I visited, a cheeky office boy opened the inquiry window in response to my timid knock. Seeing that I was only four feet (1.2m) nothing high, he said, rudely, "Whaddya want?"

"Have you any vacancies for an apprentice?" I asked.

"No!" said the boy, "'op it!" He slammed the window shut in my face.

Similar experiences met me at several other offices, but eventually I had the good luck to be greeted by a kindly old clerk who said, "Well, we haven't any vacancies just at present, but we could put your name down." He handed me a printed form marked **APPLICATION FOR APPRENTICESHIP**. I saw that it had to be signed by the parent or guardian as surety for the applicant.

That evening, I handed the application form to my father. "Where did you get this?" he demanded. I told him the name of the ship owners and added that they would probably want a boy in the not-too-distant future and would like my name to be put down on their list. Said my father, "this is what I think of your application!" Rolling the paper into a ball, he pitched it into the kitchen fire.

Try, try, try again! fancied that my father showed some signs of weakening as I kept on pestering him at every opportunity with the same old story. Then one of my school friends, who had gone to sea as an apprentice a year previously, returned home after voyage to Australia. He was bronzed, fit and well, much bigger than before, and wore his brassbound shore going uniform and badge cap, which seemed to my envious eyes the glorious garb of a hero. I invited him to our home, where my parents had to listen to the thrilling tales of his adventures. He had been carefully primed by me to avoid mentioning hardships or disasters, but he sometimes forgot the part he was supposed to play and enlarged on the terrible risks of going aloft in a Cape Horn snorter to reef the main upper topsail and the pangs of hunger endured by boys trying to exist on Liverpool pantiles (ships' biscuits) and putrid salt pork.

"There you are, Jimmy," my father would say. "I told you it is a dog's life at sea. They feed you on dog biscuits!"

Yet I felt that he was weakening. On 15th July 1898, I attained my fifteenth birthday. I had then been working for about nine months as a clerk in the office of the Anglo-American Oil Company. My father sensed that, if I didn't get the sack, I would resign, sooner or later, and clear out to sea, no matter what efforts were made to prevent me.

At the family celebration of my birthday, my seafaring uncle — who happened then to be in port — made a vain effort to convince me that life at sea was monotonous, dangerous, poorly paid, difficult, and altogether a "dead end" occupation, fit only for men who could not find anything better to do. "If I had my time over again," he said, solemnly, "I'd never set foot on a deck! The only reason I went to sea was because I was a young fool like yourself. Then, before I found out my mistake, I was too old to learn any other trade or profession. It's the same with all sailors! I never yet met a sailor who didn't want to be a farmer, with a snug crib on solid ground, far out of sight of salt water — but they're all too poor to buy a farm, and that's the only reason they keep on going to sea."

"You don't look poor, uncle," I reminded him.

"Who'd sell a farm?" he demanded and answered his own question. "Nobody! But anybody would sell a ship!"

"The Captain loves the sea," said my mother, spoiling the effect of his oration. My uncle chewed his cheroot reflectively. "Never judge by appearances, Jimmy," he countered. Then he changed the subject. "You're only a runt, anyway," he said, bluntly. "What's your height?"

"Four feet (1.2m) two," I told him.

"What do you weigh?"

"Five stone four. (34kg)"

"Huh! What use would you be, tailing on to hoist a main upper topsail? You'd be no more use on deck than a flea. You need beef and brawn, my lad, not brains, to be a tailor. Wait until you're six feet (2m) high and weigh twelve stone (76kg), before you go to sea. You're too small built, and not strong enough, to go aloft and handle sail, Jimmy. The work would kill you!"

My mother interposed, "Dr. Adams will be calling in this evening. We'll ask him to examine Jimmy. If he says the lad is too small and puny for the rigors of a sea life, that will put an end to the argument, won't it?"

As Dr. Adams had helped me into this world exactly fifteen years previously and had done the same for all my brothers and sisters and had prescribed for whatever Infantile ailments had afflicted us since, he had become a valued friend.

Presently he arrived, and the problem was explained to him, He examined me thoroughly before announcing his decision, which to me was like a peal of bells. "For heaven's sake," he said, "let Jimmy go to sea if he wants to! It will make a man of him."

With this victory, the culmination of years of effort on my part, I knew that the opposition to my desires must now collapse. Now I would see the wide world.

My father hauled down his flag. "Verra weel, Jamie," he retired. "I'll no stand in y'r way. Ye can dae as ye like! I'll look around for a shipowner to tak ye as an apprentice, and ye can go, wi' my blessing!"

I was on fire with the excitement of such a hard won victory. In every lunch hour, I continued to haunt the shipping offices, putting my name down for vacancies. My father also made inquiries and entered into negotiations to apprentice me as economically as possible, but also in the best conditions obtainable, with a firm of good repute.

Nearly three months went by in this quest, while I continued my employment, to earn my six bob a week at the Oil Company's office. At last, on 7th October 1898, I went with my father to the offices of William Thomas & Co., Ltd., shipowners, of 14 Water Street, Liverpool, to be indentured as a sea apprentice, at the age of fifteen years, two months, twenty-two days; and my seafaring career began.

*Signing the Indentures — A Millionaire with a Brass Stud — Terms
and Conditions — 'Ol Apprenticeship — "No Washing" — The
Barque "County of Pembroke" — A Welsh Captain — Getting Ready
for Sea — Serious Discussion in the Saloon.*

WILLIAM THOMAS & CO., LTD., shipowners, were a Welsh firm, with a fleet of sailing vessels, operating mostly from Liverpool. The Company's office was in Oriel Chambers, 14 Water Street. Arrived there, my father and I were conducted by the office boy into the sanctum of the head of the firm, William Thomas himself, a man of great weight in shipping circles, who was reputedly a millionaire. I was overawed, but a little disappointed to find that this important person was dressed in a drab suit of clothes, with baggy trousers, and no sign of a millionaire's opulence in his garb. Far from that his shirt collar was fastened with s brass stud, of the kind that could be bought for a penny. His inner office was small and plainly furnished. On a peg was his black billycock hat, the only visible sign of his importance.

He shook hands with my father and gave me a penetrating look of appraisal. Then, without wasting time or words, he plunged into the business in hand. "Have you the certificates?" he asked. "Yes," said my father and placed on the table a medical certificate of my health, and a certificate from the Liverpool office of the Board of Trade to show that I had good eyesight and that I was not colour blind. William Thomas glanced at these and nodded. Then he said, pointedly, "And have you brought the money?"

"Yes," said my father again, and proceeded to open his purse and count onto the table twenty golden sovereigns out of his hard earned savings. The millionaire's eyes glinted, as though reflecting the gold, as he nodded again and said with a smile, "That's good!" Then he rang a little bell on his desk. A clerk entered, bringing with him two rustling pieces of printed parchment, eleven by fifteen inches, headed **ORDINARY APPRENTICE'S INDENTURE**. This document, ready to be signed in duplicate, was in the form approved by the Board of Trade (which at that time controlled conditions of employment on British seagoing vessels).

I sat wriggling with excitement, my ears buzzing, my eyes nearly popping out of my head, as the clerk read the indenture aloud, gabbling the words, which were familiar to him but wonderful to me. The document was an indenture agreement between myself as an apprentice, of the first part; William Thomas & Co., Ltd., as my master, of the second part; and my father as surety, of the third part.

The indenture witnessed that I voluntarily bound myself apprentice to William Thomas & Co., Ltd., for four years. I covenanted that, during this term, I would faithfully serve my master; obey his lawful commands; keep his secrets; give him true accounts of his goods or money which might be committed to my charge or come into my hands; and that I would not do any damage to my master, nor consent to any such damage being done by others, but would "if possible, prevent the same, and give warning thereof"; that I would not embezzle nor waste the goods of my master, nor lend nor give them to others without his permission; that I would not absent myself from my master's service without leave, nor "frequent taverns or alehouses," unless upon his business; nor play at unlawful games.

In consideration of all this, my master covenanted to "use all proper means" to teach me, or cause me to be taught, "the business of a seaman," and to provide me with "sufficient Meat, Drink, Lodging, Washing, Medicine and Medical and Surgical Assistance."

As the clerk read this, the millionaire owner interrupted him. "No washing!" he said, briskly. "Indeed to goodness, on my ships boys can do their own washing. Cross it out!" "Very well," agreed my father, reluctantly. The clerk put a pen through the word "Washing," and continued reading the next vital words, already inscribed in ink, in the space left for them on the printed document. These specified that my master would pay me "Three pounds for the first year; four pounds for the second year; five pounds for the third year; and eight pounds for the fourth and last year" of my apprenticeship.

So, in four years at sea, I could earn a total of twenty pounds "and keep"; but the indenture further stipulated that I should provide tor myself all sea bedding, wearing apparel, and necessaries (except Meat, Drink, Lodging, Medicine and Medical and Surgical Assistance)," and that If my master provided me with any "necessary apparel or my bedding" the value of such items could be deducted from my pay.

Finally, the indenture witnessed that my father, as surety for my performance of my part of the bond, bound himself to pay a penal sum of twenty pounds if I failed to carry out my obligations. This sum he lodged in cash, to be forfeited in the event of my failure, but with the right to have the matter determined by a magistrate if a dispute occurred.

On the other hand, if I behaved satisfactorily my father's surety would be refunded to him at the end of my term of apprenticeship. All this being made clear, my father, before signing the document, turned to me, and said, "Noo, Jimmy, be a good lad, and we'll get oor twenty poonds back!"

I signed the document in duplicate. Then Mr. Thomas and my father signed it, seals were affixed, our signatures were witnessed by the clerk. As an afterthought, we all initialled the word "Washing" that was crossed out from the amenities to be supplied to me by the owners. Mr. Thomas picked up and carefully counted the twenty golden sovereigns lying on the desk and locked them in a wall safe. He shook hands with me and patted me on the head. "Indeed to goodness," he said, "I hope you will like the life at sea, James!"

Having been directed to report immediately to Captain John Williams on board the barque, *County of Pembroke*, lying in the Salthouse Dock, I went there escorted by my father, wishing that he would walk more quickly.

When we arrived and I saw the three tall masts, the yards and the rigging of the barque towering high over the wharf sheds, I could scarcely speak for excitement. "My ship, father!" I stammered. "Isn't she a beauty?"

He shook his head, sadly. "There has never been a sailor in the family before. Why should yott want to be the black sheep of the flocks" he grumbled. "Aweel, we maun mak' the best o' it!"

The *County of Pembroke* was a vessel of 1,036 tons net and 1,098 tons gross register, built by Doxford of Sunderland and launched in 1881. She had trim lines, a steel hull, planted decks, and steel masts and yards. She was 221 feet long, 35 feet (10m) beam, and 20 to 29 feet (6m – 9m) deep. She had a low poop deck, known as a "monkey poop."

Although it is not nautically correct to describe a barque as a "ship" — since a ship is square rigged on all masts, while a barque is square rigged on the fore and main, but fore and aft rigged on the mizzen — this distinction cannot be rigidly applied in nontechnical talk or writing. According to the Oxford Dictionary, the word "ship" may be applied to "any seagoing vessel of considerable size." It is applied to steamers, warships, and other vessels which have no sails whatever. If therefore I occasionally in this narrative refer to the *County of Pembroke* as a "ship," instead of as a "vessel" or a "barque," that term will then be used in its general and not in its particular sense. The word "ship" was and is often used by seafaring men, loosely, when referring to ships, barques, barquentines, brigs, brigantines, schooners, sloops, scows, and even steamers and motor vessels, unless the occasion requires an exact reference to the rig. It can scarcely be avoided in compound words, such as shipboard, shipowner, shipbuilder, shipwreck, shipmate, shipload, shipshape, and the like.

The *County of Pembroke* was low slung amidships, and, as she lay at the wharf, her monkey poop and fo'c'slehead were visible, but her main deck was below the level of the wharf planking. A gang of about ten riggers were aloft, bending sail and getting her ready for sea. My father and I stood for a few minutes looking at her. A plank stretched from the wharf to her bulwarks, serving as a gangway. We crossed this and jumped down to the deck in the waist.

A tubby little man, rotund and rubicund, with twinkling blue eyes, appeared on the poop and came forward to meet us. He was dressed in a blue

County of Pembroke

State Library of South Australia The 'County of Pembroke' in an unidentified port
[PRG 1373/13/52]

serge suit with slightly bellbottomed trousers and a high white collar and wore a black billycock hat perched on his head at a rakish angle. He spoke in a Welsh accent, tilting and precise, but rather difficult to understand. "I'm Captain John Williams, of Pwllheli in North Wales," he began. "What might be your business on board my ship?"

My father, with equal formality, explained who and what we were and why we were there. Captain Williams gave both of us, especially me, a searching look, then said, "Indeed to goodness, is that so? Come down to my cabin, and we will have a talk about it."

We followed him to the poop deck. Its planks had been holystoned as white as a hound's tooth, the teak rails varnished, the brass shining, but now, after a month in port, she was looking a bit grimy. I stared at the cabin skylight, the wheel, the binnacle, and up into the maze of rigging, and the yards nosed on the masts. The Captain beckoned and we followed him down a short companionway from the poop to his cabin. This was the first time I had ever been in such a holy of holies, and I was struck dumb with wonder. The cabin, or "saloon" was panelled entirely in bird's eye maple, highly polished.

If I could not take in all the details then, at a first glance, I had plenty of opportunities to do so later, when it became part of my duties to keep the maple, and everything else in the saloon, as spick and span as spit and polish could make it. In the centre was a polished table, with a bench on each side. "Be seated," said the Captain courteously. This was the first and last time I would sit at the table. At sea only the Captain and the officers dined there. In port, the splendid show was for business visitors.

Above the table a large, polished, brass oil lamp swung from the beams overhead by three brass chains. There was a brass swinging tray, with tumblers and coloured wine glasses in slots and a sideboard with a marble top and a brass rail around it; and the ship's medicine chest, of oak, lashed to the white scrubbed deck.

A barometer was screwed to the bird's eye maple bulkhead. Across the after end of the saloon was a red velvet settee and abaft it, a set of polished transom lockers, where small stores were stowed. At each side was a door. These led to the officers' cabins and the other compartments under the poop, including the sail locker, lamp locker, pantry, and steward's cabin. The grey light of a Liverpool autumn filtered through the skylight overhead.

"Will you take a drink with me?" asked Captain Williams.

"I willna say nae," replied my father cordially. The Captain reached for a bottle of rum and two tumblers. They clinked glasses and drank each other's health. Then, ignoring my presence, they talked about my future for a long time, with occasional refreshers of the rum. I learned now that the barque was already partly loaded and would soon be sailing with a cargo of general merchandise for Melbourne, Australia, around the Cape of Good Hope, without putting in at any intermediate ports on this outward run of nearly 12,000 miles (19,312 km). At Melbourne we were to load grain or whatever other cargo was offering there, and then return to England around Cape Horn, thus circumnavigating the globe.

The voyage, the Captain estimated, would occupy about ten months, or perhaps a year. The barque carried a complement of twenty-one hands, all told, comprising himself, Mr. Owen (First Mate), Mr. Slater (Second Mate)— all Welsh; three apprentices (the other two being in their third year); a cook steward; carpenter; sailmaker; and twelve seamen.

The Captain gave my father a list of the equipment I would require, beginning with a wooden sea chest, a canvas sea bag, three suits of working dungarees, a suit of oilskins, sou'wester, leather sea boots, a leather belt with a sheath and knife, three suits of woollen underwear, and — most important, as I considered it — my shore uniform with brass buttons and a badge cap.

The badge consisted of a monogram of the four letters W.T.C.L., which stood for "William Thomas & Co., Ltd." — lent a sarcastic seaman later informed me that the letters meant "Welsh Thieves and Colonial Liars!"

At the prospect of all this expense, for clothes which I would quickly outgrow, my father's face lengthened a little, but his optimism was restored with some revivers of the rum. As the conference continued, the Captain listed more articles that I would need, including three blankets, an enamel plate and cup, a knife, fork and spoon, straw filled mattress and pillow (known as "donkeys' breakfast"), a good supply of soap, and a gross of boxes of matches — since one of the tasks of apprentices was to light the binnacle lamp and other lights, also to trim and relight them if they went out.

My father wrote down this list, adding items that occurred to each of them, such as plenty of woollen socks, old shirts, a muffler, a guernsey, and I wondered how my gear could all be fitted into one sea chest and a sea bag. Then, with a grand gesture, my father opened his depleted purse and took from it two golden sovereigns, which he handed to the Captain for my pocket money — "verra sparingly, or in an emergency, ye ken, but dinna gie him too much o't!"

The rum bottle showing low tide and the business completed, my father and his now good friend Captain Williams shook hands cordially and went up on deck. There my father successfully walked the gangplank to the shore. I followed him, overjoyed at the wonderful events of the day. This was the only time I ever saw my father take a wee drappie too much, but the occasion was an important one. We walked the three miles (4.8 km) from the docks to our home in Cambridge Street. When we got there, we were very hungry, but mother had a good meal waiting for us. The exhilaration had somewhat worked off, and she was given a sensible account of the day's proceedings. Fortunately, my father did not have to attend choir practice that evening.

*My Outfit — First Days on Board in Port — The Half Deck —
Bending Sail — Taking in Cargo and Stores — Fond Farewells — A
Parting Gift of the Good Book — "Bring Back a Parrot!" — My
Shipmates — Sailing day — Towing Down the Mersey — A Cure for
Seasickness —the End of a Day at Sea.*

MY mother immediately took in hand the practical matter of buying and preparing my outfit. For two days I went with her to various shops, to be fitted with wearing apparel of the smallest size — but allowing a reasonable number of inches for my growth. It made me feel grateful when I realized how much of their hard saved money my parents were obliged to spend to send me to sea; but, having taken the decision, they did this willingly.

The outfitters tried to sell us all sorts of things which were not on my list, including a bos'n's lanyard and whistle, a cracker hash bag and mallet, a ditty bag with sail needles, marlinspikes, serving boards and other articles which they assured us were necessary; but, as we did not have these on our list, my mother very wisely would not buy them. In my opinion, the important thing was the badge cap. When this was bought, I put it on immediately, at the correct rakish angle, and walked home wearing it.

On the third day, I was out of bed in the dark at 4.80 a.m. and, garbed in dungarees and with my badge cap, sallied forth at 5 a.m. to walk the three miles (4.8 km) to my ship, to begin work. I was one of the world's workers! The streets of Liverpool, before dawn, were thronged with many such, some wearing hobnail boots or clogs which rattled on the cobbles like horses galloping, and mill girls in shawls, but none so eager as I to begin that day's toil. I was so anxious not to be late that I half ran most of the way and arrived a quarter of an hour early.

When I went on board, the Mate, Mr. Owen, a big, burly, bearded man whom I had not seen before, gave me a hurried look and said, "Huh? The new apprentice? Lay along there forrard and do what the other boys tell you to do."

A few minutes before 6 a.m., two youths in dungarees came on board and spoke to me. They were the other apprentices, Bill Huxley and Tom Sawyer, Liverpool lads, seventeen years of age, both in the third year of serving their time. They shook hands with me and took me into the half deck. The riggers and stevedores came on board when the Mate began bawling, "Turn to!"

In the *County of Pembroke*, the home of the apprentices, known as the half deck, was not under the poop, as in some larger vessels, but was part of the forward deckhouse, which contained the fo'c'sle, the half deck, the

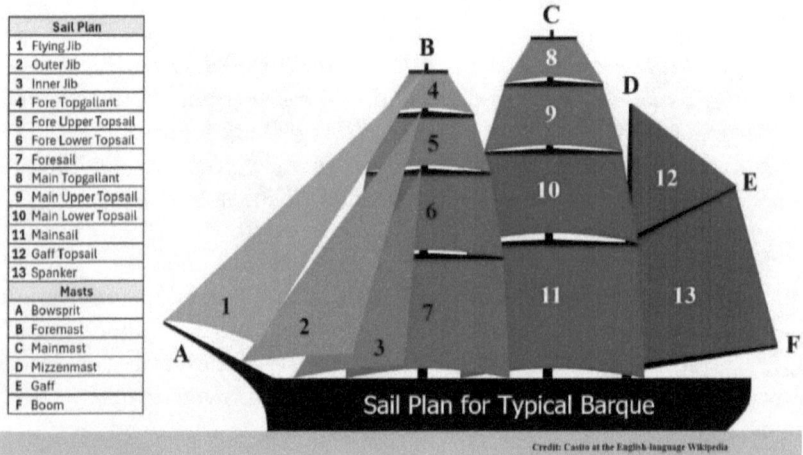

Sail Plan	
1	Flying Jib
2	Outer Jib
3	Inner Jib
4	Fore Topgallant
5	Fore Upper Topsail
6	Fore Lower Topsail
7	Foresail
8	Main Topgallant
9	Main Upper Topsail
10	Main Lower Topsail
11	Mainsail
12	Gaff Topsail
13	Spanker
Masts	
A	Bowsprit
B	Foremast
C	Mainmast
D	Mizzenmast
E	Gaff
F	Boom

Sail Plan for Typical Barque

carpenter's shop and the galley (working from forward).

The half deck had six bunks — two each side, fore and aft, and two in the middle, athwartships. Each bunk was six feet (2m) long and two feet (.6m) wide. A door on each side led onto the main deck just abaft the fore rigging. There were six open lockers for the eating utensils, and a five-gallon drum for fresh water. Our sea chests served as seats. As there were only three apprentices on this voyage, the carpenter ("Chips") and the sailmaker ("Sails"), lived with the apprentices in the half deck.

Adjacent to the half deck was the fo'c's1e, with bunks for twelve seamen. At this time the crew had not yet been signed on. The riggers and stevedores, who lived on shore, came on board daily to get the vessel ready for sea and to load the cargo. The officers, the apprentices, the cook, carpenter, and sailmaker — constituting the "afterguard" and the "tradesmen" — were paid off in the terminal port, but, when required, worked on weekly wages until the time came for signing articles again; whereas the seamen were discharged at the end of a voyage, paid off, and left to lend for themselves on shore. They, or others, were engaged again for a new voyage, a few days before sailing.

On the stroke of 6 a.m. the Mates began bawling orders and stirred all hands to activity. The riggers went aloft, to bend sail and overhaul the standing and running gear. The apprentices were told to help the sailmaker get sails on deck. As winter was near — the season of gales in the North Atlantic — the suit of hard weather (heavy canvas) sails was bent on the yards before we left port.

Some horsedrawn lorries arrived alongside, and the stevedores began stowing cases and packages of cargo in our hold. We carried about 1,200 tons of general merchandise, including, as I noticed, many cases of whiskey, beer and stout, a large number of bags of salt, and many other kinds of goods. All was bustle and activity, with much yelling of orders, which I enjoyed, for the time being, as nobody expected me to do anything, except to hop around with Bill and Tommy and try to help them in whatever they were doing. Later that day and the next day more lorries came alongside, with ship's stores for a twelve-month voyage. These were in great variety, and included paint, tar, sails, ropes, wire, and spun yarn, besides casks of flour, sugar, peas, rice, biscuits, salt pork, and salt beef. These were handled on board by the apprentices and stowed in lockers and the lazarette under the poop. The beef and pork were stowed in the 'tween deck. At noon we knocked off for an hour for dinner. We had our own lunches with us and went on shore with the riggers and stevedores to a "cocoa room" where we could get a large cup of tea or cocoa for a halfpenny. These "cocoa rooms" were at frequent intervals all along the Dock Road.

From one o'clock until six o'clock we went on with our work —in all it was an eleven-hour day. Then, hungry and dirty, I walked home three miles (4.8 km), arriving there about 7 p.m. The family studied me with astonishment, wondering when I would grow tired of this hard life; but, though I had some misgivings, I kept them to myself and said that I was enjoying myself thoroughly.

In a way this was true, as the work on board was full of novelty and interest. I was the most insignificant person in the *County of Pembroke*, but I felt that she belonged to me and that I belonged to her. I listened to everything that was explained to me, picking up the nautical terms and learning my way about; and I listened, too, to some tall tales of adventures at sea and in port, which appalled me, as they were intended to do. A few times I was allowed to practice going aloft. I was not expected to do anything there, except to keep out of the way of the men at work on the yards and to watch the right sailor's way of doing things; but I gained confidence and found the view of the docks and the city, from a hundred feet (30m) up, fascinating.

Most of my work was on deck, helping to haul and stow the stores in the lazarette, 'tween deck, sail locker and rope locker, and shovelling in coal for the galley. This was stowed in the lower fore poop. After three days of this, we were ready for sea. All hands were ordered to be on board by midnight on 11th October, and I had leave to stay at home until then on that day.

My mother now had all my things overhauled, laundered, mended and neatly packed — though this with some difficulty — into my sea chest and sea bag. During the afternoon I went with these, and my straw mattress and pillow, in a four-wheeled horsedrawn cab (fare: two bob) to the dock and delivered them into the half deck. Then I walked home for my last meal with the family for many a day.

We had ham and eggs, as a special treat. My father presented me with a Bible, inscribed, "To Gordon, on the occasion of his going to sea." It was only on very important occasions that he called me "Gordon," my second Christian name. "Be sure to read the Good Book," he said, "and never part with it!" He also gave me some sound and final advice on the need to avoid bad companions and strong drink. As the hour of my departure drew near, my mother put the four younger children to bed, after they had kissed me goodnight and goodbye. I began to feel now that I was going to my certain death in the morning. My mother's eyes were filled with tears as she put her arms around me and said, "Be a good lad, Jimmy, won't you And wear wool next to your skin, and don't catch your death of cold with wet clothes!"

"Yes, Mother," I promised.

My father clapped his hat on his head and looked at his watch. It was ten o'clock. " 'Tis time to go!" he announced, like the crack of doom. I kissed my mother for the last time and found the tears contagious. Then, with my badge cap on my head and firmly grasping my Bible, I set out with my father and my elder brother, David, to walk to the ship.

About 11 p.m., we stood together on the wharf, at the head of the gangplank. My father put his arms around my shoulders and said solemnly, "Dinna forget, Gordon, to write letters home, and read your Bible, and say your prayers every day!" My brother clapped me on the back and said heartily, "And bring home a parrot or a monkey!" They turned and walked away.

In the darkness and silence, I stood listening to their departing footsteps echoing in a cobbled street that led from the quayside. I thought that if only they'd turn around and come back and say to me, "Give up this foolish idea of being a sailor, and come home to your warm comfortable bed," I'd have swallowed the anchor then and there — but they didn't come back!

I crept down the gangway to the silent and dark deck. All hands, except an old watchman, were still ashore for a last fling. I felt my way along to the half deck, undressed in the darkness, and, tumbling into my bunk, began to cry myself to sleep. Presently I became aware of crawling things — cockroaches. Ugh! I began to think that I would get dressed and go home, to face the scorn of all who knew me, rather than sleep on straw with cockroaches for a year. At this moment the door was flung open and my pals, the two senior apprentices, jovially entered. They stumbled around in the darkness until they found the stump of a tallow candle and lit it. Then they threw their things into their bunks and, being old hands at the game, tried to cheer me up. I turned my face to the bulkhead to hide my sobs. A few minutes later they blew out the candle, turned in, and began snoring like a couple of young pigs. The door opened again. Chips and Sails came in, merry after an evening ashore; they lit the candle and lurched about for some time before turning in and dowsing the glim. It was now after midnight. I had heard the clock on the Customs House striking the hour. From the fo'c'sle next to us there were loud shouts and drunken songs. The sailors, having been thrown out of the pubs, were coming on board.

I had not yet seen any of the crew who had been signed, on that day, but they were evidently a rough lot, or so it seemed to me from their boozy noises. When their row at last subsided, I dozed off. It seemed no time at all when there was a loud bang on the half-deck door. The Mate put his head inside and bellowed, "Wake up, you sleepers! All hands on deck to unmoor ship!"

It was 5 a.m. and pitch dark. Bill and Tommy jumped out and lit the candle. Bill went outside and had a look at the weather. He returned and announced, "It's blowing and fleeting and as cold as charity!" He shook me by the shoulder and said, "Turn to quick and lively, or the Mate will come and kick you out. Get into your oilskins and sea boots for a dirty day!"

Putting on the unfamiliar rig of oilskins and heavy boots, shop-new, I followed Bill and Tommy onto the deck. The mates were rampaging about, trying to get some life into drink-drugged sailors to unmoor the barque and warp her to the river lock gate. I had no idea what was happening. I saw the crew trudging around the capstan in the waist on the main deck, abaft the mainmast and heard them singing a shanty. "Keep with me," said Bill, "and do what I do, and you'll be all right." In the uproar and darkness, I did as bid, feeling that I had never been so cold and miserable in all my life as the rain and sleet froze my face end fingers.

When Bill pulled on a chain or rope or wire, I pulled to, adding my puny weight, without any idea of what it was all about. I could see that we were slowly moving from the wharf. I was tempted to jump ashore and run home at fast as my legs could carry me, but by the time I decided to do this the strip of dirty water between me and the wharf was too wide to jump — especially in heavy boots.

As daylight grew, I saw that we had moved from the dock to the river lock gate. "We're waiting for high water, to pass into the river," explained Bill briefly. Then he added, "It's time for breakfast. Go to the galley and get it." As I was the junior in the half deck, this was my task. I took the bread barge (a box) and two tin kids (basins) to the galley. The cook was a German of stocky build, with t close cropped head and a waxed moustache — actually a fine human who had been in the German Navy. He wore a woollen singlet, black woollen trousers held up by leather braces, and boots. He was a man of iron, who never wore any other clothes than these in the coldest or hottest weather.

He gave me coffee, fried meat, and some baker's bread, This was apportioned among the five inmates of the half deck, as we sat on our sea chests. I began to feel better with something in my belly and went out on deck to see what was happening. The seamen had headaches, but they knew their work. They were a mixed lot. Eleven were rated Able Seamen and one was an Ordinary Seaman. Five were Welsh, two Liverpool Irish, two Germans, one Norwegian, one Greek and one Maltese. Seamen from North European countries were known on shipboard as 'Dutchmen' and those from Southern European countries as 'Dagoes.' The mixture of nationalities in the fo'c'sle was usual in sailing ship days, when seamen joined and left ships almost at random in all ports, but especially at a big terminal port.

There was never any difficulty in picking up a crew at short notice from the Board of Trade shipping office, as hundreds of good seamen were to be found there at any time, or were drifting around on shore in a state of destitution after spending their pay, usually on grog. Some in desperation would make a "pierhead jump," that is, they would wait at the end of the pier to jump on board if the Mate beckoned to them if he needed another man or two. These men usually had nothing except the clothes they stood up in — known as a "parish rig." The Master would sign them on and supply them with an outfit from the slop chest, the value to be deducted from their pay at the end of the voyage.

A seaman had the right to allot a month's or two months' pay to his dependents, by a note which was negotiable only after he had duly sailed in the vessel in which he was articled. As the pay of an Able Seaman was three pounds a month, his dependents had little to subsist on while he was at sea.

Our two Irish seamen were married men who had made an advance allotment to their wives. In the bleak morning light, we saw four women in drab overcoats, black shawls over their heads, standing in the drizzle and sleet on the pierhead. They were the wives and mothers, or mothers-in-law, of Murphy and Casey. The two younger women held babies in their arms, wrapped in the shawls.

"Goodbye, Mick! Goodbye, Pat!" they wailed. "And God be with you"

At we were a long time at the lock gates, the women were Shivering with cold; but they would not go away while Pat and Mick were in sight. After a while one of the older women noticed me. I felt as miserable as they, especially When I heard her say shrilly, pointing to me, "Look at that poor little devil! Sure, and he'll never come back!" Our two German seamen, Hans and Fritz, were a pair of "characters," who had come aboard in parish rig, all that remained of their possessions. Prime seamen, they had been paid off a ship a week or two previously and had gone on the spree.

According to the story they told us later, they had spent all their hard earned pay in Liverpool's pubs and dance halls. One evening Hans, the more thoughtful one, had said "Vat you say, Fritz, before our money all gone, ve buy for boots, monkey pea yackets, undervair, varm clothes, soap and matches, den ven ve broke ve are ready for der pierhead yump!"

"Ach, by yiminy," replied Fritz, "to hell mit der monkey pea yacket! Give us a tune on der Yarman flute, und ve sing and dance!"

Now, on the fo'c'slehead, standing by the capstan, Fritz cocked a weather eye to the stormy sky and, chilled to the marrow in his dungarees wet with

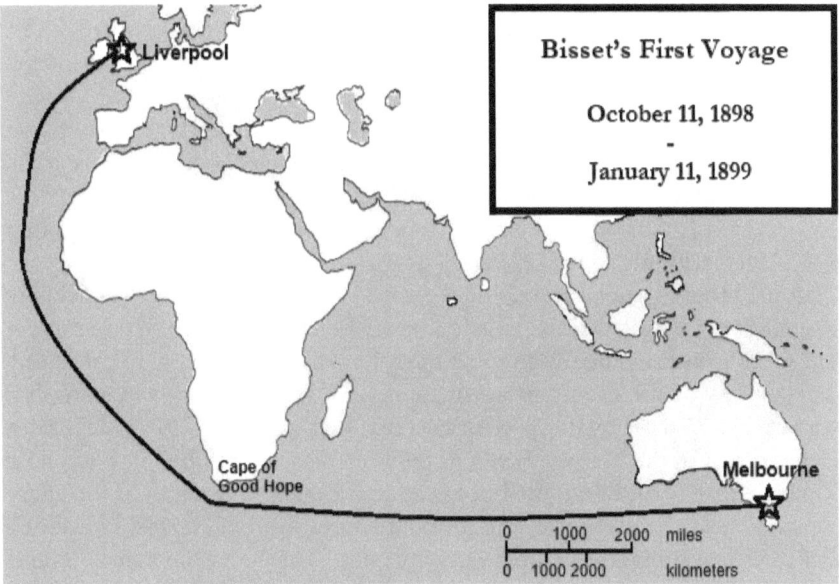

sleet, felt mighty forty for himself. "Blow yently, souvester," he moaned. "I vas only yoking in der public 'ouse!"

Though all our crew spoke English with various accents, they could understand orders given in the nautical terms which were the Esperanto of the sea. As the tide rose, the tug which was to tow us down river came nosing fussily along, and the lock gates were opened.

"Lay forward to make the tug fast!" roared the Mate. We hauled in her wire, put it over the bitts, and started to move slowly into the river.

I was ordered aft to the poop, where I wouldn't be in the way. There I saw the shivering; weeping womenfolk waving forlornly to Pat and Mick and heard the dock workers calling out "Good voyage!" That was all our sendoff. The dirty Mersey water widened between our stern and the dock gates, and I felt that the land was receding from me forever. As we dropped down with the tide, Liverpool's landmarks passed astern, and my heart sank into my sea boots.

The only person on deck, apart from myself, who appeared to have nothing to do was a man in civilian clothes who was strolling around, smoking a cigar and moodily staring at the shore. He was our solitary passenger, Dr. R. Hilton, who was quartered in a spare cabin under the poop, taking a sea voyage to recover his health.

"All hands lay aft to pick watches," bellowed the Mate. Our crew assembled at the break of the poop, as the First Mate and Second Mate picked six seamen and one senior apprentice each. Being the only first-voyager, the smallest, the most useless, and the odd man out, I was picked last of all and put into the First Mate's watch.

By this time, I was too miserable to care what happened to me. The barque began to pitch in the swell as at noon we neared the mouth of the Mersey. All hands were ordered to dinner, before we got sail on her. I went to the galley with the mess kits for the half deck's issue of a watery soup and a chunk of greasy boiled mutton and some spuds boiled in their dirty jackets. This was shared between the five of us. I drank my soup but could not face my chunk of mutton and spuds, which my shipmates divided among themselves, with my full approval.

Added to my general feeling of misery, I had a terror of being seasick; my imagination probably helped to bring on an attack of the very thing I feared, and soon I was retching my soup up over the rail. In later years, I heard pony explanations of the causes of seasickness, and suggestions for its cure; but nothing bettered my own experience on that first day when I lost equilibrium at the mouth of the Mersey. Being in the Port Watch (the Plate's), I was now on duty, from noon to 4 p.m., but as the ship began filing about in the angry sea when we cleared the bar, the formality meant nothing to me. Homesick and seasick and thinking I'd never be missed, I crept into the half deck end threw myself into my bunk, hoping to die; but the mate came in and, grabbing my feet, hauled me out on deck like a sack of coal.

"Seasick?" he growled. "I'll cure you!" Then, taking a tin pannikin from the galley, he filled it with sea water from the scuppers, as a sea came over the lee rail and bathed across the deck. "Here, drink this!" he ordered, holding me by the scruff of the neck and forcing the pannikin to my lips.

I drank the lot, hoping that it would kill me. The powerful emetic worked. Strangely enough, in about half an hour I was better and actually feeling hungry. I have never been seasick from that day to this; but I have always hesitated to recommend this old fashioned remedy to passengers in luxury liners.

As we drew away from the land, the master of the tug ahead gave a succession of quick toots on his whistle, meaning, "Stand by to slip my wire."

Some of the seamen were ordered aloft to loosen sail and others forward to slip the towline while I was told to stand by on the poop with the Captain, under the weather cloth which was secured to the mizzen rigging; it was my duty to mark the passage of time by striking the proper bells every half hour.

The land was now out of sight, and the slipping of the towline was the severance of our last link with home. We acre under sail. As darkness fell and the lights were lit, the gale was increasing in the Irish Sea. At eight o'clock, at the end of the second dog watch, I was sent below, to fall into a deep sleep of utter exhaustion and misery.

At one bell (a quarter to twelve midnight) I was awakened by Tommy bawling in the half deck, "Oh! Oh! Oh Ho there, you sleepers! One bell! Show a leg, show a leg!" He kept on maddeningly, until Bill and I turned out and got into our damp sea boots and oilskins to go aft at midnight (eight bells) for the change of the watch. No sooner had the Second Mate sung out, "Relieve the wheel and lookout," than the Mate roared, "All hands on deck. Reef the main topsail!"

So, instead of going below, the starboard watch had to turn to for a nasty job. The sail was lowered and the men raced aloft to make the reef. I was ordered to stay on the poop under the weather cloth and strike the bells, and also to relight the binnacle if it was blown out.

The weather was as black as the inside of a cow and blowing a full gale from the southwest, with a heavy sea running. I could hear the men shouting and cursing on the topsail yard, but I could not see them. I marvelled how they could work and hang on under such terrifying conditions. I felt sure now that I would never be a sailor and that my going to sea had been a big mistake.

About 2 a.m., the Captain, who was standing under the weather cloth and was evidently anxious about the barque's position, grabbed me by the arm and shouted in my ear above the roar of the wind, "How would you like to be at home now, Jimmy, sitting beside the fire?"

He meant it kindly, but I could not see the joke and broke into tears. Seeing this, the Old Man said, "Go and sit in the companionway, out of the wind, and try to stop your teeth from chattering."

At the change of the watch at 4 a.m., I went below and slept the sleep of the utterly wearied. So ended my first day at sea; but, strangely enough, when I was aroused at 8 a.m., to face another turn on watch, I had lost all feelings of seasickness and was ready to meet with confidence whatever discomforts or joys a life on the ocean might bring to me, in the days and years that stretched ahead.

*Under Sail — The True Peace of God — The Trade Route to
Australia — Lessons in Seamanship — Nautical Lingo — The
Sailor's Working Week — Consolations of Seafaring — Hungry
Days — "Wind Puddings" — The Board of Trade Scale of
Provisions — "Harriet Lane" — The Lime juicers — The
"Whack" — Dandy Funk and Cracker Mash.*

"**THE** true Peace of God," Joseph Conrad has written,
"begins at any spot a thousand miles from the nearest land."
We met with variable winds in the Irish Sea and in the
"Chops of the Channel," with some north-westerly and south-
westerly Atlantic gales. These were not of long duration, but they tested
the seamanship of the crew, as all hands were called out on deck several
times to take in or set sails as the changing conditions required.

In this heavy weather I was not allowed to go aloft with the other
apprentices and the seamen. Lifelines were rigged fore and aft along
the deck. The lee rail was often under water as seas broke on board,
the water seething and surging along the deck, to flood into the
scuppers and empty through the washpots. At such times the seamen
working on deck waded knee deep in water, holding on to anything
handy, or made their way along the deck clutching the lifeline.

I spent most of my watch on deck on the monkey poop, or
polishing the bird's eye maple and brass in the Captain's cabin, or
trimming and filling lamps, or doing other odd jobs designed to
keep me out of harm's way. I had to learn early to watch for the
seas coming on board amidships and to hold on to the lifeline if I
had to wade, with my short leg's thigh deep, along the main deck

between the poop and the half deck in the forward deckhouse.

I was drenched in every watch and soon found it impossible to carry out my mother's instructions to avoid wearing damp clothes. All my changes of clothing were wet, and for the time being there was no way of getting them dry. Despite this, even though I turned into my bunk in wet clothes, I did not catch my death of cold. I had very little time for sleep, as the watch below was often called out as soon as I dozed off. In these conditions, too,

I had no time to carry out my father's instructions to read my Bible and say my prayers every day, as I was dog tired after my watches on deck. However, though life was uncomfortable in this zone of the ocean, I had so much to learn and to observe that I had

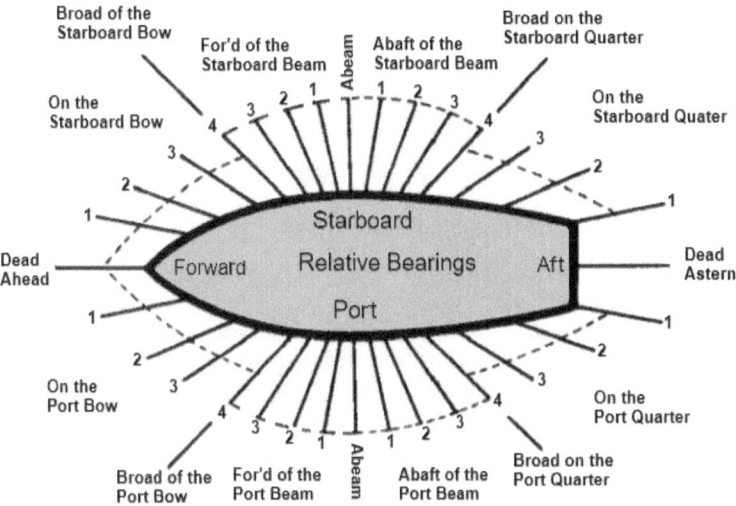

little time to feel sorry for myself. On the contrary, I was enjoying the experience to the full.

Now, after ten days at sea, we had reached the fine weather latitudes and picked up the northeast trade wind beneath a sunny sky. This wind to us was a fair following breeze, so we rolled along at eight or nine knots, on a south-westerly course, with dry decks — and dry clothes. On the first day of sunny weather, all hands and the cook and our passenger, Dr. Hilton, hung out their damp clothes to dry on lines stretched fore and aft and thwartship, making sure that they did not foul any of the running gear.

When we reached the fine weather latitudes, all hands were called on deck for a full day's work changing the suit of sails. This meant that all the hard weather heavy sails, or "storm canvas," had to be unbent and sent down on deck, to be stowed in the sail locker, and sails of lighter canvas sent aloft and bent and set.

The *County of Pembroke* was not a famous flyer, but she had a fair turn of speed. With favourable winds she could rail about 250 miles (402 km) in a day. On the long voyage to Australia, covering some 12,000 miles (19312 km) in three months, she averaged approximately 130 miles (209 km) a day. Such calculations of the speed of a sailing vessel on long ocean routes were necessarily not as simple as those of steamers, which can steer direct courses. The track of a sailing vessel is often a complicated zigzag, especially when headwinds are encountered, and frequent tacks are necessary to make headway. The total distance run by a sailing vessel on a long voyage is therefore considerably greater than the route from port to port shown on maps of ocean routes followed by steamers.

The usual route of sailing vessels from the English Channel to Australia was around the Cape of Good Hope. After clearing the Chops of the Channel, they steered — wind and weather permitting — in a SSW direction until they picked up the NE trade wind in about latitude 35 deg. N.

Then, with this wind on the port quarter, they ran to the southward, giving the Cape Verde Islands a wide berth. The NE trade wind petered out about three or four degrees north of the equator, and the vessels entered the "doldrums," a region of calms and light variable airs with sudden thunderstorms and squalls from any direction. To work through the doldrums meant a great deal of pully-hauly, taking in and making sail and hauling around the yards to take advantage of every favourable draught in making a laborious southing across "the line."

About four or five degrees south of the equator, the sailing vessels would pick up the SE trade wind, another steady breeze, in fine weather. This was a leading wind for outward bound vessels, which meant that they were braced sharp up on the port tack to avoid being carried too far to the westward. In most cases, however, vessels making a southing were carried well out into mid-ocean in the South Atlantic.

The SE trades would last until about 35 deg. S, the region of the "roaring forties." In these latitudes, strong westerly winds or gales prevail during most seasons of the year but at some times may veer even to easterly winds. With ordinary luck, a shipmaster, on reaching the roaring forties, could count on having fair westerly winds, coming from any point in the quadrant from NW to SW. This enabled him to "run the easting down" from the South Atlantic, passing to the south of the Cape of

Good Hope and across the South Indian Ocean to Australia, a vast stretch of ocean in which gales and high following seas prevail.

In the 1890s there were still some sailing vessels carrying passengers to Australia. They put into intermediate ports, such as Madeira, the Canary Islands, the Cape Verde Islands, Ascension, Saint Helena, Cape Town, or Durban — not all of these on every voyage, but one or more, usually including Cape Town — to take on or set down passengers, mail, and freight. More especially these calls were made for health reasons, to provide the passengers and crews with fresh provisions and water and a chance to stretch their legs on shore.

It was otherwise with cargo vessels, which usually avoided putting into intermediate ports, thereby saving the owners the expense of port dues and of buying fresh provisions. Their route took the best possible advantage of the trade winds and the roaring forties and avoided some pully-hauly which might be required on short tacks in bearing up for ports.

Similarly, on a homeward voyage from Australia, sailing vessels usually ran the easting down to the south of New Zealand and around Cape Horn, taking advantage of the prevailing westerly fierce winds and gales of the forties and fifties in the South Pacific.

On this historic trade route of sail, which was discovered by mariners in the centuries before the Suez Canal and Panama Canal were opened, the continents of Africa and South America were bypassed in the only stretches of open water available, namely, at their southern extremities. The cutting of the canals was of no practical advantage to sailing vessels, as heavy towage tees would be required to get them through the narrow waters of these "short cuts." The routes around the Cape of Good Hope and Cape Horn therefore continued to be used by mariners in sail for more than half a century after the Suez Canal was opened in 1869. Old habits die hard.

On a complete voyage, outward and homeward from a European port to Australia, a sailing vessel circumnavigated the globe, on a track of some 24,000 miles (38624 km), with a call at perhaps only one port of destination to discharge and take in cargo there and to replenish provisions and water.

Allowing not less than three months for the passage each way and one month each for the turnaround in the home port and the destination port, it was in practice impossible to complete a voyage in less than eight months, but usually the time taken was from ten months to a year. This was a slow movement of cargoes under sail, as compared with the competition of steamers, especially of those using the Suez Canal route to and from Australia. It was mainly for this reason that sail in the merchant marine became unprofitable and eventually obsolete; but seamen under sail, in their long passages, out of sight of land for months, had better opportunities than those in steam to appreciate to the full the "Peace of God" in the ocean's immensities. I first became aware of this when the *County of Pembroke* reached the fine weather latitudes and picked up the NE Tradewind. Then, when we changed the suit of sails, I was allowed to go aloft for the first time; I found the experience enthralling. I was as active aloft as a young monkey. Soon I got to know the names of the sails and of the various ropes, downhauls, halyards, leech lines, clewgarnets, braces, sheets, and tacks, and how to find them all on the darkest nights. The sailors taught me knots and splices and how to make sennit and baggy-wrinkle and apply seizing.

The officers and the two elder apprentices took a kindly interest in my elementary studies of the theory of navigation. I had to learn by heart how to box the compass — learning by heart the thirty-two points of direction marked around the compass card. During night watches the Mate pointed out to me the various constellations and planets. "Planets don't twinkle — stars do!" he explained. I had never in my life been in a position to see the night sky all around the horizon; but very soon I was able to pick out Polaris, the Plow, Orion's Belt, the Dog Star, and many more; and the planets; and to appreciate the immeasurable majesty of "the spacious firmament on high."

The lore of sail has become obsolete in our mechanized age, but part of its fascination was in the romantic and sometimes inexplicable names of every part of a sailing vessel and of all the gear and equipment. The nautical lingo made sailors of all nations a race apart from landlubbers. This Esperanto of the sea had evolved, during centuries of usage, from sources almost impossible to trace, passed on by word of mouth from generation to generation of seamen, most of whom were unable to read or write; but they knew unerringly the meanings of hundreds of technical terms that had a power of enchantment.

At times their very lives and the lives of all on board a vessel might depend on the correct and instantaneous response to an order given in that nautical jargon which was gibberish to a landsman but of vital reality to a sailor. Many of these words have now passed out of use among seafaring men in mechanically propelled vessels, who have specialist vocabularies of their own and can afford to be less watchful of wind, weather, and seas than the old time sailors had to be. Much of what I learned in sail was of little use to me in mechanically powered vessels; yet, after more than fifty years, the magical old words I learned as a boy came back to me, as I think of the buttock shrouds, vangs, dead eyes, gaskets, buntlines; or of goose-winging a topsail, or steering by the wind or full and by, or using a handy-billy; or I recall scraps of weather wisdom I learned in the *County of Pembroke*:

> *First the rain and then the wind:*
> *To the yards your canvas bend;*
> *Or*
> *Topsail halyards you must mind.*
> *First the wind and then the rain:*
> *Let your flying kites remain....*

and much more of the same that modern sailors scarcely need to know.

Some of the nautical expressions were intended to be funny. One of these, "Splice the main brace" — an order issued by the Captain for a tot of rum to all hands and the cook, as a reward for special effort after the crew had been aloft for hours handling sail in heavy weather — gained its meaning from the fact that the main brace is the name of a strong rope which is very rarely spliced. Though sailors were notorious for their drunken sprees in port, at sea they were necessarily sober and practically teetotallers, for months on end. Any grog that might have been brought into the fo'c'sle at the beginning of a voyage would be finished on the first or second day out, if not previously confiscated by the Mate. Then the only alcohol allowed in the ship apart from any that might be well buried in the cargo — was under lock and key in the Captain's cabin, for emergencies only. The men who worked aloft, at heights of up to 150 feet (45m) above the deck, balancing on a swaying footrope, perhaps in the darkness of night or in a blizzard, when one slip would mean certain death, were compelled to be sober, if only by their lack of access to any supply of grog.

It was not surprising then, that "Jack ashore" tried to make up for lost time; but seamen at sea lived and worked hard and cleanly and kept their wits unfuddled(sic), as they needed to do to survive. The shore folk in ports saw them at their worst and never when they were at their best, in their own element.

Irishmen were a source of wit, afloat as on shore. A dead calm was known as "Paddy's hurricane." Frayed ends of rope or yarns, blowing about in the rigging, were known as "Irish pennants." Any self-respecting officer of the watch would react to these like a bull to a red rag; on noticing them, he would at once send an apprentice aloft to cut them free.

In heavy weather, when the crew wore oilskin coats and trousers, they tied strands of rope yarn around their waists, ankles and wrists, to help keep the water out. These yarns were known as "soul-and-body lashings." Some seamen always went barefoot in fine weather. In very wintry weather, if they had no socks, they wrapped their feet in small squares of burlap before putting on their sea boots, as a precaution against frostbitten toes. These foot wraps were known in British ships as "Prince Alberts," in honour of Queen Victoria's husband, the Prince Consort; but I never discovered how the royal name came to be applied to them.

As seamen worked watch and watch — four hours on and four hours off, with the dog watch of two hours interposed in the afternoon to provide a fair alternation of day and night work for each watch throughout the voyage — no sailor in either of the watches could have more than three and a half hours of effective sleep at one stretch in his bunk, at any time throughout the voyage. This applied also to the officers of the watches and to the apprentices. We worked an average twelve-hour day, seven days in the week, with no time off for Sundays or holidays. This was equivalent to an eighty-four hour week, worked in what would be called on shore "broken time." The dog watches meant that on alternate days one watch had fourteen hours and the other ten hours on deck in each twenty-four hours.

Workers on shore, in mines, factories, or mills, had three shifts of eight hours, if production went on for twenty-four hours a day, and usually no Sunday work; but sailors averaged a twelve-hour day for months on end and accepted this as normal. In heavy weather or other emergencies, the watch below would be called out to help the watch on deck with reefing or making sail, or other work, with no thought of being paid overtime.

The pay for an Able Seaman — "able bodied," able to steer, and able to do anything in a ship"— was three pounds a month, and for an Ordinary Seaman one pound, ten shillings a month; with quarters and food (of a sort) provided, but not clothing. The working garb of dungarees, oilskins, sea boots, and woollen singlets or guernseys, and other items such as tobacco, soap and matches, could be purchased from the Captain's slop chest, on one day each week at a fixed time; the value would be debited to the seaman's wage account, to be settled at paying off time at the end of the voyage. Seamen could obtain goods from the slop chest only when their accounts were in credit, not otherwise.

With these deductions, and with cash advances to the seaman's dependents or to the seaman himself for a spree in the destination port, there remained a pitiably small sum of money for him to draw on his discharge in his home port, at the end of a voyage, as payment for ten months' or a year's work, or sometimes even longer periods of up to three years. No wonder, then, that Dr. Johnson remarked, "No man will be a sailor who has contrivance enough to get himself into a jail."

But Dr. Johnson was a landlubber, who never experienced the lure of the ocean solitudes which Conrad called the Peace of God — the feeling which every sailor knows of being insignificant in immensity. There, a thousand miles (1609 km) and more from land, men, especially those in a sailing vessel, become aware of the scintillating rotation of the universe in a way that the landbound can never know.

Even though sailors on watch are supposed never to be idle for a moment, each man has time to think, and is almost compelled to observe every mood of the sky and the sea in the ever changing pageant of colour and light, at every hour around the clock, by night and by day, in fair weather, storms, and calms, as the horizon forever recedes ahead and closes in astern, with the ship in the centre of that progressing circle.

According to scientists, all life began in the sea and later crept on shore. The sea is full of primal energy; to be in harmony with the sea is to be in contact with the elemental forces of nature. This was well understood by the Psalmist, who remarked that in "the great and wide sea are things creeping innumerable, both small and great beasts," and added: "There go the ships, and there is that Leviathan whom thou hast made to play therein"" (Psalm 104:26 KJV.)

Whether the Leviathan was a whale or a sea serpent or a creature of

A forest of masts, sailing ships waiting for cargo at a British Port (Bisset)

imagination, it symbolizes the elemental force that conquers the mind of sailors when they are far from the land and enables them to endure discomforts which they could never tolerate on shore.

In the *County of Pembroke* nineteen men and three youths were confined for three months within the restricted deck space of a barque only 221 feet (67m) long from stem to stern, existing on unpalatable food, and "with nothing to see but the sea," having no alcohol (except a rare occasional tot), no contacts with femininity, no news of the world, no organized recreations, sports or entertainments, no luxuries of any kind, no milk or eggs, no fresh fruit or vegetables, no holidays, and working an eighty-four hour week. It might be thought that they would find the life unbearably monotonous and would be worse off than men in jail (as Dr. Johnson imagined sailors to be).

The fact of the matter was that tens of thousands of sailors, knowing that these conditions were to be expected, went willingly to sea and had done so in all the centuries of deep sea sailing. They knew well that life at sea, though often uncomfortable and at times dangerous, was never sure, since no man knew what lay ahead of him, in the next week, the next day, the next watch, or the next hour or minute, in the ever changing conditions of wind and weather and the vessel's geographical position.

Far from being monotonous, life and work at sea were of ever changing variety, at the caprice of the elements or of the officers — who could find a thousand different tasks for seamen to do — to keep the vessel shipshape, when they were not actually handling sail. In most of these tasks, a sailor had to use his brains as well as his muscles. He had to be constantly alert, not only for his own safety, but for the safety of the whole company on board.

Unlike convicts picking oakum or breaking stones, or factory workers repeating one process, the sailor had to apply a wide variety of skills to a great number of practical tasks each day. He was kept too busy to become discontented or bored. Even the men on lookout or at the wheel in fine weather mid-ocean did not dare to daydream too long, before the ship herself, "walking the waters like a thing of life," recalled them to reality.

Life under sail appealed to men of a roving disposition, who sought, in the freedom of the wide oceans and in the constant movement of far voyaging, to get away from restrictions of a home life on shore or the monotony and sometimes sordid greed of shore jobs. Though they soon found that life at sea had many disadvantages, they became aware also that ii had many moments of beauty, not only of scene but of action, which appeal to man's romantic or poetic instincts. This was the compensation for all the discomforts that had to be endured. It was the reason why men had gone to sea from time immemorial and continued going to sea: the reason why sailors who deserted their ship signed on in another after a short spell ashore.

After we had been at sea for a week or ten days our provisions of fresh meat and vegetables, taken on board at Liverpool, were finished or had gone bad. For the rest of the voyage, we had to live on hardtack (biscuits) with salt beef, salt pork, tinned mutton, coffee, and tea. There was no refrigeration in sailing vessels; no electric light; and only a very restricted amount of fresh water, carried in tanks below deck amidships and drawn from a pump in buckets once each day.

I began to feel tarnished every day. One day I told a seaman I felt hungry. "Never mind," he said, "you can always get a good feed o' wind puddings."

Thinking I had been missing something, I asked, "What are they?"

"Put y'r 'ead over the t'gallant rail," he said, "an' take a few good gasps o' ozone. Them's wind puddings!"

The Board of Trade scale of provisions in 1898 was known to seamen as "the pound and pint," because these words appeared several times in the text. The ration Was known as "the whack," this term being applied to the issue of fresh water as well as of food the daily ration of meat was three quarters of a pound of salt beef or half a pound of salt pork.

The beef in tierces and pork in casks were put into ready use "harness casks," lashed to the poop deck rail, and weighed out from the harness casks to be whacked out from the cook's galley after being cooked. We had beef on Mondays, Wednesdays, and Fridays, and pork on Sundays, Tuesdays, and Thursdays. On Saturdays the ration was varied with Australian tinned mutton.

This was a novelty in those days when the art of canning was in its infancy. The mutton, shipped at Melbourne, was in seven-pound cans, which bore a label containing the words "Harriet Lane." This might have been the address of the distributors, but some sailor man with a gruesome imagination had started a rumour which many, including myself, believed. According to this yarn, a lady named Harriet Lane, when visiting the cannery, had fallen into a vat of boiling mutton. Rather than waste the boiling, the Canners had canned Harriet with the mutton. Nobody which cans contained Harriet. This made the ration Harriet Lane mutton an interesting lottery.

For the first few weeks of the voyage, we had, while the supply lasted, a whack of boiled salt fish on Fridays. As we got into warm weather, the fish smelled so high on that it was taken to the maintop and lashed there securely in a box until required. As the voyage proceeded, the pork and beef in the harness casks also smelled "high," but sailors had stomachs of leather and could not be choosers.

Onions were used to flavour the stew, but they sprouted in the tropics and soon disappeared from the menu. Potatoes were issued with the meat at midday dinner for about a fortnight after leaving port. Most of the "spuds" then want rotten and were thrown overboard. We had no other vegetables and no fresh fruit throughout the voyage.

Soon after we left port and began using salt provisions, the cook issued the compulsory Board of Trade ration of One fluid ounce of lime juice per man per day. Containing vitamins (as they are nowadays called), the lime juice was a preventative of scurvy and beriberi.

Compulsory in the Royal Navy as well as in the Merchant Marine, the lime juice enabled British ships to remain at sea for prolonged periods without need of putting into ports — and incurring the expense of port dues — to obtain fresh fruit or vegetables. For this reason, British sailing vessels were known as "lime juicers." The cook mixed the lime juice with water and a little sugar and doled it out in pannikins. A man would be fined three pence a day for not drinking it, but I never saw anyone refuse. In hot weather it was a palatable drink.

According to the Board of Trade scale, each man was given a ration of one pound of "bread" per day. This usually consisted of five hard baked biscuits. Each biscuit had forty-two holes in one side, to let the heat of the oven bake it as hard as concrete. The other side was smooth. The biscuits for the day were kept in a wooden box, called a "bread barge," which was hung up to the deckhead, in the half deck and fo'c'sle, to prevent rats from getting at it.

Twice a week our German cook baked soft bread, from white flour. These loaves were known as "rooties," which I believe is a Hindustani word, adopted from the olden days of the East India Company's merchantmen. After we had reached the tropics, the rooties became inedible, as the yeast went mouldy. One of our sailors complained to the cook of this. "You couldn't cook hot water for a barber's shop!" he said.

German Charlie promptly hit the sailor on the point of the jaw and knocked him out. "By shiminy," he bellowed, "you vill eat der rotten rooties or go mitout!"

As the voyage proceeded, the ship's biscuits became weevilly. The weevils hid in the forty-two holes. The game was to thump the biscuits on the deck, with the holed side downward, to knock the weevils out. Paddy Murphy scorned to do this. "Eat the weevils and all," he advised me. "Sure, and they're fresh meat!"

Once a week, on "whack day," each man was given a ration of three quarters of a pound of tinned butter, three quarters of a pound of jam, and one pound of sugar. In the tropics the butter was a yellow oil. Each man and boy kept his week's supply of butter, jam, and sugar in tins or basins in his locker. Some guzzled the lot in a couple of days and went without for the rest of the week. It was an unforgivable crime and practically unheard of for one man to touch another man's whack.

Some mixed the butter, jam, and sugar together into a "spread," to put on the biscuits. This made it last longer, especially if it was spread on the plain side of the biscuits, so that none got into the holes. When the ration of sugar was used in this way, we had none left to put in our tea or coffee.

Small quantities of beans, peas, rice, and dried fruit, a few ounces per man per week, were included in the Board Of Trade scale. These were weighed out to the cook for the whole crew and served up cooked with meals. The beans and rice were used in soup or stews and the dried fruit in the once-a-week plum duff on Sundays — the only day when we had a dessert, and the plums in the duff were aged and far between.

Each man was given a ration of three quarts of fresh water per day. This was doled out by the Second Mate from the pump abaft the mainmast. From each man's whack two quarts were deducted for the "cook's whack," for making tea, coffee, and soup and for cooking our meat.

That left each man one quart of water per day, for drinking, ablutions, and laundry. As the voyage lengthened, the water in the

A serving of hardtack, salt pork, and tea (AI)

storage tanks became smelly and stale in taste. When rain fell, we rigged buckets, tubs, or tins, to catch fresh water which dripped from the sails and deckhouse roofs.

The meat ration and soup or potatoes (while these lasted) were served at the midday dinner. We had only one meat meal a day. For breakfast, we had coffee, rooties or biscuits, and a spread of "whack." For the evening meal, tea, rooties or biscuits with "whack" (while it lasted), or a scrap of meat saved, according to individual self-control, from the midday meal.

After rooties disappeared from the menu, the weevilly biscuits were our staff of life. Soaking them in coffee or tea scarcely softened them. The coffee and tea were served black, but tins of condensed milk could be bought (while the supply lasted) on credit from the slop chest.

In attempts to make the biscuits palatable we placed them in a canvas bag, pounded them to powder with a belaying pin, moistened the mess with water, added jam and a piece of fat, mixed all well together in a tin, and have it to the cook to bake in the oven. This was the recipe for "dandy funk."

Another recipe, according to individual fancy and the ingredients available, consisted of broken biscuits mixed with leftover pea soup, scraps of fat pork, and anything else obtainable, and baked in a tin. This was "cracker hash."

The recipes varied on different vessels, in accordance with the old saying, "Different ships, different long splices," — or different fashions, which means the same thing — and this applied not only to the recipe for cracker hash, but to ways of doing everything on shipboard. Though methods differed on different vessels, the results were about the same on all. Cracker hash and dandy funk were desperate attempts to make hard and weevilly biscuits palatable. The monotony of diet, when a vessel was keeping the seas on a long voyage, was by far the most disagreeable aspect of life under sail.

Making Our Numbers — My First Trick at the Wheel —
"Breakers Ahead!" — Hearing the Log — "The Chinaman" —
Some "Don'ts" for First Voyagers — Learning the Ropes — The
Doldrums — The Key to the Keelson.

HUNGER made me feel homesick, but otherwise I took to my new career like a duck to water, and gradually I became convinced that I could learn to become a sailor, if I kept on trying hard enough.

One afternoon in the dog watch, as we were bowling along placidly in the trade wind, I opened my sea chest and rummaged in it for soap to wash my dirty dungarees. Hungry in usual, I was overjoyed to discover that my dear mother, without telling me, had stowed among my clothes some bars of chocolate, a few apples, and a pound of tea! I don't mind confessing that, when I turned into my bunk that night, after my watch on deck, as I chewed a piece of that doubly delicious chocolate, I shed a few secret tears, thinking of my kindly parents and the comforts of home. But the homesickness, like the chocolate and apples, did not last long.

I was usually so dog tired when I turned into my bunk that I fell instantly into deep sleep to be awakened only too soon by the apprentice in the other watch, warning me to tumble out for my watch on deck. In fine weather, especially during the hours of darkness, when there was little work to be done in handling sail, the officer of the watch paced the weather side of the poop. An apprentice paced the lee side, with the duty of watching the clock in the companionway and sounding the ship's bell with the right number of strokes at the passing of the half hours.

Then the voice of the lookout man, stationed on the forecastlehead or on top of the forward deckhouse, would be heard singing out, "All's well and lights burning brightly." If the port and starboard lights or the binnacle lamp on the compass were burning smokily (sic) or blown out, it was the duty of the apprentice to trim and relight them and, if necessary, refill the lamps with oil.

Occasionally the voice of the lookout would be wafted aft, announcing the lights of another vessel in the vast darkness ahead of us, or to port or starboard, or, in daytime, the thrilling call, "Sa-a-il Ho!" usually indicating that the skysails, royals or topgallants of some other vessel were visible coming up over the horizon. The officer of the watch would at once bring the telescope to bear and examine the stranger, to ascertain her course, rig, speed, identity, and to read her signals.

While she remained within our circle of vision, the stranger was an object of intense interest to us, as we were to the men in her, not only to avoid collision, but also because, in those days before radio, visual signalling between vessels was the only way of reporting and recording maritime movements in mid-ocean.

When ships came in full view of one another, they "made their numbers," that is, hoisted combinations of two, three, or four flags on their gaffs, identifying themselves by their numbers in the international codebook; and sometimes added information about their ports of departure and destination and the number of days they were out from port; or asked one another, "What is your longitude?" In emergencies other signals, such as those of distress, starvation, or need of medical aid, might be hoisted at these encounters and had to be carefully looked for.

The signal flags were selected by the officer of the watch end, on his orders, hoisted by a seaman or apprentice. The Captain was usually called up to the poop deck to eye the stranger and always found something wrong with her rig or the way in which she was being handled, as the Captain in the other vessel did with regard to our rig and handling, on spying us.

As we drew away from the main lanes of shipping in the north Atlantic, we sighted few vessels, for the ocean is very wide.

One fine day when we were bowling along in the NE trades, with a spanking breeze on the port quarter and all sails set and drawing nicely, a great event in my life occurred. I was scrubbing the wheel-box gratings with sand and canvas while one of the Welsh seamen,

Looking forrard from the mainmast head with all sails set to a quartering breeze. (Bisset)

Johnny Jones, was at the wheel.

The Captain came on to the poop in a jovial mood, and said to me, "Have you ever steered a ship, Jimmy?"

"No, sir," I stammered, excitedly and hopefully. "Never!"

"Can you box the compass?"

I had already learned to repeat, like a parrot, the thirty-two points of direction. "Yes, sir," I said, "I can box it."

"Well, box it now," the Captain ordered.

Staring aloft, I began reciting in a sing-song voice, "North; North by East; North-Northeast; Northeast by North; Northeast." Then I drew a deep breath and continued, "Northeast by East; East-Northeast; East by North; East; East by South . . ."

"All right," the Captain interrupted, "you can box it, I see! Now, what's the opposite to Northeast by North?"

I closed my eyes, swayed on my feet, and, with a mighty effort of memory, blurted out, "Southwest by South, sir!"

"Good, m'son, we'll make a sailor of you, yet. Now take the wheel, and let's see what sort of a job you make of it." Then he said to the helmsman, "Keep an eye on him."

I was as proud as a dog with two tails. The Captain went below, and Jones said to me, "The course is South by West. Now, look into the binnacle, Jimmy, and you'll see that the Lubber Line on the side of the bowl is foreninst[1] S by W on the card, and you must keep it there, as near as possible. Now, you have to remember that the Compass Card does not move. It is fast to its magnetic needle, with its North point bearing North. The Lubber Line moves with the direction of the ship's head, so you have to keep your eye on that, and keep that Lubber Line on the course. Understand?"

With a few spokes this way and that he steadied her on S by W, then handed the wheel over to me. The glory of it! Actually, steering a three-masted barque with all sail set in mid-ocean! I was so overcome by the thought that, before I knew what was happening, she had strayed a couple of points off course. Johnny Jones, a patient man, said, "Indeed to goodness, Jimmy, are you trying to write you name on the wake?

Steady now, give her a few spokes to port, and she'll soon settle down. Keep your Lubber Line on S by W and never mind dreaming!"

After ten minutes or so I had the feel of the helm and was able to steer a straight course. Thereafter, while the weather was fine, I was often allowed to steer, with an A.B. standing by.

After a fortnight at sea we were nearing the latitude of the Cape Verde Islands. I noticed that the Captain and the Mate conferred when they took a sight of the sun at noon, comparing results. Then the Captain went below to lay off our position on the chart. He came on deck again presently and said to the Mate, "Keep a sharp lookout this afternoon and tonight, Mister. I reckon that on this course we should pass thirty miles (48 km) to the westward of the islands. Warn the lookouts to keep their eyes peeled!"

No matter how confident the Captain might be of his position, he was

On a barque looking aft from the mainmast head onto the poop, a quartering breeze in the trade winds. (Bisset)

taking no chances of piling the barque onto a reef, during the hours of darkness when we would be bowling along at a nice speed, with all sail set to the royals, in a fair wind.

"Aye, aye, sir," said the Mate. At the changes of the watch during the afternoon, he went forward with the Second Mate to the forecastlehead and spoke especially to the lookout man. They scanned the southern and eastern horizons with the telescope but saw nothing of land. The senior apprentice was sent aloft on the foremast, at sunset, but reported no land in sight.

Night fell suddenly, and it was pitch dark at the change of the watches at 8 p m when the Mate's watch took over. Our first duty was to "sweat her up," which meant hauling In the slack caused by the slight

The wheel at the helm of the ship along with compass (AI image)

stretching of halyards and other lines under the press of sail in the steady breeze — a routine task at the change of the watch in the trade winds. While this was still in progress and the watch below had not yet turned into their bunks, the newly posted lookout man on the forward deckhouse suddenly sang out at the top of his voice, "Land ho! Breakers ahead!"

At this dread cry every seaman on board knew that we were in peril. The men of the watch below ran out on deck, to join the others peering ahead. Sure enough, from dead ahead to about four points on the port bow a crescent of gleaming white lay on the dark surface of the seas, not more than half a mile (800m) away.

The Captain had come up to the poop at the change of the watch and was still there, gazing at the stars in the velvety darkness. He instantly reacted to the lookout's warning, and his orders rang out crisply, "Hard up the helm! Stand by the fore and main braces! All hands on deck!"

There was a pandemonium of bawled orders as the two mates got their watches tailed on to haul the yards around, the men also singing out hoarsely as they hauled on the braces. As the barque paid off before the wind and gradually came to on the starboard tack, she ran into the edge of the gleaming white area and shipped some heavy dollops of water over the lee rail.

Instantly the decks were lit up, as with bright moonlight, by dozens of phosphorescent jellyfish slopping about as the vessel lurched and righted herself. The Captain was the first to comprehend what had happened. We had run into a dense mass of jellyfish floating on the surface. When seen from a distance by the lookout man in the darkness of the night, the luminescence they emitted had resembled breakers on a hidden reef.

"Belay everything!" roared the Captain. "Keep clear of those jellyfish, or they'll sting you!"

The threat of impending disaster had turned to farce as the barefooted seamen, in the ghostly light, nimbly dodged the shining, flopping jellyfish, shouting with laughter and relieved emotions as they saw what had caused the false alarm of shipwreck peril. In a few minutes the jellyfish had slithered out through the scuppers and washports. The phosphorescent mass gleamed ghostly on our lee, extending for about a mile (1.6 km). We stood away to the westward for two hours, and the phosphorescence soon faded astern. The Captain intended to be quite sure that we were giving the Cape Verde Islands a wide berth, and nobody could consider his decision unwise after the fright we had received.

Chronometers carried in sailing vessels were often inaccurate. There was always some doubt of a vessel's longitude, even if the latitude was accurately fixed. The senior apprentices said next day that the Second Mate had told them that our encounter with the jellyfish had occurred exactly in the latitude of the Cape Verde Islands, but about thirty miles (48 km) to the westward, according to the Captain's reckoning.

I have never since seen such a dense mass of marine phosphorescence as on that occasion. The jellyfish "reef" was so extensive, and the shining creatures in i t so numerous, that it was like a floating luminous island. There must have been millions of them crowded together in a gigantic swarm, for some freakish natural reason which I cannot guess.

Three weeks after leaving port, we were about 2,500 miles (4023 km) from England. One morning the Captain came up as usual to the poop deck, looked around at the sky, and said to the Mate, "Heave the log, Mister."

The Mate went below and presently emerged with a hand log and sandglass. He handed the sandglass to me. I had already been taught my duty, which was a not very difficult part in the operation of heaving the log. The other apprentice in the Mate's watch, Bill Huxley, and a teaman stood by as the log was heaved. The purpose of the operation was to estimate the vessel's speed in knots, that is nautical miles per hour. (A nautical mile is 6,080 feet (1853m), being equivalent to one minute of longitude at the mean of the Great Circle of the earth and is 800 feet (243m) longer than a land mile, or British statute mile.)

The hand log was a primitive apparatus. It consisted of a long line on a reel, with a small, cone shaped canvas bag at the end. When this bag was thrown overboard astern, it filled with water and acted as a drogue which pulled the line off the reel. The first fifteen fathoms (i.e., 90 feet or 27.4m) of line to run out was called "stray line," and allowed the bag to fill with water.

A piece of white rag tied around the line marked the end of the stray line. When this rag passed over the stern, the apprentice standing by with the half-minute sandglass turned the glass over, and the measuring of the speed began. The line was marked, at precalculated intervals, with knotted yarn, so placed that the number of these knots which ran out over the stern in half a minute indicated the number of nautical miles per hour at which the vessel was traveling through the water.

The Mate gave the reel an occasional twitch to insure that the line ran out freely. The moment the sand ran out the boy sang out "Stop!" and the men grabbed the line, holding it while the Mate noted, by the nearest mark, what speed the vessel was doing. On this occasion ten knots and a little more of the line had passed over the stern when the sand ran out.

"Stop!" I sang out.

"What's she doing, Mister?" asked the Captain. "Ten and a Chinaman, sir," replied the Mate.

The Captain went below to lay off the barque's position, on his chart, while we hauled in and reeled up the log line. I couldn't understand what a Chinaman had to do with our speed. It was clear to me that the expression meant that we were doing a little more than ten knots and less than eleven, and that everyone understood what was meant except me.

Later in the day Bill Huxley explained the matter to me, as he had heard it from an old shellback on a previous voyage. In the days of the smart Yankee clippers sailing from 'Frisco to China, there was in one of these clippers a Chinese cabin boy, who couldn't be taught to do anything right. One day, when the Bucko Mate was getting ready to heave the log, the cabin boy came up the companionway to the poop deck, with a bucket of slops which he emptied to windward.

The slops blew back into the Mate's face. The clipper was slipping along at a smart pace. With a roar of rage, the Bucko Mate grabbed the cabin boy, bent the end of the log line around his waist, threw him over the stern, and hove the log with him as a drogue!

After the speed had been determined, the sailors quickly hauled in the line and dumped the half-drowned culprit on the deck. At this moment, the Captain appeared on the poop and asked, "What's the speed, Mister?"

"Ten and a Chinaman, sir," answered the Bucko. Ever since then, any fraction of speed over the knot has been referred to as "a Chinaman." This story, which I believed at the time and probably still believe, had a moral, which was: Don't throw any liquid to windward, and don't even spit to windward on shipboard.

There were many other "Don'ts." One day, when I had the menial task of scrubbing out the Captain's cabin, I said to him, with appalling ignorance, "Shall I wash your bedroom floor, sir?"

He looked at me indignantly. "The floor, boy?" he said. " Never call a deck a floor. And never call a cabin a bedroom! Indeed to goodness, m'son, you talk like a sojer, not a sailor. Keep your wits about you and learn the right sea talk. Don't call decks floors; don't call bulkheads walls; don't call aft behind, or forrard in front, or you'll never be a sailor!"

I hung my head in shame. "And another thing," he continued, "never be guilty of calling a ship a boat, or your Captain a skipper! Now get on with your work, m'son, and scrub the deck in my cabin as clean as a hound's tooth!" So my nautical education steadily proceeded. It was a long time before I "learned the ropes" — which meant learning that there are very few "ropes" in a sailing vessel. The average landsman might think that the standing rigging and running gear of a large sailing craft is a "maze of ropes." In a literal sense he might be correct, as the top hamper of a windjammer consists chiefly of a complicated arrangement of wire ropes and hempen (or manila) ropes connected with the spars and sails and manipulated with tackles and other gear.

But to sailors every part of the standing rigging and running rigging had a name, and in these names the word "rope" was rarely used. There were halyards, braces, sheets, lifts, clew lines, buntlines, leach lines, downhauls, robands, gaskets, stirrups, shrouds, ratlines, stays, hawsers, springs, warps, whips, lashings, lanyards, painters, and many more, as if sailors deliberately avoided the word "rope"—perhaps because "the rope" in olden days meant "the hangman's hempen haul" or a flogging with a "rope's end."

There were, as far as I can now remember, only seven "ropes," so called, in the *County of Pembroke*. These were: (1) the footropes, on which men stood when working out on the yards; (2) boltropes, sewn around the edges of sails; (3) wheel ropes, for steadying the steering gear; (4) manropes, for safety purposes on gangways and pilot ladders (but these were known as "lifelines" when rigged fore and aft along decks awash in heavy weather); (5) bucket ropes, for hauling up buckets of sea water overside; (6) towropes for towing by tugs or other craft (alternately known as "hawsers"); and (7) boat ropes (alternately known as "painters"), for securing boats alongside or astern.

I have an uneasy feeling that some old sea dog may recall one or two other "ropes" that I have forgotten; but different ships had different long splices, and all the experts will agree that very few ropes in the windjammers were called "ropes."

So the old saying, "You must know the ropes," meant more than it seemed to mean.

One morning, when I was turned out of my bunk for a watch on deck at 4 a.m., I became sleepily aware that the barque was at a standstill except for a slight rising and falling in a gentle ocean swell. We were in the doldrums, becalmed. There was not a breath of wind, from any point of the compass. The sails hung limply from the yards. A red dawn flushed the sky, revealing a vast expanse of unruffled glassy water on all sides, in which we appeared to be stuck fast, like a fly on flypaper. Then the sun came up in full tropical power, pouring his burning rays on us and the ocean, as he climbed to the vertical at noon.

During that day and for fourteen days thereafter, the only breaths of wind were occasional cat's paw breezes, eddying unpredictably and dying as capriciously as they began. As these light airs partly filled our sails, sometimes coming from ahead and threatening to take us aback, all hands and the cook were called out to tail on, hurriedly hauling around the yards, so that we could gain perhaps a few miles of way, on one tack or another, before the fitful breeze died. By these methods we might make a southing of about 50 or 60 miles (80 km – 96 km) in each twenty-four hours.

A pull on the fore sheet. (Bisset)

This was a trying time for all on board. Nothing can be more helpless than a sailing vessel becalmed. "Ach," said Fritz, one of our German seamen, "now ve have Paddy's hurricane, oop and down der mast!"

Every stitch of sail was set to the royals and staysails, but they hung loose and drooping and lifeless for hours on end. beam on and rolling in the ocean swell, the If we were sails banged and chafed against the masts. At these times the "courses" (the mains'l and fores'l) were clewed up braided up, to prevent them from flapping. The sailors hated this pully-hauly in the tropic heat, as the sails would have to be hurriedly set again at every puff of wind. The Captain, a firm believer in old superstitions, whistled softly at intervals tor a wind and took due credit for his efforts when a breeze sometimes came in answer to his summons.

The heat softened the pitch in the deck seams. When not handling sail, we were kept busy hauling up buckets of water from overside to souse the decks. We sweated at our work. The whack of one quart of tepid fresh water for each man was insufficient to quench our thirst. My face and arms were red with painful sunburn. The burning heat of the sun was reflected dazzlingly from the ocean, and the sky glistened like burnished copper.

Sunset and sunrise were blazes of crimson. At night in the cloudless sky the stars and planets shone like brilliant jewels on velvet. It was possible to read print on deck by starlight. When a breeze stirred, the wavelets flashed with the phosphorescence of floating marine organism, so that we seemed to be floating in a bowl of light.

There is an old saying that "ships draw together in the doldrums." Though we had seen very few vessels in the preceding fortnight, when we were snoring along in• the trade winds, we now had at times three, four or five in sight, all like us crawling along fitfully in the light airs or lying inert in the calms. The caprice of the cat's paw breezes was apparent from the different set of the sails and different courses steered by vessels only a few miles apart. The frequent tacks and the slow rate of progress brought within sight of each other vessels which, with stiffer and steadier breezes, might have passed in the night at a distance and been out of sight below the horizon before daylight came. One day in the dog watch, when we were in a dead calm, Paddy Murphy said to me, as I was skulking in the shade of the deckhouse, "Mr. Owen [the Mate] wants you to fetch him the key of the keelson."

I looked along the deck to the poop. The Mate was staring moodily astern over the taffrail. "And be lively," added Paddy.

"The key of the keelson?" I asked him. "What's that, and where do I find it?"

"Ask Mick," said Paddy. "He'll tell you." I went looking for Mick Casey and found him doing a bit of sailorizing in the fore shrouds.

"The key o' the keelson?" said Mick. "You'd better ask Fritz the Dutchy. He'll tell you where to lay your hands on it."

Fritz the Dutchy was in the watch below, lying in his bunk in the fo'c'sle, reading a penny dreadful. "Der key of der keelson?" he echoed, when I asked him. "You petter ask Yonny Yones. He had der key last veek."

Worried now, I went on the run to find John J o n e s , o n e o f t h e Welsh seamen, and found him seated in the waist, busy at his hobby of putting a ship in a bottle, a task which occupied him the whole voyage. He was singing a hymn in Welsh, tunefully, as he worked.

"Indeed to goodness," he said, "go and ask Rhys Davies where it is. He had it an hour ago, on the fo'c'slehead." The Mate was still staring moodily astern, but I feared his wrath at my delay, so I ran forward to the fo'c'slehead, where Rhys Davies, a grumpy man, was posted on lookout. "The key o' the keelson!" he growled. "Haven't you got any brains? There it is!" He pointed to one of the heavy iron levers for the windlass, which were unshipped and lashed to the bitts. "Hurry up," he said, "or the Mate will brain you with it!"

I unfastened the lashings and shouldered the heavy bar, which was as much as I could carry. Jeers followed me as I staggered along the deck with it and mounted the companionway to the poop. The Mate turned and saw me.

"What the hell are you doing with that?" he roared.

"It's the key of the keelson, sir," I stammered.

The Mate's scowl changed to a grin. "Go and stow it in the fog locker," he said, and turned away. Bewildered, I retired with my burden down the companionway and again interrupted John Jones's hymn singing. "Please, Johnny," I said, "where's the fog locker?" "It's where you got that bar from, you goose," said Johnny.

Comprehension dawned as I carried the heavy bar along the deck to the fo'c'slehead, enduring the good humoured jests of my shipmates, who had combined to take a rise out of a boy. It was not until some time later that I discovered that the keelson is the heaviest girder in a sailing vessel. It is an exceptionally strong and weighty girder, secured to the inside of the keel at the bottom of the vessel, from stem to stern. To get at it, at sea, the whole cargo would need to be moved. It has no "key."

Rhys Davies supervised me as I lashed the lever secure again.

"Never mind, Jimmy," he said. "You're not the only fool in this windbag. Every man Jack who goes to sea in old Thomas's hungry ships ought to have his head read, so they needn't laugh at you for being a fool!"

CHAPTER FOOTNOTES
(1) foreninst: beside or the opposite of. (Scottish origin)

In Mid-Atlantic — Crossing the Line — Distractions in the Doldrums — "Chips" Gets a Touch of the Sun — "The Bells of the Sea" — A Million to One Chance — A True Tale of a Bar of Soap — The Southeast Tradewind — Steering "By the Wind" — We Pick up the Westerlies

ON 13th November 1898 — one month and a day after our departure from Liverpool — we were on the equator, in Long. 26 deg. W, about 700 miles (1126 km) from Cape San Rogue in Brazil and 1,200 miles (1931 km) from the coast of Africa. In the earlier years of sail, outward bound vessels usually made their first port of call for refreshments at Rio de Janeiro in Brazil, and their second at Cape Town, running the easting down across the South Atlantic; but the development of clipper design in the nineteenth century, with improvements in rig and methods of handling sail, had enabled vessels to work more directly southward.

The *County of Pembroke* crossed the line, and for several days more we made laborious progress in the doldrums. Schools of dolphins played in the clear water alongside, and occasionally schools of flying fish, chased by albacore or bonito, leaped clear out of the water, skimmed along airborne for two or three hundred yards, then dived in again, leaving the pursuers unsighted. Some flying fish landed on our decks. These were eagerly picked up, as they made good eating, tasting like fresh herrings.

One day when we were becalmed, the Captain was standing with his hands behind his back, gazing over the taffrail. The Mate picked up a flying fish on the main deck. He came up behind the Captain and, without a word of warning, put the wet fish into his hand!

Captain Williams dropped the fish as if it had been a hot iron. He spun around and glared at the Mate. He had a waspish temper when aroused, and his face was red with rage as he roared, "What the — !"

"A fish for your lunch, sir," said the Mate, hurriedly.

Controlling his temper, the Captain growled, "Did I order fish for my lunch? No, I did not! Pick the damn thing up and throw it back into the water — and, by heavens, Mister, if you put a wet fish into my hands again, I'll log you for disrespect!"

In the doldrums, our carpenter ("Chips") became moody. He was a tall, gloomy man, with sallow features, piercing black eyes and a drooping black Mustache, who spoke in a hushed, secretive way and loved to sit around spinning gruesome yarns. Though he was supposed to bunk with the apprentices and the sailmaker in the half deck, he had deserted us and rigged his hammock in the carpenter's shop. He still had his meals with us and made us all miserable with his morbid yarns of ghostly, supernatural warnings of disaster, death, and destruction. His obsession was what he called "the bells of the sea," which always tolled to prophesy calamities.

Being a tradesman, "Chips" did not have to keep watch, but did his work by day and could sleep all night, unless he was turned out by the cry of "All hands on deck" to help with handling sail in an emergency. His tradesman's work, in a vessel which had steel masts and yards and a steel hull, was not as essential as that of ships' carpenters in an earlier era of sail, when hulls and all spars were of wood, and planks and spars often had to be repaired or replaced at sea. There were some, but not many, wooden spars in the *County of Pembroke*. These included the fore and main topgallant masts, the gaff on the spanker, and a few others. He had the care of all woodwork in the vessel, including the blocks, belaying pins, rails, hatch battens and hatch boards, deck planting, furniture, and fittings. In normal times he was more ornamental than useful — and not very ornamental. In the tropics he got a touch of the sun, which sent him off his head.

He took to prowling around the decks at dead of night listening for "the bells of the sea." One night, in the "graveyard watch" (from midnight to 4 a.m.), when we were flat becalmed, he crept along to the poop, where the Mate was gazing in a reverie astern over the trail, perhaps feeling a little drowsy. The Mate did not notice that the carpenter was standing behind him until Chips leaned forward, and whispered hoarsely in his ear, "The bells! The bells! The bells!"

The Mate spun around, startled. "Hear them bells, Mister," said the carpenter in a sepulchral voice, "the bells o' the sea, ringing for the dead!"

The Mate grabbed Chips by the shoulders and shook him vigorously.

"You're going balmy," he said. "The heat has affected your brain! I've heard about you and your bells, worrying the crew. One more word from you about bells, and you'll be locked up until we reach Melbourne! Now lay forrard and get into your bunk and stay there, and don't come on to the poop unless you're sent for. If I catch you prowling about on deck at nightt i m e again, I'll give you bells! Hell's bells!"

Next morning, the Captain sent for the carpenter and made him swallow a still dose of a black draught from the medicine chest. "This will cool your blood," he said, "and you won't hear any more bells. If you do, I'll give you another dose."

Chips drank the draught at a gulp, but it did not cure him of his delusion. At noon a light breeze stirred, and the barque began to move gently forward in the shining water, at a speed of one knot or less. Suddenly Chips ran out from his shop, his eyes staring, and sang out to the men on deck, "Listen, mates, listen! Hark at them bells, the bells o' the sea! We'll never reach port, I tell ye! We're all dead men! Can't you hear them bells?"

His voice rose to a screech of horror as he climbed on the rail, holding on to the fore shrouds, and pointed ahead, fine on the port bow.

"Pull him down!" the Mate roared, running forward. "Grab him before he goes over the side and lock him in his shop!"

Three seamen and the Mate dragged the demented carpenter into his shop, next to the half deck, slammed the door, and locked it. "Stay in there and cool down," the Mate growled. Within a few minutes Chips had removed the glass panel from the door porthole. It was not much use trying to imprison a carpenter with his tools to hand in his shop. Thrusting his head out of the port, he sang out in a voice of doom, "The bells o' the sea foretell death and destruction. I can hear them ringing!"

"Shut up, you crazy galoot!" said the Mate, putting his hand over the carpenter's face and shoving him violently backwards.

In the midst of this excitement, the lookout man, Rhys Davies, came bounding down from the forecastlehead, his eyes wide with fright, his face pale, his voice hoarse as he sang out, "Mister! Mister! I hear bells! Indeed to goodness, I hear them, on the port bow, ringing over the water, and there's no ship or land in sight!"

"Have you gone mad, too?" asked the Mate, sarcastically. "It's true, Mister, it's true!"

At this, Chips put his head out again and looking like a death mask, groaned, "I told you!"

"It's true, sir," Davies insisted. "At first I couldn't believe it, but then I heard them again and again. You could hear them yourself, Mister, if you'll listen!"

"All right, then," said the Mate. "All hands to the fo'c'slehead, to listen for bells! And, by the seven holy ducks that sat on Solomon's grave, if any man hears bells that are not there, I'll knock his ugly block off."

All the crew were now on deck. The Mate led the way, and we followed him, to stand in grim silence, listening intently.

Suddenly and unmistakably, there came the deep note of a bell, tolling across the smooth, empty expanse of glittering water on the port bow. We stood dumb with fear. The bell tolled again.

"Holy mackerel!" the Mate gasped. "Nothing in sight, and we're hundreds of miles from the land! Go and call the Captain!"

One of the senior apprentices ran aft. Presently Captain Williams, who had been taking a nap in his cabin, came forward carrying his telescope. "What's all this nonsense, Mister Mate?" he grumbled.

"A bell tolling on the port bow, sir. We've all heard it. Listen, sir, and you'll hear it yourself!"

The Captain brought his telescope to bear in the direction indicated. As he looked, the bell tolled clearly again.

"Indeed to goodness," the Captain exclaimed. "It's a bell buoy! I can see it, very rusty, with no top light, but the clappers are working well enough. What's a bell buoy doing in the middle of the ocean? It must be adrift, broken loose from somewhere inshore. Bear up for it, Mister!"

He strode aft, followed by the officers. The carpenter put his head out of the door port and moaned as the Captain went by, "The bells of the sea! We'll all be dead soon!"

"Stow your gab," said the Captain, angrily, "or I'll gag you and put you in irons."

The crew were still peering nervously in the direction of the bell, but we could not see it with the naked eye. A sailor growled, "The Old Man ought to haul off, instead of running up to it. Chips is right, this means bad luck."

Some of the others murmured agreement, but the Mate and the Second Mate gave them no time to grumble, as both watches were ordered to stand by the braces to trim sail to every puff of the breeze as we slowly made headway in the direction of the bell.

Presently we could discern a round object bobbing in the wavelets ahead. Though our Old Man was superstitious in some things, he never hesitated in any emergency at sea. He went below to his cabin and came up again, carrying his rifle. By this time, we were only half a mile (800m) from the drifting bell buoy. The wind dropped to a flat calm. "If we can lay alongside it, Mister," said the Captain, "I'll try to sink it with a bullet. It's a danger to shipping!"

A cat's paw breeze rippled the surface of the water, making the bell jangle loudly but enabling us to work nearer to the buoy, before the breeze died. Now the Captain went to the forecastlehead and loaded his rifle. He handled the weapon awkwardly. The two officers kept well behind him, carefully eyeing his movements as he took aim. The crew lined the rail, and the carpenter stared haggardly out of his porthole.

A Bell Buoy (AI)

Three times the Captain fired and missed. The fourth shot hit the target and made the bell clang loudly. "Don't shoot, sir, don't shoot!" the carpenter suddenly screamed. "It's bad luck!"

"Gag him," said the Captain. "He's putting me o ff my aim!"

Helped by two seamen, the Mate opened the door of the carpenter's shop, trussed Chips up with a handy line and gagged him with some strands of rope yarn. They left him lying in the scuppers. The Captain fired some more shots, now from a range of less than 100 yards. He improved with practice. The bullets clanged into the rusty buoy, some at the waterline, and presently we saw that it was slowly filling and sinking. The bell continued to toll until it sank below the surface. The Captain strode aft with his rifle, a smile of satisfaction on his face. As he passed the carpenter, he said to the Mate, "Unbind him now."

Released, and given a drink of water, Chips stared overside at the place where the buoy had sunk. Then he turned to the Mate and said, calmly and earnestly, "Was I mad, Mister? No, sir! It was a real bell, and maybe a terrible' warning."

"You'll hear it no more," said the Mate. "We've settled its hash."

A lively breeze sprang up. "Square away the yards!" ordered the Captain, from the poop. All hands tailed on to the braces, and soon the barque was slipping through the water, with everything drawing. By nightfall we had made several miles to the southward.

What puzzled us all was how Chips had heard that bell for several days and nights before anyone else heard it.

Was it just a coincidence that we encountered a real bell on a drifting buoy in mid-ocean — a million to one chance — at the very time when Ships had gone off his head with a touch of the sun and imagined in his delirium that he could hear the sound of bells?

No wonder some sailors are superstitious, when such queer things happen at sea — especially in the doldrums.

Rhys Davies was another man who had an obsession. His grievance was that he had been robbed of five shillings — the last money he had in the world — at a boarding house in Liverpool, on the day the *County of Pembroke* sailed. He never wearied of telling this story to anyone who would listen to it. He had been on the booze in Liverpool, he said, but he was sure that he had five shillings left in his on the day he signed on for the voyage.

"A half-crown piece I had," he insisted, "and two shilling pieces and a sixpence. I put them on the washstand while I had a wash and packed my bag. Then I went out of the room for a few minutes. When I came back to the house my money was gone! I suppose the dirty boarding keeper pinched it. Anyway, I got even with her. I took the bar of soap from the washstand and stowed it in my bag. Not worth five bob, but better than nothing!"

One day, as we were working through the doldrums, there war a heavy shower of rain which filled the tubs and buckets hurriedly put out to catch the precious downpour. some of the crew, including Rhys Davies, decided to wash their clothes. He rummaged in his sea bag and brought up the bar of soap he had taken from the boarding house. On deck, he rubbed the soap on his dungarees in a bucket.

Suddenly he gave a yell of astonishment. "My money! Look,

shipmates, I've found my money!" He held up the bar of soap. Embedded in it were a half-crown, two-shilling pieces, and a sixpence. Rhys scratched his head in wonderment. "That woman," he said, "pushed the money into the soap, thinking I wouldn't take the soap, but she made a big mistake. Now I've got my money and her soap as well!"

After these distractions, we at last got through the doldrums and picked up the 5E trade wind in Lat. 5 deg. S. The wind blew fresh and steady day after day as, braced hard up on the port tack, we made a speed of eight or nine knots with all sail set, running almost due south for ten days, beneath sunny skies. In these conditions I was sometime sent to the wheel with A.B. Jones "Look now," he said, "she's braced sharp up, with the wind on the bow. The order for steering is By the Wind. D'ye what that means, Jimmy?

"No," I said. "I don't!"

"Well, it means to keep the sails full o' wind and steer by the wind, not by the compass. Indeed to goodness, you'll never be a sailor if you can't steer By the Wind. We have to steer as near into the eye o' the wind as damn it, without being taken aback. Understands This is a SE breeze, and we want to make southeasterly, but we can't steer dead into the wind. Your common sense, if you have any, must tell you that. So we're braced sharp up, and the man at the wheel has to keep her as near to the wind as possible without ripping the sticks out of her! Do you follow me?"

"I think I do," I said.

"Heaven help you if she's taken aback when you're at the wheel, Jimmy! The Captain will knock seven bells out o' you, and he'll never let you man the wheel again, so take good care of what you do. Never mind the compass, just keep your eye on the weather leach of the main royal. Keep that shaking gently, and, the way the yards are trimmed, all the sails below the royal will be filled."

I took the wheel and soon discovered that a nice touch was necessary. If the head of the barque ran off a point or two, the main royal bellied out, and my tutor said, "Too full!"

If she came to, a point or so, the royal was nearly aback, so it became a skilled job, requiring constant watchfulness, to keep that sail trembling, as it were on a fine edge. I had practice at this art in all my watches on deck for several days while we were in the SE trades. Then the wind lost its strength for a few days, in the "horse latitudes," and the skies clouded over.

All hands were now ordered on deck for another long day's work, changing the suit of sails and bending our "storm canvas" on the yards. In this work I was now able to go aloft and lay out along the yards with the seamen, balancing on the footropes in confidence and feeling that I was a real sailor, at last!

On 4th December, when we were in Lat. 35 deg. S and Long. 20

deg. W, a north-westerly gale came roaring down upon us, out of a murky sky, and we squared away to begin running our easting down.

High combing seas rolled up astern. Lifelines were rigged fore and aft along the decks, and everything was snugged down for the heavy weather to be expected in the high latitudes of the Southern Ocean.

*Running the Easting Down — The Joys of a Sailor's Life —
Winds and Weather — Driving on with Decks Awash — High
Following Seas — A Purler Over the Stern — Hove to in a Gale
— Splicing the Main Brace — Christmas Far From Home —
Sixteen Bells for a New Year — "Sail Ho!" — A Clean Pair of
Heels — Closing in on the Land — Cape Otway and Port
Phillip — A Smart Passage*

RUNNING the easting down was a thrilling and at times frightening experience for a first voyager, with many discomforts and much hard work and some danger; but, on the whole, this was one of the supreme satisfactions of a sailor's life — to drive on day after day, week after week, for thousands of miles across the open ocean, with strong following winds providing the mighty propulsion of natural force captured by man's ingenuity. Our barque was only a speck in the immensity of sea and sky and the men in her of puny strength, compared with the forces of wind and water that roared and surged and bore down upon us, threatening us with destruction for daring to venture into their realms of uncontrolled fury; yet for all their unleashed and elemental power, we, like all other sailors, had full confidence that the combined skills of shipbuilding and seamanship and our constant alertness would enable us to gain a victory against the hostility of the ocean's immense forces and to use those forces for our own purpose — of reaching a destination.

This was the glory of life under sail: men taming and making use of the power of the wind, which was the sailor's worst enemy and best friend. In all shifts of the wind, in its varying velocities, we caught it in our sails and made it propel us in the direction in which we wanted to go. We were never at its mercy, except when it sulked and becalmed us or headed us off. Any wind that blew was our servant, not our master; yet, like a wild and dangerous beast, it had to be constantly watched, or it would turn on us and destroy us.

From the moment the towrope was cast off on leaving port, a sailing vessel had no other power than that of the winds to propel her for thousands of miles on the ocean routes to her destination in a far country. Though never completely at the mercy of the winds, we were dependent on their caprices for the rate of progress we could make; but while any wind stirred, from any direction, we could sail with it or into it, with appropriate changes of course. The outlook of mariners in sail was therefore quite different from that of those in steamers (or, later, in motor vessels), who, with mechanical propulsion, can maintain their course and speed almost — but not quite — regardless of wind, weather, and currents; under sail every change of the weather had to be watched for and promptly met.

This was the essence of seamanship: the constant alertness. To neglect it — for example, by carrying too much canvas aloft in a gale — could mean a disaster, such as dismasting; or, in high seas, with unskilful handling — a vessel could broach to and perhaps founder. On the other hand, by carrying too little canvas when running before a gale with high following seas, a vessel could be overwhelmed by a heavy sea crashing over the stern, with danger of damage on deck and to the lives of men. These conditions applied especially when running the easting down. To surmount them was a great satisfaction, increased by the exhilaration that comes from driving on with a strong following wind, ln high seas, for day after day and week after week, in man's triumph over nature's blind fury.

We had picked up the westerlies in Long. 20 deg. W, about 1,700 miles (2735 km) westward of Cape Town, and 300 miles (482 km) westward of the "lonely island" of Tristan da Cunha in the South Atlantic. From that point to our destination at Melbourne, in Long. 145 deg. E, we had to make our easting through 165 degrees of longitude, equivalent in the latitudes in which we sailed to a distance of about 7,500 nautical miles, or 8,636 statute miles (13898 km and all of these figures are approximations only).

On picking up the westerlies in Lat. 35 deg. S, Captain Williams set our course to the south-westward, giving Tristan da Cunha a wide berth, until we reached Lat. 40 deg. S. We then ran almost due east, between Lat. 40 deg. S and Lat. 42 deg. S, passing about 300 miles (482 km) to the south of the Cape of Good Hope.

We had begun to run the easting down on 4th December; this was the midsummer season in the southern hemisphere, when the westerlies are of variable force, but seldom as severe as the winter gales in these latitudes.

Nevertheless, we ran into heavy weather, with gales and squalls of rain and sleet, high following seas and grey skies, and only rare intervals of sunshine and winds of moderate force.

Like most other masters in sail, Captain Williams believed in "cracking on," with as much press of sail as possible, to make a smart passage; his pride of seamanship insisted on this. At the same time, he used his judgment, from hour to hour and minute to minute, to avoid carrying so much sail that the masts might be sprung, or the sails blown out of their boltropes or split to tatters. He was on deck at every change of the watch and at many other times throughout the day and the night, to eye the weather. He took his naps in "forty winks" in his cabin below, fully dressed and, as the saying goes, with one eye on the

Taking a purler over the side. (Bissett)

barometer all the time.

The winds veered from NW to W and SW, and all points between, with squalls of rain and sleet. We were making on average from eight to ten knots, even under reduced sail. In these conditions the watch below was often turned out to help the watch on deck with taking in, reeling, or making sail. We turned into our bunks fully dressed, and usually in damp clothes, for snatches of sleep, knowing only too well that we would be turned out again at any moment by the cry of "All hands on deck!" Then we would have to go aloft in a howling gale with squalls of rain, sleet, or hail, and sometimes in the pitch darkness of the night, to balance on swaying footropes, up to 100 feet (30m) or more above the deck. There we would handle the heavy, wet and at times frozen canvas, and then scramble down to the deck for pully-hauly, wading in ice cold water up to our waists.

The *County of Pembroke,* being low slung amidships, had a freeboard of not more than six feet (2m) from the Plimsoll mark to the bulwark rail. Most sailing vessels were designed in this manner, low amidships (as compared with the high superstructure of steamers), this being necessary to enable the mainsail and foresail to be set low on the masts, where the masts were thickest and strongest. In consequence of the low freeboard, seas were shipped over the lee rail when the vessel was sailing on a tack in heavy weather; and sometimes the lee rail was "under" for minutes on end. As the vessel righted herself, the water surged along the main deck, emptying through the washports and scupper holes.

When we were running before high following seas, the rolling combers from astern occasionally broke over both rails amidships, filling the decks with foaming water. The discomfort of flooded decks was one of the worst adversities of a sailor's life. Most of the lines for handling sail were belayed along the rails amidships. There was no alternative to wading in the flood of surging water on the main deck when the yards were being braced up or hauled around in heavy weather.

We developed an almost instinctive knowledge of the barque's motions in the seas, anticipating the moment when water would be shipped and ducking under the rail to avoid being drenched from head to foot. When emerging from the half deck, we paused and judged the right moment to open the door so that water would not swirl in over the sill. But all such precautions were of little use. Though my sea boots were thigh high, water usually got into them, and I slopped about with wet feet and cold toes for hours, on deck or aloft, until a chance came to empty the water out of my boots and perhaps to change my socks — if I was lucky enough to have a dry pair of socks in my kit.

When not handling sail with the seamen I was stationed on the poop with the Mate and the helmsman during my watches on deck. There, it was a terrifying experience to look astern at the following seas, combers forty feet (12m) from trough to crest, gigantic walls of water which seemed poised to crash down and send us to kingdom come.

Then, as if by magic, the barque usually lifted her stern to ride up the precipice of water, which broke and surged along her sides; yet even the most experienced officer of the watch or old salt at the wheel showed anxiety at such moments. Well they knew that one of those seas, towering higher than usual, could be a "purler over the stern," to crash on the poop deck, with disastrous results.

Though scientists say, as a matter of theory, that "waves" (which sailors call "seas") only undulate up and down and do not move forward, sailors are well aware that the high rollers of the southern latitudes, whipped by westerly gales, have a progressive as well as an undulating motion. The movement of a sailing vessel across these hills and valleys of water would be a nice calculation for a mathematician specializing in relativity. Propelled by the wind aloft in her sails, she moves, or should move, faster than the following seas, to ride over those ahead of her. Yet, as she surmounts each crest, to plunge into the trough in its lee, as if into an abyss, that crest astern curls over and threatens instantly to engulf her in the chasm of the waters.

When we were passing the meridian of the Cape of Good Hope, the westerly gale increased to hurricane force, and the seas became very threatening. During the Mate's watch on deck, from 4 a.m. to 8 p.m., we were running under lower topsails and a reefed foresail, in the grey light of a heavily overcast dawn sky. The Captain, who had been up most of the night, stood by the Mate, looking grave and anxious. They realized that the following seas had increased to such a height that they threatened to overrun us. "All hands on deck!" the Captain ordered. "Go forward, Mister Mate, and get that foresail in. We will have to heave to."

The Second Mate, followed by German Charlie the cook-steward, came up the companionway to the poop as the cry was taken up forrard, "All hands on deck!" The men of the Second Mate's watch, with the carpenter and the sailmaker, tumbled out of their bunks and stood under the fo'c'slehead, waiting for further orders.

The officers ran forward, and very soon, with a tremendous flapping of canvas and shouts of the men as they hauled, the reefed foresail was clewed up, and the men raced aloft to furl it — a job that took all of one hour. The Captain ordered me to stay on the poop and said to me, "If a sea comes over the stern, m'son, jump into the rigging and hold on for your dear life."

The manoeuvre of heaving to meant that a dangerous moment would occur while we were bringing her into the wind, when we would be beam on to the high rollers. At such a moment, if steering way were lost, the vessel could broach to and take heavy seas on her beam.

The Captain, looking worried and restless, stood by the helmsman as we continued to scud under the lower topsails. He hoped that the wind might drop a little, enabling him to continue running before it. But his luck was out; the gale increased its fury.

When the foresail was furled, the Mate came aft again and stood by the wheel with the Captain. Suddenly the Captain sang out, "Jump for it!"

He and the Mate and I sprang into the mizzen rigging at a gigantic greybeard purler crashed from astern onto the poop. Though I climbed ten feet (3m) above the deck, I was submerged there by the seething sea which surged around and above me as I clung desperately to the shrouds, holding my breath.

After a minute which seemed like an hour, the wall of water swirled forward, foaming onto the main deck. I took a deep breath and saw that the Captain and the Mate, also clinging to the rigging, were shaking themselves like spaniels as they jumped down on deck again and grabbed the wheel.

The helmsman, Hugh Evans, had been caught by the water, washed over the forward rail, and dashed against the base of the mainmast. There he lay, unconscious and half drowned, with a broken leg and head injuries. He was picked up by the Second Mate and some of the seamen and carried through the swirling water to the fo'c'sle.

The purler had fortunately not broken the wheel, but it had stove in and carried away the teakwood and glass cabin skylight, the companion, and the 'binnacle. Water had poured in through the openings, to flood the compartments and alleyways under the poop to a depth of several feet.

Our passenger, Dr. Hilton, who had been in his bunk, came up the companionway wearing a long flannel nightshirt, dripping wet. "A man is injured," said the Captain, pointing to the deck forrard. The doctor waded to the fo'c'sle, holding on to the lifelines.

The Mate at the wheel kept the barque steady, to prevent her from broaching to. The moment of chaos had passed but the Captain, thoroughly shaken, could hesitate no longer. Another purler, with the skylight opening uncovered, and the vessel would be in immediate danger of foundering. His voice rang out above the roar of the gale: "Stand by to heave to!"

All hands struggled along and stood by the braces. After a giant sea there is usually a series of smaller seas. Watching for his opportunity, the Captain gave the order, "Hard down the helm! Slack away the port braces!"

This means hauling in the starboard braces, but with all hands on deck and only the lower topsails set, there was ample muscle power available. The Captain said to me, "Lay forrard, m'son, and tail on." I waded along the main deck, up to my armpits in water, and added my weight, for what it was worth, to that of the seamen. The purler had filled the main deck from rail to rail.

By God's mercy the barque came slowly into the wind on the port tack and lay hove to, without further damage. She lurched and pitched violently as she lay with the seas five or six points on the port bow but was now in a position to ride out the gale in comparative safety.

The crew were then ordered aft, to batten down the gaping holes in the poop deck, and to bail out the water from the cabins and storerooms under the poop, using buckets hauled up on lines. The carpenter had now become an important man. For the rest of the voyage, he would be busy repairing the damage. In the meantime, he had to make a splint for the broken leg of Hugh Evans, which was set by Dr. Hilton. The unfortunate seaman had concussion and an injured skull. He was lashed into his bunk and attended by the doctor. It was merely a fortunate chance that we happened to carry a passenger who was a doctor. In ordinary circumstances, the Captain treated injuries and illnesses, with the aid. of a book entitled *The Ship Captain's Medical Guide*.

The work of battening down the openings in the poop deck, bailing out the water, and saving whatever stores could be saved after the water damage kept all hands at work throughout the whole day. Toward four O'clock in the afternoon, the gale moderated. Soon afterwards we were ordered to get sail on her again, and we resumed running the eastward as night closed in. The crew had now been at work fourteen hours without rest or hot food, so the Captain gave the order, "Splice the main brace" — a tot of rum for all hands, except the apprentices. We were given a tin of condensed milk!

Alter this day of near disaster, we made good progress to the eastward with strong westerly winds and squalls and some days of sunshine. It was now mid-December. We had not sighted land since leaving port two months before, and we had sighted no other vessels since leaving the doldrums, more than three weeks before. I realized now how vast and lonely is the ocean and began to wonder if we would ever reach Melbourne.

On Christmas Day we were in Lat. 40 deg. S, Long. 90 deg, E, still driving on, with a moderately strong following Wind, and all sail set to the topgallants, beneath a sunny sky, The Mate heaved the log and announced that we were doing "ten and a Chinaman." It was my first Christmas away from home — and so far away, thousands of miles! I knew that my home folk would be thinking of me and wondering how I was faring. I thought of them, too, with my mouth watering for a piece of my mother's plum pudding and wishing they could know I was alive and well.

German Charlie put some plums in our duff that day, but not many. The salt pork was going high, the biscuits were weevilly, and the water in the tanks was stale and smelly. To celebrate Christmas, the Captain ordered the main brace to be spliced. In the dog watch the Welsh seamen sang Christmas hymns in Welsh, the Captain and the Mates joining in.

Seven days later, on New Year's Day, 1899, at midnight, sixteen bells were struck at the change of the watch — eight for the old year and eight for the new year — in accordance with sea custom.

On the following day we passed the meridian of Cape Leeuwin, the southwestern cape of the continent of Australia, in Long. 115 deg. E, but we were about 300 miles (482 km) to the southward of the land. Late that afternoon, the lookout man raised the cry of "Sa-a-il Ho!" and we could see the topgallants of a vessel barely discernible on the horizon ahead of us, making eastward. "We're overhauling her," remarked the Captain. "Keep an eye on her during the night, Mister!"

The stranger was of intense interest to us, but night fell before we

A sailing ship in heavy seas. (AI Image)

could identify her. During the night her lights became visible. At dawn she was well in sight — a full rigged ship, but evidently no flyer, as we were overhauling her rapidly, coming up on her starboard quarter at ten knots. Our Captain cracked on, and presently we came abaft the stranger's beam, about half a mile (800m) away from her, and made our numbers. She was the ship *Verbena*, 1,719 tons, from Liverpool, bound for Melbourne. She had left Liverpool on 27th September, fourteen days before our departure. The fact that we had overtaken her gave our Old Man obvious pleasure. He sent us aloft to set the royals, and we surged ahead, showing the *Verbena* a clean pair of heels before sundown. Next day we similarly overhauled and passed two Russian vessels, the barque *Hellas* and the ship *Endymion,* which were wallowing along in sight of one another, with their topgallants and royals furled. We showed them our heels, too, and felt very pleased with ourselves.

Now, as we closed in toward the land, approaching the western entrance of Bass Strait, we sighted to the northward other vessels, including steamers, plying on the coastal route between Adelaide and Melbourne.

On the afternoon of 10th January 1899, when we were ninety days out from Liverpool, the lookout man raised the thrilling cry of "La aa-nd Ho!" and those of us who had nothing better to do sprang into the rigging to feast our eye on the marvellous sight of a solid reality — the shore! We had made our landfall at Cape Otway, sixty miles (96 km) from the entrance to Port Phillip, our destination. At Cape Otway we made our numbers to the signal station, which reported the movements of shipping by means of a land telegraph line to Melbourne. We now raised the anchor cables from the chain lockers, ranged them on deck abaft the windlass, and shackled the ends to the anchors.

During the night, under reduced sail, we stood in toward Port Phillip Heads, in the lee of the land. At dawn we were standing on and off the heads, flying the signal for a pilot.

We had not long to wait; but, when the pilot came on board, he advised our Old Man to take a tow through the Heads and up the harbour to our anchorage in Hobson's Bay; a northerly wind was blowing offshore, which made navigation of the entrance and the channels of Port Phillip difficult.

As a tug was already standing by, the Captain, after some bargaining, agreed, and her towrope was soon made fast. In the meantime, the Mate had kept all hands busy forrard since dawn unlashing the two old fashioned heavy iron anchors on the forecastlehead and getting ready to let go.

This was work that the crew did with a will, singing as they worked. It was the first time in my life that I had made port or taken any part in coming to anchor. As I gloatingly looked at the shore and its houses, I was thinking that soon I would be feasting on sweets and cakes and fresh fruit and walking on paved streets and looking in shop windows and seeing women and children and horses and enjoying all the other sights so familiar to people on land.

But, as we towed in through the Heads, there was no time for dreaming. All hands were ordered aloft to furl the sails. We moved slowly up the thirty-mile (48 km) stretch of landlocked water in Port Phillip's spacious basin, from the Heads to Hobson's Bay. Toward noon we moved to our anchorage, a mile (1.6 km) offshore, near the mouth of the Yarra-Yarra River. As we cast off the towrope, the Captain sang out, *"Let go the anchor!"*

With a rattle of the chain, the starboard anchor plunged to the bottom. It was the moment of triumph. We were snug in port, after a smart passage of 91 days.

We were boarded by Customs officials, immigration officials, health officials, shipping reporters, port officials and a representative of the agents, James Bell & Co., who came out in a steam launch. They plied the Captain with questions and gave him news of the world, of which we had heard nothing for the three months since we had cast off the tug outside the Mersey Bar in the Irish Sea.

The experiences of a first voyage remain in the memory of every sailor, for no voyage is as memorable as this one, when everything has to be learned. Many a time I have come to anchor or to berths in many a port, since that sunny day in the long ago in the port of Melbourne, when the mud hook of the *County of Pembroke* plunged to the bottom with a splendid splash. I was the most insignificant person in that barque, and what had happened on the voyage out was not very remarkable or unusual, except to my imagination, which saw every incident in the glow of adventure.

The first voyage, like the first love, is the best, the most thrilling, the longest remembered.

James Bisset, at the age of 16, home from his first voyage as an apprentice in the County of Pembroke (Bisset)

In Port at Melbourne — Our Cargo — Shore Leave — Limited Pocket Money — A Feed of Grapes — The Seamen's Mission — Bourke Street on Saturday Night — A Ri p-roaming down — Loading Wheat at Williamstown — Pianist at a Dance Hall — Homeward Bound — A Cure for Dysentery — Arithmetic and Pharmacy — The Howling Fifties in the South Pacific — Cape Horn.

WE were twenty-six days in port at Melbourne, from 11th January to 6th February 1899. That was not considered a slow "turnaround" for a sailing vessel in a destination port, discharging and taking in cargo. In some ports there were delays of up to three months before a vessel obtained a cargo and cleared out; but our agents, James Bell & Co., made arrangements for our cargo to be handled fairly quickly, so that we could put to sea again without undue waste of time.

On the day after our arrival at Robson's Bay, we were towed into the Yarra River and berthed at a wharf in Victoria Dock, about four miles (6.4 km) upstream, at the edge of the city of Melbourne. There our cargo was discharged by the labour of stevedores — and a strange assortment of merchandise it was!

The list of items, published in the Melbourne *Argus* of 12th January 1899, showed that we had brought to the thirsty colonists, among many other things, 2,170 cases of stout, 50 cases of ale, 2,595 cases of whiskey, 20 cases of champagne cider, and 25 quarter-casks of brandy!

This hard liquor was only a small part of the merchandise that came out of our hold. There were 5,160 bags of Cheshire salt; 50 tons of rock salt; 60 bags and 100 kegs of borax; 400 kegs of sulphate of copper; 40 kegs of potash; 13 cases of magnesia; 100 drums of caustic soda; 15 kegs of soda ash; 17 drums of calcium, and 916 kegs of bicarbonate of soda.

A port in the busy days of sail (AI Image)

Building and construction materials we brought to Melbourne included 61,800 slates; 12,000 firebricks; 1,550 cases of tin plate; 1,064 bundles of hoop iron; 262 cases of window glass; 275 fire tiles; 10 tons of pig iron; 259 reels of wire netting; 116 kegs of nails.

Sundry items included 10 bales of hemp cord; 94 bundles of sheets; 26 cases of mangles; 316 cases of paper; besides, as *The Argus* reported, "a large quantity of iron, steel, general soft-goods, and unspecified merchandise."

This was a typical mixed cargo of manufactured goods, not of a perishable or urgent nature, exported to Australia from Britain in those days of cargo carrying under sail. As a sailing vessel has only one hold, the stowing of such a mixed cargo required forethought and skill, to avoid shifting or breaking of the packages. The return cargoes, which were usually of wheat or bales of wool, could be more easily stowed.

While the cargo was being discharged, the crew, including the apprentices, worked a ten-hour day, from 6 a.m. to 6 p.m., with an hour off for breakfast and lunch. We were kept busy chipping rust overside and scraping grass and barnacles from the hull as the lightened barque rose in the water; painting overside; overhauling the running gear and standing gear; serving and blacking down the rigging: sails for the sailmaker to overhaul, and again; greasing down the masts; painting the boats and deckhouses; polishing brass and woodwork; and doing anything else that the ingenuity of the Mates could find to keep the crew from idleness and to make the vessel shipshape and Bristol fashion and get her ready lor the homeward voyage.

In the evenings and on Saturday afternoons and all day Sunday, the crew had shore leave. If their accounts were in credit, the seamen got small cash advances from the Captain and went on the spree. Some absented themselves for a few days, but none deserted, as "crimping" was not a well-organized industry at Melbourne at that time.

There were about twenty other sailing vessels in port while we were there, but most of the shipping trade of Melbourne was in steam, coastwise and on the route to Europe via the Suez Canal. The heyday of sail at Melbourne had passed. Seamen who deserted there might be stranded for weeks or months. A shipmaster who needed men had no difficulty in picking them up. The situation was different at ports on the west coast of America, and at the Australian coal port of Newcastle, where sailing vessels were tied up for months awaiting cargoes, and many seamen deserted, or were enticed by "crimps" (boarding house masters), made blind drunk, and put on board vessels which were short- handed and ready for sea — the crimp being paid "blood money" by the Captain; but, as our stay in Melbourne was of short duration, our crew remained 'on the articles and had little inducement to desert.

My credit in the slop chest was practically non-existent, my pay was only three pounds a year, and I had served only three months; but Captain Williams held the two pounds which my· father had given him for my pocket money, to be used "verra sparingly ye ken." Each Saturday night when I went ashore, he gave me two shillings and warned me to keep away from "wine, women, and song."

The warning was scarcely necessary, in my circumstances. The seamen were not much better off, as the Captain limited their advances to five shillings a week, but this went a long way, with shandygaffs at two pence per pint and prices of other luxuries in proportion. I spent most of my money on fruit, especially grapes, which could be bought off street barrows at two pence per pound. This price seemed a fantastic bargain, as grapes were practically unobtainable in England. I ate them, seeds, skin, and all, with reckless gluttony, in large quantities.

On the Captain's advice, the two other apprentices and I spent most of our evenings at the Seamen's Mission, near the docks. There we met boys from other ships, including the cadet ship *Hesperus* of the Devitt Moore Line, the *Loch Linnhe*, the *Loch Tay*, the *Loch Lomond*, the *Verbena*, and the *Dumfriesshire* barque; the boys all had tall tales to tell of the remarkable adventures and dangers they had encountered.

The volunteer lady helpers at the Seamen's Mission were motherly and kind and gave us a reminder of home, with singsongs around the piano, concerts, and especially with the tea and cakes they provided free for ever hungry boys and homeless or stoney broke sailors. Theirs was a noble work of practical Christianity, but most of the hardened fo'c'sle hands preferred boozing in pubs to the temperance attractions of the Mission.

My brassbound uniform came out of my sea chest wrinkled and crumpled, mildewed from damp, and its buttons green with Verdigris. When I put it on, the trousers had crept above my ankles, and I could scarcely button the jacket! Despite the diet of salt provisions and weevilly pantiles, I had grown taller and bigger on the outward voyage, under the influence of hard work, sunshine, and ozone. This was embarrassing, but I polished the buttons and swaggered ashore, for the first time in my life, with the confident feeling that I was a real sailor now, after all.

Saturday night was a big night in Melbourne as at Liverpool. From our berth it was a walk of about two miles (3.2 km) through the long, wide, straight streets of Melbourne, lined with imposing public and commercial buildings, to Bourke Street, the main centre of attraction. At this time there were no motorcars or electric trams. The streets were filled with horsedrawn vehicles of all kinds — buggies, sulkies, gigs, carts, drays, wagons, hansom cabs, "growler" cabs, horsedrawn buses and horsedrawn trams with men and women riding on horseback. Crowds promenaded on the wide pavements in the fine summer weather. Most of the men wore beards or moustaches. The womenfolk had ankle length dresses, tight laced busts, and big hats adorned with feathers or flowers.

The street scene was gay and animated. Shops and pubs were open until eleven o'clock. There were fruit barrows aplenty, under naphtha flares, the barrowmen loudly calling their wares; street singers; soapbox orators; Salvation Army meetings; and the bars of the brightly lit pubs, wide open, were crowded with noisy, jostling drinkers, presided over by flashy barmaids, with plenty of drunks and fights, and all the other signs of a rip-roaring town.

Bourke Street on Saturday night made a scene unequalled, in its way, anywhere in the world The population of Melbourne was half a million, and it seemed that the majority of inhabitants made a point of going to Bourke Street on Saturday night, for an outing or to do their weekend shopping at the Eastern Markets there. The street, exactly one mile (1.6 km) long and ninety-nine feet (2.7m) wide, perfectly straight, was one big bazaar, lined with brightly lit shops, pubs, theatres and dance halls, and the street itself was crowded with tens of thousands of people, in festive mood, making their own fun.

In the shops and market stalls were many Chinese, selling vegetables and fruit and fancy goods imported from China. Among the crowds were hawkers with trays of nicknacks. Gangs of "larrikins" from nearby suburbs, with gaudy "donahs" on their arms, pushed their way through the crowd, giving cheek and looking for fight, challenging rival "pushes." The vitality of the people, happy and carefree as they were in their roistering mood, in the cool of the evening under the open sky, made a remarkable impression of the joy of life, in which everyone shared. It was a "free show" — which suited impoverished apprentices. After walking up and down Bourke Street for a couple of hours, eating grapes, we could go back on board the *County of Pembroke* feeling that we had thoroughly enjoyed ourselves.

When all the cargo was discharged except for the tiles and bricks — which were left in as ballast — we were towed down the river and across Robson's Bay to a wharf at Williamstown to load wheat from railway trucks run alongside. There we remained about ten days. The first job we had was to clean out the hold, to remove any traces of chemicals or other spillage of the outward cargo which might affect the wheat. Then some bagged wheat was loaded in, and the tiles and bricks were discharged. The stevedores then filled the hold with 14,305 bags of wheat, to a total weight of some 1,200 tons. The wheat was stowed in bags by strong men who shouldered it from chutes and stowed it in such a way that it was a compact mass, on an even trim. Though Williamstown was connected by rail with Melbourne, the train fare was more than we could afford, and we had to seek such pleasures in the evening as could be found in this small outport, which had a population almost entirely concerned with ships and shipping. There was a

Seamen's Mission here, but not much else of interest to a boy except the fruit shops, where I spent most of my money on grapes.

One night, as I was going down to the wharf late, I heard music and laughter coming from a low down dance hall in a tavern. Timidly I crept inside to have a look. The air was thick with tobacco smoke and beer smells and with the noisy hilarity of drunken sailors and wild women.

Suddenly the pianist fell off his stool in a drunken stupor, and the dance stopped. Some of the sailors from the *County of Pembroke,* who had seen me enter, asked me if I could play the piano. Foolishly, I admitted, "Yes, a little bit — by ear." "Come on, then," they shouted. "Let her go, Gallagher!" and I was hustled across the room to the piano, which had half a dozen empty beer glasses on top of it, the cause of the pianist's downfall. They shoved the drunk out of the way. I sat down, and soon I was giving it all I knew and greatly enjoying myself in the very unaccustomed surroundings. The piano was awful, but no worse than my playing. The audience was anything but critical, and the fun went on, fast and furious.

Then came a hush. I looked around to see what was the matter, as a large and heavy hand fell on my shoulder. It was the Captain's hand. With him was the Mate. They had looked in out of curiosity, as I had done. "What are you doing here?" asked the Captain. Without waiting for an answer, he and the Mate hustled me out of the room and in.to the street, followed by a chorus of groans and curses from the revellers.

As we walked the short distance to the wharf, and went on board, the Captain lectured me heavily. "Don't you know it's sinful to go into such a place?" he said. "And besides, you've broken the terms of your indenture, which forbid you to visit alehouses and taverns. I'll have to report you to the owners, and I'll tell your father, too. No doubt your indentures will be cancelled when we get back to Liverpool. Now you'll have no more shore leave, m'son! You'll stay on board until we sail!"

This sounded hypocritical, but the Captain was doing the right thing in the circumstances. I had no means of knowing that he had no intention of carrying out his threat to report me. He only wanted to scare me and succeeded for the time being. The prohibition on going ashore was no great hardship, as we were due to sail in a few days. My shipmates generously brought me some grapes, but by that time my appetite for them was nearly satisfied.

On 3rd February 1899, we were entered out, and on the 6th, we cleared out from Melbourne, homeward bound, via Cape Horn, to "Queenstown for orders."

We towed out of Port Phillip and set sail to the south-eastward, in fine weather. At sundown, Wilson's Promontory, the southeastern corner of the Australian continent was abeam, the last land we would see for many a day. At nightfall its light winked astern and gradually dipped below the horizon.

For ten days we continued to sail southeasterly, on the starboard tack, with westerly breezes increasing from moderate to fresh and strong, until we were in Lat. 50 deg. S, well to the southward of New Zealand. There we squared away for Cape Horn, running before westerly gales with high following seas. The distance from Melbourne to Cape Horn is 5,862 nautical miles (9433 km), across the South Pacific Ocean, the widest and wildest and loneliest stretch of open water in the world, far from inhabited shores.

On the day we left port, I was taken ill with dysentery, caused — as I now suppose — by eating too many grapes. The symptoms were much worse on the second and third day. The Captain dosed me with chlorodyne twice a day for a week, with no good effect, until the chlorodyne bottle was empty. This bottle was Number 15 in the medicine chest, to correspond with numbers in *The Ship Captain's Medical Guide*. I had eaten nothing since leaving Melbourne and had grown thin, weak, and pale. I thought my last days had come.

The Captain said to me, "Well, m'son, I don't know what to do with you. According to the book, Number 15 should have cured you, but now the bottle is empty, and you are no better. I think I'll give you some Number 10 and Number 5. That adds to fifteen!"

I was too sick to care what he gave me. It happened that Number 10 was a brown powder with a nasty taste. It was a diarrhoea mixture. Number 5 was a syrupy cough mixture. The Old Man mixed these two in a glass, diluted them with a little water, stirred vigorously, and I swallowed the dose. Almost immediately I felt better. After two more doses, I was cured. I don't know if the application of arithmetic to pharmacy worked equally well in all cases; but Captain Williams was a resourceful man who never let any practical problem beat him.

For four weeks we ran before the westerly gales with shortened sail, in the "howling fifties," with decks full of water and high following seas. The gales freshened to strong and heavy, with frequent hurricane squalls and precipitous seas. This was a time of continual anxiety, hard work, broken sleep, and discomfort of cold and wet clothes, as we waded on deck or climbed aloft to take in or reef or make sail, with numbed fingers raw with chilblains from contact with icicles on the rigging or with broken fingernails from gripping heavy folds of wet canvas frozen half-stiff with sleet, and faces lacerated with needles of hail which at times made it impossible to look to windward in a blizzard. Yet every man knew that he must carry on, as the safety of the barque, and of every person in her, depended on instant obedience to the orders of the Captain and the officers and on their judgment of the amount of sail to be carried, at every change in the force of the wind, to keep her running before the following seas without being demasted.

Forty days out from Melbourne we passed the meridian of Cape Horn, about 100 miles (160 km) to the southward of that land's end of dread renown. We had not sighted a sail since leaving Wilson's Promontory, but now, as we drove on in a heavy gale, we occasionally glimpsed ships hove to and headed westward, battling into the teeth of the gale, outward bound on the route from Europe or the eastern states of the U.S.A., to the west coast ports of North and South America.

Full identification of these vessels was impossible. We glimpsed them like ghostly apparitions as we drove on into the scud, with spindrift and foam obscuring visibility, so that there was not time to make our numbers; but we could see from their rigs and merchant flags that some were Yankee "Down Easters," and others British, German, French, Russian [Finns], or Scandinavian.

The route around Cape Horn was the last great sailing ship route in the world. Before the Panama Canal was opened it was the only seaway (apart from Magellan Strait) from the Atlantic to the Pacific. Few, if any, steamers made the long haul around the Horn. They avoided the stormy weather off the Cape by going through the narrow, winding channel of the Strait of Magellan, which, being landlocked, was not practicable for sailing vessels; but even this passage was a very long haul for steamers voyaging from Europe or the eastern U.S.A. to San Francisco or other west coast ports, and there were practical problems of obtaining bunker coal at intermediate ports along the route.

On that long haul sailing vessels could compete success- fully with steamers, taking out cargoes of coal or general merchandise and returning with wheat from California, sugar from Hawaii, or nitrates and guano from South American west coast ports. The route around the Horn, going eastward, was also frequented by sailing vessels from Australia and China. All this would be ended by the opening of the Panama Canal in 1914, which gave steamers the tremendous advantage of a short cut from the Atlantic to the Pacific and sounded the death knell of sail; but in the 1890s the "windbags" still carried on valiantly. While they lived, the Cape Horn route, despite the difficulties and dangers of its terrific westerly gales, remained one of the world's main seaways.

10

*A Hurricane Squall off Cape Horn — Demasted! —
Clearing the Mess — A Cape Horn Calm — How to Catch an
Albatross — We See an Iceberg — "Growlers" and "Calves"
— The Aurora Australis — Into the Atlantic — Furbishing
Ship — A Dust Storm in Mid-ocean — Queenstown for
Orders — My Irish Suit — Towing into Antwerp — Paying Off
the Crew — Sailors and Harpies — Home to the Mersey —
First Voyage Ends*

AT midnight, as we drove on past the pitch of the Horn, the Captain
came onto the poop and eyed the weather. He said to the Mate,
"The wind is easing, Mister, and the glass seems to be on the rise.
Go forrard and shake the reef out of the foresail. We'll set the topgallants
shortly, if the wind is still easing."

"Aye, aye, sir," said the Mate.

"Keep an eye lifted to windward. There's still a lot of wind in some of
these squalls!"

With these words the Old Man went below. Warned by his barometer, his
long sea experience, and his "sixth sense," he well knew, as did the Mate, that
as the wind dropped it would be necessary to carry more canvas to keep the
barque running before the very high quartering seas. He knew, too, that in
this season, in the month of March, the westerly gales off Cape Horn
sometimes dropped to a dead calm or veered even to the eastward.

He wanted to make as much easting as possible while the wind was fair.
The Mate soon had the watch on deck aloft, casting off the reef points and
reef earrings, and before long the full foresail was sheeted home and drawing
well. Then, after a heavy rain squall, he decided to set the main and fore

topgallants.

At eight bells the Captain came on deck and approved the situation. We were preparing to turn into our bunks below for a snatch of slumber when suddenly, as though from nowhere, a howling squall came up in the darkness, with a long line of white spume gleaming on the crest of a huge comber that towered twenty-five feet (7.6m) higher than the other seas, which had been moderating under the influence of the heavy rain.

This happened just as the Second Mate was taking over, and all hands were on deck. As the squall struck well out on the quarter, she shuddered and heeled over. The Captain sang out, "Run her off a couple of points!" and then to the Mates, "Get the topgallants off her again. She won't stand it!"

The Mates and all hands hurried forrard; but, before anything could be done, there was a frightful ripping crash aloft, and the fore topgallant mast — a wooden spar about fifty feet (15m) long — snapped off sheer just above the fid and crashed to the deck and over the bulwarks on the lee side.

The Captain took one quick glance forrard and at the sky, then stood by the man at the wheel and said in a steady and matter-of-fact way, "Get all hands forrard, Mister, and clear up the wreck! Haul in the spars if possible and save everything for future repairs."

At this moment the barque was in extreme peril, and the Captain well knew it, but at any such time of crisis he showed no fear or hesitation. The chief danger was from the steel royal and topgallant yards, crossed on the fallen mast, which were battering against the barque's side with a frightful clatter as she rolled wildly in the confused cross current raised by the hurricane squall. This battering threatened to make a hole in the hull plates, or to spring the rivets, near or below the waterline. A small leak could let enough water into the hold to destroy our wheat cargo; but a bigger hole in the plates could sink us if the storm continued for long.

"Look lively there, men," sang out the Mate, as he and the Second Mate waded forward to the scene of chaos and confusion.

In the darkness the crew worked desperately with knives und axes to cut free the tangled mess of wires, ropes, canvas, wood, and iron hanging in the shrouds and stays und over the bulwarks. Some of the men made lines and chains fast to the fallen yards and the broken mast trailing overside and, after almost superhuman efforts, got them inboard and lashed so that they could do no harm to the hull.

At a time of crisis such as this, the value of expert knowledge of seamanship, so laboriously acquired in long years of experience, was demonstrated. The officers sang out their orders hoarsely, working with the men as all responded with a will to clear the tangled mess, but each man knew what to do and how to do it. At intervals the barque lurched sickeningly to leeward, burying her bulwarks in a sea which washed inboard in a foaming cascade over the rail where we were working. Then, up to our necks in water, we would hold on to the rail or anything else handy — to resume work instantly as the water left us to go sweeping across the deck on the roll, while everything on deck and aloft seemed to be groaning, rending, ripping, and tearing as she rolled to windward as if in agony to rid herself of the clinging menace.

Everything had to be done urgently. If the hurricane squall had continued for long, other sails might have split, or the masts which bore them might have crashed down, to add to the chaos; but, by the Mercy of Providence, the squall passed within a few minutes. Thereafter the wind rapidly moderated, but the sea remained confused and angry for some time, making the barque roll, tumble, and lurch, shipping seas in great dollops which fell thudding on the decks from either side, while we worked frantically to clear the wreck.

As the wind dropped, the Captain, leaving Paddy Murphy at the wheel, came forward and watched the weary crew at work hauling the spars inboard. Dawn came in greyly, as the wind dropped almost to a calm, and the seas moderated to a long oily swell. By this time, we had freed most of the frayed and broken wires and let them slither overboard, but the Captain sang out, "Save any good lengths you can, Mister. We'll be able to use them later!"

As daylight grew and the weather improved, the Captain and the carpenter inspected the wooden mast and, seeing that it was not split but only broken off sheer near its base, the Old Man ordered us to lash it along the deck, in a good position for repairs. The yards were fortunately undamaged.

By the time this was done it was 8 a.m., and another watch had gone by. The seas subsided and the decks were dry, and the sun struggled through a lifting bank of cloud. We were becalmed, in fine weather, off Cape Horn! Hundreds of albatrosses, Cape Pigeons, and molly hawks circled around us or sat on the gentle swell, white dots on the water as far as we could see. Most of the men had bleeding cuts and gashes on their hands, fingers and arms, from handling frayed wire. We were hungry, cold and utterly exhausted.

"Lay aft!" said the Old Man. All knew what this meant. He was going to splice the main brace. He went below and presently emerged with a demijohn of rum, serving a tot to everyone — except the apprentices. We had a tin of milk to put in our breakfast coffee.

In the meantime, the carpenter had been working on the topgallant mast stretched on the deck, trimming its splintered base and in other ways getting it ready. The Old Man had decided to send it aloft immediately, while the calm weather lasted. All hands therefore had to remain on deck for the difficult feat of seamanship, to send the long and heavy spar aloft, rerig it and stay it, fidded(sic) into the topmast cap.

This was putting a heavy strain on the wearied flesh and blood of the crew, but the Old Man's decision to rerig the mast immediately was a wise one, as every man knew. At any moment stormy weather could come up again, and the vessel was unbalanced in her sail capacity with the fore topgallant mast down. The crew therefore turned to with a will, and the work was accomplished by the unremitting labour of all hands with the yards also sent aloft and crossed on the mast, in eight hours' hard toil.

Something perhaps unprecedented then occurred, as the Old Man again spliced the main brace, for the second time that day, at 4 p.m., but the weary crew had well-earned it and went below in the dog watches to fall instantly asleep. The Cape Horn calm continued all that day and night. Next morning a light breeze stirred. It was from the northeast — a rare phenomenon in that region but occasionally encountered.

We went aloft and bent sail on the rerigged fore topgallant mast. Then, with all sail set to the royals, we had a "pleasure cruise" in fine weather, making south-eastward on the port tack. The Captain reasoned that the northeasterly breeze would not last long, but he wanted to make headway and get into a good position for a run to the Atlantic, around the Falkland Islands, when westerly weather came again, as come it must.

The easterly breezes lasted for three days. In that time, we sailed up to 58 deg. S Lat., about 300 miles (482 km) SE of Cape Horn. The crew, in fine fettle now after our narrow escape from disaster, amused themselves by catching albatrosses. This was much easier than a novice might think possible. The giant birds have snow white plumage with black upper-wing surfaces, yellow legs and feet, pink beaks, and black, beady eyes. With a wingspread of from twelve to fifteen feet (3.6m – 4.5m), they soared around the barque for hours, without moving their wings, examining us with apparently intense curiosity, as if they understood everything about sailoring.

Paddy Murphy explained to me, in perfect seriousness, that when a sailor dies and is buried at sea, he is reborn an albatross. It would therefore be murder to kill an albatross, and very bad luck as well, but it was a kindness to the soul of a dead sailor to catch one and give him a chance to walk a deck again.

To catch an albatross, a sail hook, baited with fat salt pork, is veered astern on a line. The birds peck at the pork, but do not swallow the hook. A bird is held when his upper mandible — which is curved — catches in the sail hook. The line is then drawn taut and kept that way, so that he cannot unhook himself. Several men are required to haul him in, as he spreads his huge wings and big webbed feet in the water, offering strong resistance. At last, he tires and is hauled to the deck. There he is let go free, but cannot fly away, as he has no means of getting up enough speed to be airborne.

Sometimes we had as many as six on the deck, squatting there, seemingly quite contented and philosophical, or waddling about with quaint dignity on their big, webbed feet, their short legs unaccustomed to bearing their weight. They made no attempt to bite, scratch, or counterattack when handled, but, to our amazement, a few minutes on deck made them seasick; and much to the Mate's disgust, they would vomit on the deck. When we parted their feathers, we could see that their bodies were infested with black insects, like fleas. After watching their antics for a while, we would pick them up and dump them into the sea overside, when they would immediately spread their magnificent wings, thrash along the surface, paddling furiously, then volplane away is if nothing unusual had happened to them.

A lone albatross has been known to follow a ship for a thousand miles, but I do not believe the story that they never follow a Scottish ship!

On the morning of the third day of this spell of excep-tional fine and sunny autumn weather, the lookout man sang out, "Sa-a-a-il Ho!"

As we were then in Lat. 58 deg. S, the Captain guessed what kind of sail this might be. He focused his telescope, and sang out to the lookout man, "It's not a sail, it's an iceberg!"

This was the season when bergs break loose from the Antarctic ice fields and slowly drift northward, melting as they drift. As the berg was dead ahead of us, in fine weather in the forenoon, the Captain ran up to within half a mile (800m) of it before we altered course and bore away northward.

The Mate, who prided himself on his mathematical skill, took measurements of the berg by sextant angles and announced that it was 187 feet (57m) high and 380 feet (115m) across its base at the waterline. As ice floats in salt water with only one eighth of its bulk showing above water, we could guess at the hidden dimensions. The berg was a beautiful but terrifying sight, its pinnacles gleaming with prismatic colours in the sunshine, and patterns of purple shadow in its crevices. Any vessel which collided with such a "floating island," in a gale or in the darkness of the night, would have practically no chance of surviving.

When we neared the berg there was a growling sound from our hull plates as small pieces of floating ice scraped along the plates. These were known as "growlers" for that reason. They are thrown off as outliers to a disintegrating berg, and are one of the few indications, apart from direct visibility, of a berg's proximity.

While we watched, the berg began cracking and splitting with loud reports, and presently a great piece of ice parted from its peak and crashed into the sea, throwing spray high into the air. The broken off piece drifted away in a process known, in the lingo of old time whalers, as "calving."

When the calf parted, the mother berg partly rolled over in the water to a new equilibrium, and presently some more pieces broke away. I was fascinated, but hated the sinister thing, and had good reason to dislike icebergs in some later incidents of my sea career.

On our new tack, the *County of Pembroke* rapidly drew away from the floating island of ice, but it remained visible until after sunset, dipping below the horizon in the twilight, when a beautiful play of the aurora australis lit the whole southern sky with shimmering beauty.

During the night the easterly breeze dropped, then veered around to the southwest, working up to a fresh gale. With this fair wind we drove on to the eastward of the Falkland Islands and into the Atlantic. There we were headed off by contrary winds for many days but eventually picked up the SE trades and bowled along steadily, with the wind on the starboard quarter.

Now was the time to furbish ship, to make a good show for the owners on our arrival in our home port. We spent every daytime watch holystoning the decks as white as a hound's tooth, sand-and-canvasing the teakwood fittings, and washing the paintwork. This went on daily, as we laboriously worked our way through the rainy, humid, and damp doldrums.

A "holystone" is a piece of sandstone, which gets its nautical name probably from the fact that seamen had to go down on their knees in a prayerful attitude to use it for cleaning and smoothing decks. The larger stones, weighing three or four pounds, were known as "Bibles" and the smaller ones, for getting into awkward corners, were "prayer books."

There was an old jingle:

> *Eight bells had struck. The watch came from*
> *below to bend the knee and neck;*
> *Though not in prayer, but to curse and swear*
> *and holystone the deck.*

Each man provided himself with a block of wood and a piece of canvas to kneel on. Sand and water were sprinkled on the deck planks, then, getting into line in kneeling position, we began working the holystones to and fro, with the grain of the wood, for hours on end — until the Mate gave the order to "flete" back.

About five degrees north of the equator, we picked up the NE trade winds. Then, braced sharp up on the starboard tack, we stood away to the NNW and could look forward to a couple of weeks' steady breezes and fine dry weather. Under such favourable conditions, the Captain decided that the masts and yards should be given a fresh coat of white paint. Next morning all hands were called out early and sent aloft, with brushes and pots of paint, intent on making a job of it in one day. That evening, when we had finished, she looked a picture, and even the Mate was satisfied.

During the night the breeze freshened a little. We were then not less than 900 miles (1448 km) from the shore of Africa. I was on deck with the Mate at sunrise in the 4 a.m. to 8 a.m. watch, when he suddenly said to me and the helms-man, "Look at the sun striking on those yards! Makes them look all red, doesn't it? It's the new paint glistening. She's a sight for sore eyes!"

A few minutes later, he noticed a little drift of reddish dust swirling in the corners of the poop deck. "What the hell's this?" he said suddenly. "Where did that dust come from?" He picked some up and rubbed it in his fingers, then, swearing like a trooper, raced aloft, to look more closely at the glistening red masts and yards.

A stream of astonishing profanity disturbed the morning's peace as the Mate saw that the wet paint was smothered with a fine coating of red dust, which could not be rubbed off or washed off. The Captain heard the commotion and came up on deck. "A ruddy dust storm, sir, during the night!" said the Mate, in a voice of incredulity and despair.

Many a ship has been lost to icebergs (AI Image)

"Dust storm?" said the Captain, taken aback.

"We're nearly a thousand miles from land!"

He went aloft and saw for himself that the unbelievable had occurred. The only logical explanation was that a whirlwind from the Sahara Desert had carried a cloud of dust high in the air and had transported it 1,500 miles (2414 km) or more, to deposit some of it in mid-ocean on our new paint! To make the tragedy more awful, from the officers' point of view, there was not enough white paint left to give the masts and yards a new coat. "We'll have to go home this way," lamented the Mate, in the voice of one who feels himself utterly disgraced.

The crew laughed behind his back at this humbling of the Mate's pride, but they too were disappointed at having a good day's work ruined in such an extraordinary way. For days afterwards the Mate was to be seen moodily staring aloft, cogitating on ways and means of getting the dust out of the paint, but there was nothing whatever to be done. "No one will believe that we ran into a ruddy dust storm at sea," he lamented.

I may add that this is the only time that I ever saw paintwork spoiled by dust in mid-ocean; and I have not heard of it happening in any other ship.

After losing the NE trades we made very slow progress, through meeting contrary winds in the North Atlantic. On 11th June, 125 days out from Melbourne, we sighted the Old Head of Kinsale on the Irish coast and, that evening, dropped the killick in Queenstown Harbor, snug in that fine haven sheltered by Erin's green hills.

The Old Man went ashore to report our arrival by telegram to the owners and to receive their orders. Brokers' agents then came on board and took samples of our wheat cargo, which they sent to London to be valued. We lay ten days at Queenstown before orders came that we were to proceed to Antwerp to discharge.

Among the various bumboats visiting us at Queenstown was one owned by a tailor and outfitter, who had a good business supplying shore clothes to seaworn sailors, if their accounts were in credit. By arrangement with the Captain, the men signed their names in the slop chest book for articles they purchased from the tailor or the grocer or other bumboat salesmen, the value of the purchases being deducted from the men's pay at the end of the voyage pay off.

As I had now grown out of my clothes, I asked the Captain for some money to get a new suit to go home in. I had served nine months and had earned two pounds five shillings in wages in that period, and the Captain still had a little of my pocket money left. He told the tailor that I could spend two pounds and no more on a new suit.

With this the tailor was well content. He measured me, and, the very next day, came off with a blue serge suit which had a velvet collar and bellbottomed trousers. This, he assured me, was a perfect fit and the very latest fashion among sailor men (. With it I got also, after consulting the Old Man, a wide awake hat for four shillings. The suit was probably the worst fitting garment ever known in the history of tailoring, but I thought it splendid and gladly signed my name for it. This outfit cost me the earnings of my first nine months at sea.

When orders came at last for Antwerp, we raised the anchor and set sail toward the Straits of Dover. There, off Dungeness, we met baffling headwinds and were accosted by several Antwerp tugs, cruising in search of prey.

They sheered up on the quarter, one after the other, each tugmaster assuring our Old Man that the easterly wind would last for at least another week and quoting a fair and reasonable price — as they called it — for towing us into port. Captain Williams engaged in long arguments with each tugmaster, trying to beat down his price, and most of them sheared off in disgust. However, as night closed in and we were headed off in a narrow track of shipping, he at last accepted the cheapest price obtainable, and sang out, "All right, give us your rope."

The crew heard this with great delight. In a trice one watch raced aloft to furl sail and the other watch ran forward to the forecastlehead with the Mate to make the tug fast.

Next afternoon we arrived in Antwerp and moored, alongside a dozen other windjammers, in Sailing Ship Harbor, with our bowsprits sticking out over the quay and nearly into the windows of the houses opposite.

The following day, the voyage being completed, the sea-men were paid off. In nearly ten months they had earned from twenty-five to thirty pounds each, less deductions for advances, allotments and purchases from the slop chest. Under Board of Trade regulations, men paid off in foreign ports were given traveling warrants to their home port in Britain, plus one pound cash for current expenses, and could draw the remainder of their pay through the post office on arriving home.

Three old sea dogs, who elected to remain in Antwerp, were paid off in cash. They went ashore for a couple of days' debauch, got fleeced by the waterfront harpies of their money and everything else they possessed, and within a week were outward bound in another lime-juicer which lay next to us in the tier.

We apprentices watched her unmoor, and waved good-bye to our former shipmates as she slowly moved astern into the river. Drink sodden and bleary eyed, they were heaving round the after capstan, picking up the stern moorings, and feebly joining in the time worn chanty:

Away, Rio!
Away, Rio!
So fare you well, my pretty young maid;
We are bound for the Rio Grande.

Truly, the life of a seaman under sail was a hard one, and the wonder is that so many men kept on at it — perhaps because they could think of nothing better to do; yet, with all the hardships and follies, the old shellbacks thought themselves well rewarded for months of hard work, danger, and sobriety by a few days' glorious debauch in port, and looked forward only to repeating the experience in some other port, they did not care where.

The *County of Pembroke* lay at Antwerp for three weeks before our cargo was discharged and ballast taken in, for a tow around to Liverpool. Some "runners," or temporary hands, were engaged to work the ship on this short voyage under tow. These were mostly old salts, who worked as riggers and were available for short runs from port to port about the British coasts. They knew their work thoroughly but had a conscientious objection to doing anything except actually working the ship when she was under way.

We were under tow three days from Antwerp to the Mersey, with sails stowed and very little to do except make our numbers to passing vessels and signal stations on shore; but the Old Man kept the apprentices hard at work polishing brass, swabbing decks and polishing the bird's eye maple in his saloon.

On 8th August 1899, we entered the Mersey, a wonderful sight to me after an absence of ten months.

As soon as we were berthed, I was given leave to go ashore. After collecting what remained of my pay — about five shillings — from the Captain, I dressed in my Queenstown outfit, put my sea chest and sea bag into a cab, and. drove home in style. I approached the front door with a regular western ocean roll in my gait.

My mother opened the door. It was a joyous welcome, with many exclamations of wonderment that I had grown so much bigger and stronger and that I looked so fit and well; but when the excitement died down a little, she said, "And where in the world did you get that awful suit?"

Next day I was hurried down to a tailor and got another suit, which, my mother said, made me "look presentable." So ended my first voyage, on which I learned that a sailor's life is not all beer and skittles; but I learned, too, that seagoing, despite its discomforts and risks, offers the attraction of ever changing scenes and new experiences such as land folk seldom know. Though sailors when at sea often wish they were ashore, the reality seldom corresponds with imagination; and when they are ashore, they wish they were at sea again.

I liked being at home; but I liked even better being at sea. Experience had not cured me of that desire but had strengthened it.

THE *County of Pembroke* lay at Liverpool thirty-eight days, loading a new cargo. Everyone was paid off except the Captain, the two Mates, and the apprentices. We were allowed to go home to sleep but had to be on board for work at 7 a.m. daily, except on Sundays when we had the whole day at home. For a few days the barque was put into dry dock to have her bottom scraped and painted. Afterwards our work consisted chiefly of chipping and painting overside, cleaning out and painting inside the hold, painting the bulkheads and deckheads of the compartments under the poop, and painting inside the deckhouse.

At home I had opportunities to enthral my brothers and sisters and some former schoolmates with heroic tales of my adventures; but I was careful — especially if my parents were listening — not to talk of discomforts and dangers, for I did not want to worry them. Before long I convinced myself, from my own narratives, that life at sea was glorious, and I forgot about its miseries. This was a matter of stubborn pride, as I could not now back out from a sea career without loss of self-respect. I was determined not to give my father any chance of saying that he had been right, and I wrong in my choice of a career. Apart from that, I now really believed that I was cut out to be a sailor and that the sea life, with all its disadvantages, suited me better than any career that might be open to me on land.

On 15th September 1899, we towed out from the Mersey and set sail, bound for Port Adelaide in South Australia, with a cargo of general merchandise. On this voyage we had four apprentices in the half deck. An Irish lad, Jack O'Connor from Drogheda, was with us, making his first voyage. I took pity on his ignorance and, from my vast experience, showed him the right sailor's way of doing things. As I was now sixteen and he was only fifteen, I felt that he had everything to learn.

Once again, I was in the First Mate's watch, with the senior apprentice, Bill Huxley, and six seamen of mixed nationalities — one Irishman, one Finn, one Cockney, one Greek, and two Welshmen. The Second Mate's watch also had two Welsh seamen and four others. On "Hungry Thomas's" ships preference was shown for a proportion of Welshmen in the fo'c'sle and also in the afterguard. This created some national solidarity fore and aft, which might be useful in allaying discontent in a crisis.

Our route and routine were the same as on the previous voyage. By the time we had worked our way through the doldrums and picked up the SE trades in the South Atlantic, every man knew every other man's peculiarity, and we were a harmonious company of shipmates. I was able to go aloft with full confidence to work on the yards with the seamen. I was now expected to do a man's work, but still for a boy's wages, and with only a boy's strength.

One sunny afternoon in the dog watch, as we were ghosting along in the trades, I sat on the deck with the six seamen off duty, listening to their talk, as I often did; but on this occasion I heard two yarns that impressed themselves on my memory, along with thousands of other tales of old salts that made up the unwritten lore of sail unwritten because the men who told these narratives of their experiences were usually unable to read or write, and when they died their stories died with them.

The first yarn was from Mick Mulligan, an elderly but agile man from Bantry. After rubbing a fill of 'baccy between his horny palms and lighting his clay pipe, which he called his "dudeen," he spat over the rail to leeward and began.

"The best Captain I ever sailed with," he said, "was Captain John Mulcahy, a regular bluenose. He was master of the full rigged ship Kingsport, launched at Kingsport in the Bay of Fundy, and that was twenty years ago. She was wooden built, of rock elm, red pine, and oak, and towed to Saint John's in New Brunswick, to be masted and sparred. I joined her there as bo'sun for her maiden voyage, and she was as fine a looking craft as ever I set eyes on, but she had a weakness. She didn't have enough iron bolts and tree nails to hold her hull together!

"The builders had run short o' bolts, but the owners wouldn't wait. They said she was good enough and decided to have her sent under sail to England to be finished. They had a cargo of lumber lying on shore out in the open for months in sawn baulks and boards and battens, in a stack that had no cover on it, and 'twas bitter winter weather, with snow and ice and frost thick on the ground and on the stack, cold enough to freeze the ears off a brass monkey. Yes, mates, them boards was full o' frost, as hard as a shipowner's heart, but the owners decided to ship them to England in the Kingsport on her maiden v'yage, to take a good price that was offering. It was nigh on Christmas and sleeting colder than charity. The lumbermen loaded them deals into our hold and filled her up from keelson to deckhead, packed so tight there wasn't room for a match- stick in the hold when they finished.

"Three days after Christmas we sailed, and the fo'c'sle hands were groggy and inclined to lay down on the job, but old Mulcahy and the Mates, with a little help from meself, soon knocked the Christmas spirit out o' them bozos, and they turned out to be a mighty good crowd o' seamen.

"With a living nor'wester under the starboard quarter we soon ran out o' the Bay o' Fundy and rounded Cape Sable well to the southward. After a few days, the wind fell light, then came away with a bang and drove us into the Gulf Stream. The Kingsport was a beautiful ship to handle, but after a few days in the warm Gulf Stream weather our troubles began. The frozen timber in the hold started to thaw, and, as it thawed, it swelled! Well, mates, as the hull was not properly fastened, the pressure from inside opened her seams, and she began to leak like a basket.

"We manned the pumps in every watch, and soon it was· all hands to the pumps, until we pumped half the western ocean out of her, but the water was gaining. The decks began opening up, and we could see the oakum washing out of her overside seams as she rolled. She was bursting her sides! Old Man Mulcahy didn't fancy losing his ship in that way on her first run, but he wouldn't fly a signal o' distress. Not him! 'All hands lay aft,' he sang out, 'belay everything and 'vast pumping!'

"He mustered us at the break o' the poop. 'Now, men,' he says, 'the ship's waterlogged, and pumpin' won't do any more good. Ye can see for y'rselves she can't sink, on account o' the cargo o' lumber, but if it keeps on swelling, she'll bust her sides and fall to pieces under our feet. There's only one thing to do, and that's to lash her together. We'll put the anchor chains round her, and there'll be no watch below till the job's done, so, if ye want to save y'r hides, turn to with a will, and look lively.' "

Mulligan puffed at his pipe, then continued, "We worked hard and lively, I can tell ye, getting a length o' the anchor cable ranged on deck, and unshackled. Then we passed a line underneath the ship's bottom and tailed on with the heavy tackles to haul the end o' the cable around underneath and brought the end up to the deck on the other side. Then we passed a wire lashing through the two ends o' the cable and hove it bar tight on the capstan and made it fast. We put one length round her by the foremast, another by the main and a third by the mizzen. That was nine hours' work for all hands, and good work at that, though I say it meself, as by this time she was both rails under and wallowing like a turtle. Then the Old Man says, 'Lay aft,' he says 'for a tot o' grog, and well earned, men! She's all Sir Garnet now, and we'll make port under our own sail. She can't sink and she can't bust open now, but the hold's full o' water and the deck's full o' water, and 'twill be hard driving to make port, but we'll make it! She's only a raft under sail, men,' he says, 'so be careful none o' ye goes overboard.'

"That was true enough, shipmates. She was rails under, with only the poop and the forecastlehead showing. The galley was washed out, and the fo'c'sle was belly deep in water, but we carried on, making about two knots, and in thirty-two days we made Holyhead, sixty miles (96 km) from Liverpool, the port we were bound for. By this time the position was desperate. We were forty days out from the Bay o' Fundy, and living on dog biscuits, as the harness cask was empty. Every man had saltwater boils, and we were as weak as kittens. A Mersey tug hailed us, and, seeing the trouble we were in, offered to tow us up for a hundred and fifty pounds.

"I'll give you seventy-five,' says our Old Man, 'and not a penny more, or we'll sail up. " 'Sail up?' says the tugmaster. 'Why, Captain, you're sinking, an' there's a gale blowing up tonight.'

"'Who says I'm sinking?' says Old Man Mulcahy. 'She's an unsinkable raft. I've sailed her a thousand miles (1609 km) like this, so I can sail another sixty to the Mersey Bar.'

" 'All right, then,' says the tugmaster, 'I'll make it a hundred and twenty-five.'

"'Eighty,' says Mulcahy, 'or ye can sheer off.'

"'I'll stand by,' the tugmaster sings out. 'Ye're in no condition to be on the high seas, Cap'n, and ye won't make port in this coming gale.'

"Gale my foot,' says the Captain. 'The fair weather will hold."

Mulligan relit his dudeen and continued. "The tug sheered off, and our hearts sank into our sea boots, but he kept us in sight until sunset. Then he came up again on our quarter. 'A hundred pounds, Captain,' he sings out, 'and it's my last word, or I'll have to leave ye. I'll report ye when I get in. The wind's getting up, isn't it, Captain?' " 'Robbery,' says Mulcahy, 'but I'll take your line at that.' "Well, shipmates, I give you my word we weren't long a passin' her a rope. We towed into the Mersey and anchored, and it was a great wonder to everybody to see us arrive, with chains around us and all. The hands were paid off with nothing extry, except the extry time on the v'yage, but the underwriters presented Cap'n Mulcahy with a gold watch and a purse of sovereigns, for holding a ship together with chains hove round her hull, the only time I ever seen that done!"

After Mick Mulligan had finished his yarn, our Finn seaman, Yonny Helsing, said, "Shiver my timbers, Mick, dat vas a close shave. Reminds me von time ven I first vent to sea, and ve had a more close shave dan dat."

"What happened then, begorrah?" asked Mick.

"I vas in a Rooshian ship, from Revel, and ve loaded veat at 'Frisco for Hamburg. Our Captain he vas a tamu fool from Cronstadt, didn't know fore from aft. Ve had a good run from 'Frisco, until ve ran into dirty veather near Cape Horn. Six days der Old Man had no sight of der sun, as ve stood on southward in vesterly gales. Den he reckons ve was south of der Horn, and he gives der order to square away der yards and run east.

"That night I vas on lookout, and der Mate he says to me, 'Yonny,' he says, 'keep y'r eyes peeled. Der Captain he tinks ve are sout' of der Horn, but mebbe he ain't right!' '"Vot you mean, Mister?' I says. 'You tink ve might run up on der land?'

"'Mebbe, Yonny,' says der Mate, 've ain't far enough sout' yet to square away, and ve might see land ahead, der coast of Chile, and Gott help us if ve run ashore there, Yonny. It's an ironbound coast, like der Norway fjords, but no lights on it, and no people living dere, no animals, no trees, no nothing. Suppose ve get wrecked dere, Yonny, and ve reach der shore, ve must eat von another to live!"

"Vell, mates, der vind she blew up to a full gale, and der night she vos as dark as inside der belly of a cow, so I could see nothink. Ve drove on under topsails, vith big seas astern and decks full of vater. I vas properly frightened. At midnight all hands vere on deck and dey all vere frightened too. Dey thought somethink terrible might happen. Vell, sure enough, a few minutes after midnight, in der pitch dark, der sea and der vind dey suddenly dropped to a dead calm! Ve could see nuttings, and hear nuttings, but der ship she lost vay and she lay so still like she vos dead. 'How can dis be?' ve all said. Der Old Man he sang out, 'Cast der deep sea lead, Mister, and get a line bent to the kedge anchor. Dere's something mighty queer going on.'

"Der Mate handed der lead. line, and der Second Mate's vatch began getting der kedge anchor overside, but der Mate he sang out, 'Eighty fathom, hundred fathom,' and no bottom. A Rooshian seaman he said, 'Gott save us, ve have sailed into der mout' of Hell!' "Der Captain he said nuttings, but der Mate he sang out, 'Hell be tamned! Dere's no vater in Hell! Haul der lead line in, sving der boat out on der davits, and all hands stand by forrard, until ve see vot's vot.'

"Four hours ve vaited in der terrible quiet dark, and den daylight came, and vot you think ve see? Der ship she sits still like a duck, in der middle of a big fjord, vit' high mountains all around, and ve can see no vay to get in, or out to sea again! Der Captain's hair vas turned snowvite in der night mit der fright he got!

"Der boat ve put over and pulled two miles (3.2 km) to der vestward to find der mout' of der fjord. Sure 'nough, ve rounded a headland, and saw der open sea, vit an entrance half a mile (800m) wide. Outside, der gale vas still blowing. 'A miracle!' says der Mate. 'Ve sailed in here before der vind in pitch dark, vere no man would try to sail in, even in full daylight! Gott was der Man at der veel, but how in Hell can ve get out o' here in dis vesterly gale?' "Ve pulled back to the ship, and lowered der kedge to der bottom in 120 fathoms, but she vos not drifting! So ve lay still as a rock in der fjord, under lee of der land, in vater like a looking glass. Den der gale outside dropped, and Gott sent an easterly breeze offshore, so ve could sail out again, safe and sound.

Finn's tale of waking up with his ship in a storm free fjord. (AI)

"Ve rounded der Horn, but der Captain he vos a sick man. Ven ve reached Hamburg, he left der ship and never vent to sea again. Now, vat you think, shipmates, dat vos a close shave, hey?"

"Maybe you dreamed it," said Mick Mulligan. "No," said Yonny. "It vos all true!"

Having heard many "tall" tales of this kind from old shellbacks, I see no reason to disbelieve them, as every sailor knows that there are more things in heaven and on earth — and on the sea — than are dreamt of in landsmen's philosophies.

I later verified the story of the Kingsport from dock officials at Liverpool, who remembered her arrival in the Mersey lashed together with her anchor cables. They said that the incident was reported as remarkable in the newspapers of the time. As for the Finn's story of the ship that ran into a fjord on the Patagonian coast of Chile in the darkness, I can't imagine how Yonny Helsing could have invented the details. He was a stolid fellow, who never had much to say, but perhaps he had a good imagination and enjoyed spinning a good yarn.

About ten days after hearing these tales of narrow shaves, I had something happen to me which I hesitate to put into print, lest it should be disbelieved; but as it did happen, I must include it here. The *County of Pembroke* was running her easting down in the roaring forties, after passing the Cape of Good Hope, when the wind shifted a few points, and she took a big sea over the lee rail. I was tailing onto the main brace with the other men of the watch, when my feet were swept away from under me by the surge of the water, and in another instant, I was washed overboard! Encumbered as I was with thigh boots and oilskins, I had little chance of swimming, but luckily, I managed to hold on to the loose end of the brace, which was trailing overside with me, washed there by the same sea that had carried me over the rail.

As I grasped the line, the barque rolled to windward, and I hung on, gasping for breath and trying to yell for help, but my shipmates, who had ducked under the rail when the sea was shipped, had not seen me go overboard and my voice was lost in the roar of the wind and waters. The barque rolled to leeward again, shipping another sea. As I struggled and kicked, holding grimly on to the line, the sea washed me over the rail inboard! This time I made no mistake. I flung both arms around the fife rail at the base of the mainmast and clung on. My shipmates stood gaping at me. The Mate said, "Where did you come from?"

I spat out a mouthful of salt water and answered, truthfully, "I was washed overboard by one sea, sir, and washed back on board by the next!"

The Mate was the first to get over the general surprise at this astonishing statement. "The next time you do a thing like that," he said, "I'll log you for attempting to desert ship!"

On 17th December, ninety-three days out from the Mersey, we made our landfall in South Australia, sighting land at Kangaroo Island. We sailed through Investigator Strait in hot midsummer weather, with a fair breeze, and into St. Vincent Gulf, bearing up for Port Adelaide. Off the entrance to the port, a paddlewheel tug took us in tow and berthed us in a dock with several other sailing vessels. The first news we heard on our arrival was that Britain was at war with the Dutch "Boer" Republics of South Africa, the Transvaal, and the Orange Free State. W:ar had been declared on 11th October, while we were at sea.

As sailors know nothing of politics, we had heard only vaguely at Liverpool that trouble was brewing.

At that time the six Australian colonies were not federated into an Australian Commonwealth. Each colony, including South Australia, had its own naval and military forces, and all the colonies had offered troops to help Britain. Already two detachments had sailed from Adelaide, one of infantry on 28th October, and one of Mounted Rifles on 2nd November. Another detachment of Mounted Rifles was being got ready. It was to be embarked on 28th January 1900.

We spent Christmas Day of 1899 — my second Christmas away from home — drearily at Port Adelaide. The port, four miles (6.4 km) from the city, had few attractions to offer boys, as its shore buildings consisted mainly of pubs and wharf sheds; but the good ladies of the Seamen's Mission gave us tea and cakes and tried to make us feel cheerful. We did not visit the city of Adelaide, as the fare of one shilling was more than we could afford. After discharging our cargo and taking in stone ballast, we sailed from Port Adelaide, bound for Port Pirie on the shore of Spencer Gulf, about 250 miles (402 km) away. Our orders on leaving Liverpool had been to proceed from Adelaide to Port Pirie to load bagged ore. With a pilot on board we made slow headway, with frequent short tacks, up Spencer Gulf, seeing several other windjammers on the passage. At that time Port Pirie, the port of the fabulously rich Broken Hill mine, 225 miles (362 km) inland, was a regular rendezvous of windjammers, which brought coal there from Newcastle in New South Wales — a haul of some 1,200 miles (1931 km) around the Australian coast — and lifted bagged ore and ingots of lead for European destinations. Smelting works had been established at Port Pirie in 1889.

On arrival at Port Pirie, we anchored with twenty-five other sailing vessels waiting to go alongside the jetty. The Captain ordered the four apprentices to man the gig, to row him ashore. While he conferred with the agent, we examined the town. It was known as "Bag Town" because many of the men employed in the smelting works lived in hessian huts on a flat piece of ground, which was a marsh filled in with ballast brought in sailing ships from many lands.

I sometimes wonder how the geologists of the remote future will explain the many kinds of stone they will find on the foreshores of harbours that were sailing ship ports in the nineteenth century. Steamers, being weighted with their engines, bunker coal, and water ballast, seldom required ballasting with stone; but in sailing vessels, with their tall top hamper, ballast was essential to avoid capsizing. Great expense and loss of time were entailed by taking it in and discharging it, even for short movements from port to port or from one berth to another inside a harbour. When ballast was discharged, it was sometimes stacked handy to wharves, to be used in another vessel, and sometimes dumped along the foreshores by municipal councils, for filling in low lying places, as was done at Port Pirie.

When Captain Williams returned to the gig, which was tied to the jetty, he was a little excited, having had a few drinks with the agent. He told us that we were going to Port Germein, twenty miles (32 km) north of Port Pirie, to load flour and hay under government charter for the military forces, and that soon we would be bound for South Africa! These orders had come to the agent by telegraph while we were in transit from Port Adelaide. In consequence, we remained only overnight at Port Pirie and next morning heaved up the anchor and sailed, with the pilot on board, to Port Germein.

This little port had a long jetty stretching out over a mud flat, and only two or three buildings on shore. It was originally a loading port for schooners taking wool brought from the interior on camels. We were sent there to take in our cargo of flour and hay for the second detachment of the South Australian Mounted Rifles then preparing to embark at Adelaide. By going to Port Germein, we were able to tie up immediately at the mile-long (1.6 km) jetty, instead of waiting our turn, possibly for weeks, at Port Pirie.

The flour, in hundred- and fifty-pound bags and the hay in pressed bales and some other military stores came by rail to Port Germein, but we had to load it and stow it with the aid of a dozen wharfies, plus the labour of our own crew- hot work in that arid region of red soil and little rainfall. There were few attractions on shore — one grog shanty, a police station, and a camp of ragged Aborigines, who begged for 'baccy.

After a fortnight's sweating, we had our cargo well stowed and trimmed, and we battened down the hatches. A small "Puffing Billy" tug towed us slowly clear of the jetty, and we set sail, on 19th January 1900, bound for Algoa Bay in South Africa.

After two days' difficult and slow sailing in Spencer Gulf, we rounded Cape Catastrophe into the teeth of a strong westerly gale.

It was one thing to run the easting down to Australia, but quite another matter to sail into the teeth of the westerlies on that route, as we soon enough discovered. For several days we were hove to, in the Great Australian Bight, making scarcely any headway until the gale abated. Then we sailed south-westerly on the starboard tack for a week, before wearing ship, to sail on the port tack, clearing Cape Leeuwin, and across the Indian Ocean to the vicinity of Mauritius. From there we picked up fair winds on the old East India trade route, and dropped the killick in Algoa Bay on 19th March 1900, sixty days out from Port Germein.

Congestion at Algoa Bay — "Muddling Through" in the Boer War — Rowing the Old Man Ashore—Fire in the S.S. "Mariposa" — The Swimming Pig—In Ballast to Newcastle, New South Wales—Long Delays in Ports — A Coal Cargo for the West Coast — We Arrive at Carrizal — Lightering and Loitering — "There's Always Tomorrow."

ALCOA BAY is at the southeastern corner of the African continent, 420 miles (675 km) by sea eastward of Cape Town. It is a crescent shaped bay, forty miles (64 km) wide at its mouth, facing southeast, and therefore sheltered from the prevailing westerly weather, but offering no protection from easterly or southeasterly winds. When we arrived, there were over forty sailing vessels and a dozen tramp steamers anchored in the bay, all loaded, like our barque, with military stores, and waiting their turn to discharge their cargoes with the limited lighterage facilities available.

The town of Port Elizabeth, on the shore of a cove in the lee of Cape Recife, at the southwestern end of the bay, had a pier and limited wharf accommodation, inadequate for the sudden increase of shipping that converged on Algoa Bay with troops and war supplies from Britain, Australia, and India. This port was nearer than Cape Town to the scene of hostilities in the Transvaal and the Orange Free State; but in the early stages of the war, as historians agree, there was much muddle and "absent mindedness" in Britain's conduct of the military operations, including the organization of supplies. Though ships of all kinds had been sent to Algoa Bay, no one had thought of the need for increased facilities for unloading cargoes. With up to sixty vessels in port, only two or three could be berthed at the pier, and more were arriving almost every day.

Australian Light Horse detachments, impatient at delays, put their horses overside and swam ashore with them at low tide for distances of a mile and more. The *County of Pembroke* was anchored two miles (3.2 km) from the pier. We lay there in idleness for two months before we could obtain lighters to begin discharging our cargo; and that was possible only because the hay and flour we carried were urgently demanded by the Australian troops on shore.

Other ships which had arrived before us had been lying at anchor for four or five months without being able to obtain lighters. It was out of the question for a sailing vessel to be berthed at the pier, unless she carried troops, and then she was berthed for only a few hours while they disembarked. Priority in discharging cargoes, either at the pier or by lighters, was given to steamers, because of the higher rate of demurrage on steamers than on sailing vessels. Moreover, the windjammers were a nuisance to the harassed port authorities, as they had to take in ballast when their cargoes were discharged. It put an extra strain on the inadequate labour resources of the port to procure, cart, and deliver the ballast to the waterfront, to be lightered out to the ships progressively as their cargoes were discharged into the lighters.

To make matters worse, lightering was impossible when easterly or southeasterly gales raised seas in the open bay where the ships were anchored, and then there was a risk that vessels would drag their anchors and be driven on shore.[1] At such times lightering was suspended for several days. In these disorganized conditions we lay at anchor for three months before we were able to discharge our cargo of 1,200 tons and take in 300 tons of stone ballast and clear out. We had some degree of priority, because our cargo was perishable, but some windjammers lay there for six months before the "absentminded beggars" of the War Office, who were proud of their ability to "muddle through," made arrangements to clear them from the port.

For the first two months, while we were waiting for lighterage, the "matelots" of the fo'c'sle had no chance to go ashore. The Mates kept all hands busy overhauling gear aloft, chipping rust, painting, and endeavouring to scrape off the barnacles which accumulated on the hull at and below the waterline. Few fresh provisions were taken in, and we had the same monotonous diet as at sea.

The apprentices were more fortunate than the fo'c'sle hands, as it was our task to row the Captain ashore in the gig whenever he had business to transact, and this was very frequently. On almost every fine day we were ordered to get the gig ready. This required an hour's work before breakfast. All paintwork had to be scrubbed. The thwarts and oars had to be sand-and-canvased "as white as a hound's tooth" (the Old Man's favourite saying), and the brass tholepins and the yoke on the rudder polished till they shone like gold.

With so many ships in port and so many critical eyes ready to find fault, all the captains vied with one another to have the smartest gig, and ours took a lot of beating. When everything was spick and span, including ourselves in clean white shirts and dungarees we would bring the gig alongside the gangway, and the Captain would embark and take his seat in the stern, but not before casting a severely critical eye over the boat to detect any speck of dirt or tarnish that may have escaped our notice.

The boat was a four oared gig. It would have been beneath the Old Man's dignity to be rowed ashore by less than four apprentices. Captain Williams was suitably garbed to uphold his status as a Master Mariner. He was smallish, rotund, and rubicund, with twinkling blue eyes, but had a devil of a temper when aroused. For going ashore, he usually wore a blue serge suit, with a high white collar and cravat with a gold pin and a heavy gold watch in his waistcoat pocket, secured by a gold chain across his stomach. This was a watch which had been presented to him by an underwriting firm some years previously, for a feat of seamanship which had saved them paying out a considerable amount. The Captain's trousers were bell bottomed, and on his head was a brown billycock hat, well brushed and worn at a rakish angle. We boys were very proud of him. The two-mile (3.2 km) pull to the pier was a mere "warm up," as the Captain called it, for four stalwart apprentices. His important business on shore, as far as we could ascertain, was usually to spend a few hours hobnobbing with other ship captains in a hotel near the pier. Our duty was to wait in the gig until he returned. We would make the gig fast to the pier among many other gigs from other ships. It did us a power of good to yarn with the boys in these boats, exchanging sea stories and candidly appraising our different ships, and captains.

Though our pocket money was scanty, we managed to buy some fruit and sweets from shops near the pier, but we could not venture far, lest the Old Man should suddenly return; and two boys were always left in the gig, to keep an eye on her. After he had transacted his business on shore, we rowed the Captain smartly back to the *County of Pembroke*. On some occasions he visited other vessels at their anchorages or went ashore again in the evenings. This meant that we were boatmen for much of the time far better than polishing brass and bird's eye maple in the barque, in our opinion.

One Sunday afternoon, as we were pulling the Captain ashore, we saw smoke billowing out of the afterhold of a tramp steamer, the *S.S. Mariposa*, lying at anchor. She was flying a two-flag urgent signal, meaning, "I am on fire."

"By damn," said Captain Williams, "Captain Evans is an old pal of mine. I'll lay alongside him and see if we can give him any help. A long, strong pull there, m'sons, put your backs into it!"

The *Mariposa* was partly loaded with bales and trusses of hay, which had caught alight in her hold. Her crew were pumping water into the hold, but the fire was getting out of control. As we lay alongside, Captain Evans leaned over the wing of the bridge and sang out, "I'm going to beach her. Do you want a pig? We have a big pig here, and the decks are getting too hot for him."

"Indeed to goodness, yes!" our Old Man sang out. "Throw him overboard and thank ye!"

A minute later several men appeared at the rail and threw a large, black, pig, squealing loudly, into the water alongside the gig. The pig began vigorously swimming away, and we pursued him. Our Old Man went into the bows, to secure the pig with the painter.

This proved more difficult than he expected, but we were smacking our lips at the prospect of a grand feed of roast pork that evening. In his efforts to secure the pig, the Captain forgot that he had his best suit of clothes on.

Tramp Steamer S.S. Mariposa (Public Domain, Wikipedia)

He leaned over the bow and tried to pass the line around the pig's neck. The pig struggled and splashed salt water on the Captain's suit, wetting his sleeves to the shoulders. Then his presentation gold watch fell out of his waistcoat pocket and dangled in the water, though held securely by its chain.

"Damnation!" the Captain roared. "That pig is too big to haul into the gig. Curse his hide, he's ruined my watch!"

At this moment a naval launch drew near, manned by eight oarsmen, with a Petty Officer at the tiller. They had been sent to stand by the burning steamer, to give aid if required. "Ahoy, there!" Captain Williams sang out. "Do you want a pig?"

Broad grins spread on the tanned faces of the tars as the Petty Officer said, "Thank you," and steered for the pig. In a few minutes the porker was secured and lifted grunting into the naval launch. So we saw our hopes of a good dinner disappear.

Then came a dramatic scene as the Mariposa, which luckily had steam up, slipped her cable and drove in toward the beach, with dense black smoke and flames rising from her afterhold. She gained speed, steering among the anchored vessels, and ran well up onto the shore. There, a fire brigade from Port Elizabeth and a crowd of soldiers attempted to put out the fire, but they could do nothing effective, as her decks and hull plates were red hot.

For three days she continued to burn out, and her hull glowed, making a remarkable sight at nighttime. When at last the fire died, she was only an empty shell, but strange to say the iron hull was undamaged, and she was eventually refloated.

The apprentices of the *County of Pembroke* had further opportunities of improving our skill as boatmen when Captain Williams heard that a full rigged ship, the *Brambletye*, was lying at a cove ten miles (16 km) from our anchorage with a cargo of explosives for the Army, and that she had been lying there for six months waiting to be unloaded.

"By damn," said Captain Williams, "the Master of the *Brambletye* is an old pal of mine, from the same village in Wales. I'll go and pay him a visit, as he must feel lonely, lying out there for six months! Have the gig ready overside tomorrow morning after breakfast."

It was a long pull in the hot sun, but we arrived alongside the *Brambletye* at midday and immediately noticed that she had marine growth fully eight inches thick all round her waterline. Evidently her Captain had decided not to use scrapers or chipping hammers on her hull while she was loaded with explosives. She was smothered in rust. The "absentminded beggars" of the War Office had ordered her to this remote cove and apparently forgotten her.

Her Captain and crew were in a miserable state of boredom, having no facilities for recreation on shore. Our arrival was greeted with joy, and we were invited to dinner, which consisted of pea soup, salt pork and biscuits. To our surprise, there was a lady on board the *Brambletye* — the Captain's wife — and, as she was in an "interesting condition" her husband had decided to send her to England by steamer. "We'll take you in the gig," Captain Williams offered.

So, on the pull back we had two extra passengers, and the lady's luggage. She and her husband stayed on board the *County of Pembroke* for a week, while arrangements were made for her steamer passage. On the appointed day we took them to the *S.S. Dunnottar Castle* and saw her off with a very tearful goodbye. Next day we rowed the Captain of the *Brambletye* back to his ship. Soon after, her cargo was discharged, and she made a very slow passage of four months in ballast to Newcastle, in New South Wales, to load coal for the west coast of South America.

After we had been lying at anchor for two months, lighters began coming alongside to lift our cargo. They were manned by Kaffirs, big muscular men, ebony black, who soon became covered white with flour as they handled the bags out of our hold. As the barque rose in the water, we scraped the grass and barnacles from her hull, as far under as we could reach. Then ballast was brought out in the lighters and hauled inboard with tackles and baskets. We took in and stowed 300 tons of this, while the last 300 tons of flour were being lifted. The ballast consisted of broken bricks, rubble, and cement blocks, salvaged from a demolished building, difficult to spread and stow evenly, but the best obtainable. Our Old Man viewed it with distrust, and we spent several days in the hold, tamping it down with planks and battens.

On 24th June 1900, after ninety-three days in port, we gladly heaved up the anchor and set sail, bound for Newcastle on the east coast of Australia — a run of 6,000 miles (9656 km) — in ballast, to procure a cargo of coal. I believe that, under our charter party, the government of South Australia was charged a price which allowed for a return to Australia in ballast and demurrage for our long stay in port at Algoa Bay, but such wartime charters were exceptional. In ordinary circumstances, sailing vessels often proved uneconomical because so much of their time was spent idle in port or on voyages in ballast, in quest of cargoes.

It was midwinter as we cleared out of Algoa Bay and immediately began running the easting down in the westerly gales. The Old Man drove on skilfully, maintaining a speed of from eight to ten knots. The weather was bitterly cold, and we suffered much from chilblains and "wrist boils." These latter caused by the rubbing of the oilskin cuffs, wet with salt water, on our wrists. For these boils there was no known cure. It was useless to bandage them, as salt water soaked the bandages and made the skin irritation worse. In twenty-five days' smart sailing, we arrived in Bass Strait and scudded on past Cape Otway in a gale, to turn the corner of the Australian continent at Wilson's Promontory and head northward on 18th July.

Now we were in the lee of the land, though some twenty miles (32 km) out to sea, and the westerly gales eased off. By good fortune we had southerly breezes as we made steady headway along the Australian shore, getting a fix from landmarks and lights on the coast.

At sunset on 20th July, we had Sydney Heads and Macquarie• Lighthouse abeam, and next morning we were hove to within sight of Nobby's Light, at the entrance to the coal port of Newcastle, thirty days out from Algoa Bay.

Towed in by a tug, we were berthed on the Carrington side of the harbour, opposite the city. Between seventy and eighty vessels in the port had arrived ahead of us and were waiting their turn to go under the cranes to load coal. Of these, more than sixty were sailing vessels. Newcastle, in New South Wales, was at this time one of the busiest sailing ship ports in the world. It had a thriving trade with the west coast ports of South America (Chile and Peru), where coal was in demand for domestic use, bunkering, the railways, and steam engines in the copper mines, as there were no local coal mines. Unfortunately, the trade was in one direction only, as the products of South America were not in much demand in Australia. Sailing vessels therefore often carried coal from Newcastle to the "west coast," then picked up a cargo of nitrates and sailed on to Europe, around Cape Horn; though some regularly returned to Newcastle in ballast, for another cargo of coal.

Another disadvantage of this trade was the slow "turn around" of sailing vessels at Newcastle, and also in the west coast ports. It was not unusual for a vessel to remain three months in Newcastle, waiting to be loaded. Though the actual loading at the crane berths took only a couple of days, the number of crane berths was inadequate, and vessels had to wait their turn for weeks and sometimes months. Similarly, in the west coast ports of South America, the discharging of coal by lighters with manual labour (usually of the crew) was a slow and laborious process, as was the taking in of ballast.

Modern ideas of hustle and bustle and of a quick turn-around for shipping were scarcely thought of in sailing ship days. A sailing vessel spending, say, three months in port at Newcastle, three months in port on the west coast, and two months on a voyage in ballast to return to Newcastle was incurring expenses and eating up time unprofitably for eight months in a year! In such conditions, it was not surprising that shipowners were called skinflints because of the low wages and poor provisions in their vessels. The mercantile marine under sail was becoming less and less profitable, but this was due not to any lack of efficiency in the men or ships at sea. The trouble was due to lack of port facilities and the difficulty of picking up cargoes when and where they were needed.

The *County of Pembroke* lay at Newcastle a hundred and ten days, from 21st July to 8th November 1900. Any reader who may find this statement surprising may verify it from the files of newspapers of the time, as I have done. This delay was necessary to obtain a cargo of 1,600 tons of Wallsend coal for delivery to the west coast port of Carrizal in Chile. We lay at Berth 21 on the Carrington side, along- side the Norwegian barque *Stjorn*, 1,467 tons, and next to the barque *Firth of Stronsa*, 1,211 tons, which was in Berth 22. Part of the delay in loading was due to the necessity to take in a "stiffening" of a few hundred tons of coal before our ballast could be discharged. We had to wait our turn to go under the cranes for the stiffening, then be towed across the harbour to take in the stiffening and towed back to Carrington to discharge the ballast. Then there was another long wait of many weeks to go under the cranes again for the rest of the cargo.

In these conditions, and as there were so many sailing vessels in harbour, constantly arriving and departing after long periods of inertia, the crimping industry was well organized in Newcastle. Vessels lying at the Farewell Buoys, near Nobby's Light, were usually shorthanded until crimps brought out drink-drugged sailors from pubs on shore, who were easily persuaded by the crimps, on the inducement of a few days' spree, to desert their own ships and leave it to the crimps to find them another ship!

Three or four of our crew deserted in this way and were replaced by others when we were at the Farewell Buoys.

During our long stay in port, the crew and apprentices had leave to go ashore on Saturday afternoons and evenings, with frugal cash allowances in pocket. We went by ferry to Newcastle and promenaded the streets in company with hundreds of other apprentices, eyeing the girls, though usually with little success, as the demand greatly exceeded the supply.

On weeknights and Sundays, we often spent hours in the Seamen's Mission, which was at Stockton, across the harbour from our berth, and attended concerts and dances and "socials" organized by the kindly ladies of the Mission — God bless 'em.

At last sailing day came, and we were towed out past Nobby's, well clear of the land, to set sail and run to the south-eastward, on the starboard tack, in a stiff southerly buster. This lasted for a week, until we reached Lat. 50 deg. S, to the south of New Zealand, and squared away in a howling westerly, to run the easting down.

For four weeks we drove on with decks awash, to Long. 100 deg. W, when we altered course to the nor 'east, in winds of decreasing velocity as we bore in toward the coast of Chile. We made our landfall off Valparaiso, 6,000 miles (9656 km) from Newcastle, thirty-seven days out, and then sailed slowly, in very light airs, with all sail set to the royals, beneath a cloudless sky, along the rocky and mountainous coast, northward for another 300 miles (482 km), to arrive at Carrizal on 20th December 1900.

Like all the west coast ports, Carrizal is on the shore of a wide crescent bay. We signalled for a pilot, but none appeared, so we sailed in, with very light breezes, to drop anchor a mile (1.6 km) offshore. There was no other vessel in the port. The harbour facilities consisted of a short jetty, for boats and lighters. There were only two or three lighters available. They were propelled by sweeps and manned by Chileans and beachcombers whose motto was manana, meaning, "Why hurry today? There is always tomorrow."

On "surf days" long ocean swells rolled into the bay and all lightering was abandoned. The town was a straggled collection of white painted adobe houses, its narrow streets crowded with a mixed population of Chileans of Spanish descent, Indians, Negroes, and Chinese, and "poor whites" who were mainly beachcombers or stranded sailors of all nationalities. There was little inducement here for our crew to desert. We unloaded the coal cargo with the labour of the crew, including the apprentices, filling it into bags which were swung overboard into the lighters, at the rate of about thirty tons per working day. We were covered with black dust, but some of us enjoyed a swim in the warm, clear water each evening, overside.

So, Christmas Day, 1900, arrived — my third Christmas away from home.

The voyage had already lasted fifteen months, and in this desolate spot home seemed farther away than ever it had seemed before.

But I had now completed a little over two years of my apprenticeship in sail. I had seen something of the wide world and had learned enough to know that a sailor's life was a hard one, and that I had much more still to learn.

CHAPTER FOOTNOTES:

The *County of Pembroke,* in 1904, one year after I had left her, ended her days at Algoa Bay, where she was driven ashore in a SE gale and became a total wreck.

13

*Shovelling Coal at Carrizal — The Captain's Magpie — A West
coast Welcome — Northward in the Pacific — The Columbia River
— Loading Flour at Portland, Oregon — A Change of Captains —
Sailors' Hobbies and Marine Curiosities — Putting a Ship Into a
Bottle — Homeward Bound — We Call at Pitcairn Island — I Barter
My Bible — Hidden Treasure*

NEW YEAR'S DAY, 1901, the first day of the twentieth century,
found me shovelling coal in the hold of the *County of Pembroke* at
Carrizal, with black dust in my nostrils and throat and covering all
the skin of my body, except where streams of sweat left grimy streaks. The
apprentices were required to work with the crew in the hold, to set the men
a good example.

We worked from 6 a.m. to 5 p.m. daily, with half an hour for breakfast,
and one hour for midday dinner. There was no work done on Saturday
afternoons or Sundays. On "surf days" and at other times when lightering
was slow and also on Saints' Days or "feasts," which were numerous in Chile,
the Mates could find plenty of other work to be done on board the barque.
Occasionally the Captain required the apprentices to row him ashore in the
gig — a welcome change for us from shovelling coal.

While he transacted his business with the agent, we reclined in the gig in
the shade under the pier, or caught fish, which were so plentiful that they
could be scooped up in a hand net or hooked with a "jigger," but, as we were
told that they were poisonous, we did not try the experiment of eating them.
The seamen in the barque out in the bay also caught fish with handmade lines
and hooks, but, as the fish were inedible, it was a wasted effort.

On Saturday afternoons, the seamen were allowed to go ashore, with an advance of one peso (a South American dollar). For a few cents fare, they were taken off by a boatman from on shore. There was little risk that they would be crimped at Carrizal, especially as no other vessels were in port. They indulged in sprees on pisco at a few cents a nip and perhaps on other pleasures of the port at similar bargain prices. If any men were missing on Monday morning, the Captain would know where to find them — in the calaboose, a filthy, vermin ridden hole, where the gendarmes had lodged them for brawling. He would pay their fines — the amount to be deducted from their pay — then bring them or send them on board and, in accordance with the articles they had signed, fine them a few shillings extra, for overstaying leave.

The apprentices were not allowed shore leave in the evenings; there were no attractions in Carrizal except taverns and suchlike, which we were forbidden by our indentures to frequent.

In this port the mystery of the Captain's Magpie occurred. "Maggie," as we called him (or her) was a handsome and intelligent bird — an Australian talking magpie that had been presented to Captain Williams by a friend in Newcastle. It was generally supposed on board, and asserted by the Captain, that Maggie was a male. His wings were clipped so that he could not fly. He lived in the Captain's cabin, wandering around it as he pleased, and in fine weather or in port, sometimes hopped up the companionway and sunned himself on the poop. His "cage" was an upended wooden soapbox, with a perch across the inside and no door. He was put to bed in this box at nighttime and in heavy weather. At other times, as he hopped around in the cabin or on the poop, he uttered discordant squawks, which the Captain proudly interpreted as the spoken word.

We learned from the Second Mate that the Captain spent an hour or so every evening teaching Maggie to speak Welsh. The method of doing this was somewhat original. After the evening meal was cleared away, the Captain sat with a glass of whiskey at the polished table and placed Maggie on the table in front of him. Then the lesson began, as the Captain spoke some word or short phrase in Welsh and repeated it many times, until Maggie uttered a squawk, which the Captain at once considered to be a proof that the bird was almost human and learning fast.

As the lessons proceeded, Maggie proved that he was a good mimic in another way. Noticing the Captain occasionally taking a sip from the glass of whiskey, Maggie decided to do the same. He dipped his beak into the glass and took a few meditative sips. Then, greatly to the Captain's amusement, the bird got drunk and began to slide and stagger in a comical dance around the polished surface of the table. This performance took place every evening, giving the Captain 'and the bird much pleasure. The entertainment was often seen by the First Mate, the Second Mate, and by the cook, who, as steward, lived under the poop and waited at the Old Man's table.

As the apprentices had the task of cleaning out Maggie's cage daily and removing other messes made by Maggie in the cabin or on the poop deck at frequent intervals, we were not amused. Then, one morning, there was a great hullabaloo after breakfast. Maggie was missing! Work on the coal came to a standstill as all hands were put on to search the barque, inside and out, from stem to stern and truck to keelson, and in every hole and corner, looking for Maggie.

No luck. "He must have fallen overboard," said the Captain, scanning the surface of the water, near and far. "Man the gig! I'll find him, alive or dead. A bird would take a long time to sink, and perhaps the poor fellow may be still alive."

Though still in his pyjamas, the Old Man got into the gig, the apprentices manned the oars, and we pulled around and around the barque in widening circles, scanning the waves; but there was no sign of Maggie. "Queer," said the Captain. "Perhaps he has drifted ashore."

Estimating the probable line of drift, the Old Man steered the gig for the shore, ordering us to pull very slowly, and keep our eyes peeled. But we did not find Maggie.

"Perhaps he has reached the shore," said the Old Man, hopefully. We beached the gig half a mile (800m) north of the town and for two hours trudged up and down, clambering among the rocks, searching every nook and cranny, without success. The Captain in his pyjamas was the most active person in the party, constantly calling out to us not to neglect looking under and behind every rock, near or remote. At last, as the tropical sun beat down fiercely on his unprotected head, he uttered a heavy sigh of regret and ordered us to row back to the barque, abandoning the search.

"I can't believe it," he said. "That bird has signed off. Maybe he's been crimped!"

The mystery was never solved. It is possible that Maggie fell overboard and was taken by a fish, but his (or her) death cast a gloom over us all.

After we had been in port a fortnight, a full rigged ship appeared in the offing, with all sail set in the light airs, standing in to the bay. Our Old Man ordered the apprentices to man the gig, and we rowed out to meet the newcomer. She was a ship we had seen in Newcastle. We made fast alongside her, and our Old Man, greeted cordially by her Old Man, went to the poop while we apprentices joined the crew on deck, to add our muscle power to theirs, helping to work the ship to her anchorage.

This was the usual procedure in west coast ports, where the apprentices from vessels at anchor, sometimes thirty or forty boys all told, rowed out with their captains to greet newcomers and give them any help that might be necessary if the crews in the incoming vessels were weakened by scurvy or depleted in numbers by accidents or frostbite incurred when rounding the Horn to the westward from Europe. In any case the extra manpower was useful in the fitful light airs that prevailed in the west coast bays.

The coast of Chile fringes a strip of land at the foot of the immense range of the Andes, which towers in peaks to 20,000 feet (6096m), from twenty to forty miles (64 km) inland. This mighty range of mountains has the effect of a windbreak — creating a pocket of calm or light eddying airs along the coast at its foot, extending for twenty miles (32 km) or more out to sea. The light airs prevailed, except on rare occasions when a "norther" blew, which, unimpeded by the mountains, raised seas in the open bays and at times caused vessels to drag their anchors and drive on shore.

As we lay for seventy days at Carrizal, discharging our cargo and taking in ballast, several other sailing vessels arrived during that period. On each occasion, the captains and apprentices from vessels at anchor went out to welcome the newcomer. These were pleasant interludes in the drudgery of shovelling coal; we could meet other boys and sometimes renew acquaintances made at previous ports of call. The fraternity of the sea was governed by haphazard encounters of hail and farewell. Many times, later in my life I met ships' officers whom I had last seen thirty years or so before, when we were boys together in the random encounters of sailing ship ports or as shipmates.

One day early in March 1901, we hoisted the Blue Peter and next morning, helped by apprentices from two other vessels then in port, heaved up the anchor and set sail, in ballast, from Carrizal, northward bound for Portland, Oregon, in the U.S.A. As soon as we were well under way our reinforcements· and their captains gave us a cheer and left us.

Slowly we drew away from the land, on a north-westerly course in the blue Pacific Ocean and, in a few days, picked up a fair wind in the SE trades, which bowled us along in fine hot weather at ten knots. This carried us to the doldrums in the equatorial zone. After a week of frustrations there, we picked up the NE trade wind and made good headway until we passed the latitude of San Francisco. Now in the North Pacific, we encountered variable winds and gales until, in April, we sighted Cape Disappointment at the mouth of the Columbia River. We had sailed in ballast some 5,000 miles (8406 km) from Carrizal, in five weeks.

We anchored outside the bar and a few days later were taken in tow by a stern wheeler tug, — the first sternwheeler I had seen. Her name was *Harvest Queen*. She made fast alongside us amidships and took us seventy miles (112 km) up the picturesque river, its banks densely forested. In the distance we could see high peaks on which snow lingered. This beautiful scenery, with springtime in the air, was a sight for sore eyes after our sojourn in the arid zone at Carrizal. We dropped anchor in the stream off the bustling city of Portland, among many other sailing vessels, and waited to go alongside to load a cargo of flour.

Among the vessels in port were several Yankee "Down Easters," wooden built, with a rig of skysails above the royals, famous Cape Homers of their day. They were known as "Skysail Yarders." Their crews were hard driven by Bucko Mates but were well paid and far better fed than the crews of lime juicers. In this port, as at San Francisco and Seattle, crews deserted wholesale, enticed by crimps, or to go looking for work in the lumber camps or explore the many other opportunities that thriving America offered at this time of expansion.

We lay at Portland nearly two months, and in that time several of our crew deserted, but we knew that we would have no trouble in obtaining others, from crimps, when sailing day came. At this port, too, we parted from Captain Williams, who left to take command of the four masted barque *Kate Thomas*, of the same owners. Her Mate, Edward Sager, took over the *County of Pembroke*, his first command. He was a fine seaman and well deserved his promotion.

While we lay in the stream, carpenters from the shore came out and lined our hold with planks, to keep our intended cargo of bagged flour clean. These planks would be sold as lumber on our arrival at our home port. After a tedious delay, we moved to a wharf, and our cargo of 1,400 tons of flour — in about 20,000 bags — was expertly stowed by shore labour in a few days.

Captain Sager, being a "new broom" and anxious to make a fast passage, overhauled the barque and all its gear and stores and kept all hands at work to get everything shipshape, for he intended to crack on, on the long run of 14,000 miles (22530 km) home, around Cape Horn. The apprentices had some leave to go ashore, with limited cash. This we spent chiefly on feeds of steak, priced at twenty-five cents, in hash houses on the waterfront, as we were craving a change from the scanty provisions served on board.

Eighteen months had now gone by since our departure from Liverpool. At sea we were still being served with the salt provisions taken on at the beginning of the voyage. The pork and beef came out of the harness casks green and yellow and stinking, but we had to stomach it or go hungry. The drinking water in the tanks was stale and smelly. The tanks had been filled at Newcastle six months before and we had not been able to get much fresh water at Carrizal, where there were no proper facilities for watering.

Fortunately for us, the supply of putrid salt provisions was now nearly exhausted, and the tanks were almost empty.

At Portland Captain Sager took in new provisions and filled the tanks with fresh water for our run home, on which we would be four or five months at sea.

At every port of call on this voyage, I had made a hobby of putting sand into a bottle — a harmless and inexpensive hobby if ever there was one, intended to provide tangible proof that I was a world traveller. I had a corked pickle bottle filled with water, and into this, at each port, I put a small fistful of sand, which then settled under the water in layers of different colours, white, grey, black, and red, demonstrating that I had set foot on many a foreign strand.

Another harmless hobby I had was drawing pencil sketches of ships, of various rig. I did this with primitive skill, my art being self-taught. Now I aspired to higher flights of art. At Portland for a few cents, I bought two small brushes and some oil paints. On the inside of the lid of my sea chest, I sketched a large, and, as I thought, glorious picture of the *County of Pembroke* in full sail and proceeded to colour it in oils with a vivid green sea, bright blue sky, crimson hull and white sails. The result, however garish it might have seemed to an art connoisseur, was kindly admired by my shipmates. I looked forward to astonishing my parents with this work of art not less than with my bottle of sand.

One of our sailors throughout the voyage had been working in the dog watches at putting a ship into a bottle, a task it had taken him twelve months to complete. With endless patience he had built the ship in miniature from pieces of wood, whittled with his jackknife, and had rigged her correctly with all sails to the royals on her three masts, using thin tarred twine for the rigging and carefully carved tiny pieces of wood for the blocks and tackles. There was nothing omitted. She was complete with deckhouses, wheel, binnacle, capstans, anchors, bitts, even belaying pins in the rails.

She was painted and varnished and perfect. When we arrived at Portland, the old seaman obtained a narrow necked bottle, and some putty and green colouring matter for the "sea." After rubbing the colour into the putty, he ran it into the bottle lying on its side. Then came the great moment, of putting the ship into the bottle. He cut the masts off short at the deck and hinged them, so that the whole top hammer lay down flat, in a fore-and-aft direction. Then he inserted the ship, stern first, through the neck of the bottle, and maneuverer her on the sea of green putty into a central position. When she was firmly settled there, he gently pulled on fine threads attached to the masts and yards and passing through the end of the jib boom and out through the neck of the bottle. With these threads he raised the hinged masts to a vertical position and trimmed the yards horizontally. Hey presto! A ship in a bottle! He decorated the cork and the neck of the bottle with cunningly worked twine plaiting known as cross pointing and brightened this up with a few touches of paint.

"What are you going to do with her?" I asked. "Sell her, o' course!"

"How much do you want for her?" "Two pounds o' plug tobacco."

I looked at the treasure wistfully. The price of two pounds of plug tobacco, about five shillings, was beyond my financial resources. Then suddenly I had a bright thought. Though not a smoker, I should be able to obtain the tobacco on credit from the Captain, its value to be deducted from my pay at the end of the voyage.

With some trepidation, I approached Captain Sager and explained matters to him candidly. "A ship in a bottle?" he said. "Are you sure you don't want to smoke or chew the 'baccy yourself?"

My eagerness convinced him that my only desire was to be a shipowner, and he gave me the tobacco. The ship in a bottle was mine! Carefully I stowed it in my sea chest, looking forward to the pleasure it would give my mother when I presented it to her to place on the mantlepiece at home. A real work of art, I considered it.

A ship in a bottle (AI Image)

For a few days before sailing, we lay at anchor in midstream, taking in stores, bending sail, battening down hatches, and waiting for clearance. On sailing eve, at midnight, a crimp's boat came out and delivered to us six seamen, unconscious drunk, required to complete our complement. Among them was one West Indian Negro. The Captain duly paid the crimp for the bodies, at the prevailing rate of blood money fifty dollars a man delivered on board. This amount, according to the legal fiction, was a debt owed by each man to the crimp for board and lodging on shore, for an unspecified period, and for providing a sea kit. The Captain discharged the debt in cash and deducted the amount from the sailors' pay at the end of the voyage.

It mattered little if they were sailors or sojers, the Mates would make seamen of them on the voyage. They were put into the fo'c'sle to snore on their donkeys' breakfasts. By the time they came to, a few hours later, we had hove up the anchor, to the strains of "Rolling Home," and were on our way downstream.

As we towed down river, the Captain signed them on and satisfied himself that the new hands, though bleary, were actually seamen and knew what was happening to them. In the afternoon we were clear of the land and cast off the tug, which circled around us once as we made sail, before giving three farewell blasts and a call of "Bon voyage" from the tugmaster through his megaphone. With a stiff nor'-wester on the starboard quarter, we stood away to the southward, and the light of Cape Disappointment gradually dipped astern as, toward the end of May 1901, our long homeward voyage began.

In a month's good sailing, in favourable conditions, we were in the South Pacific. One morning there was a cry of "Land Ho!" It was Pitcairn Island, that lonely spot where, in 1789, the mutineers of the Bounty had taken refuge, with their Tahitian wives, and had remained with their own form of government, undiscovered for twenty-five years. Though most of the descendants of the mutineers had been removed to Norfolk Island in 1866, some were still living on Pitcairn Island in 1901, with admixtures of recently immigrated Polynesians.

The light breeze in which we had been sailing fell to a flat calm, and a current carried us in toward the island. When we were three miles (4.8 km) offshore, we saw three boatloads of natives putting out to meet us. It was a fine sunny day, and the water was so still and glassy that we could plainly see the coral growth on the bottom. The Captain ordered soundings to be taken, which revealed that we were in twenty fathoms. To check our drift, the kedge anchor was dropped, with a three-inch manila rope cable.

Presently the boats came alongside. The natives were brown skinned, and splayfooted through wearing no boots. They spoke Kanaka and quaint English. They were eager to do business by barter, offering coconuts, bananas, man- goes and other fruits and vegetables, live pigs, fowls, eggs and curios in exchange for whatever they could get — but they chiefly wanted Bibles or prayerbooks, clothing and "timepieces." The Captain allowed some of them on board, and a lively trade developed.

The Pitcairn Islanders were Christians, and very religious people. They had no immediate use for money and wanted trade by barter. Their headman asked the Captain if he had any flour to spare. As we had 20,000 bags of flour in the hold, this was an easy question for the Captain to answer. In exchange for six bags of flour, he received two small pigs, some fowls, eggs and bananas for the saloon table.

Delivery of the flour to the natives involved a nice point of mercantile marine law. At our port of discharge, the Captain would have to account for the correct number of bags taken in at Portland, but not for their contents to the last ounce, or even the last hundredweight, as bags often burst and the contents spilled in the hold or on deck while being loaded or discharged. The Captain could spare the contents of six bags, but not the bags.

An old piece of sailcloth was spread in the bottom of one of the boats, and we emptied the contents of six bags of flour from the cargo onto it. The Captain then took the empty bags and threw them back into the hold before we battened down the hatch again.

In the meantime, the seamen and the apprentices ransacked their sea bags and sea chests for articles of barter, of which we had little to spare. For an old shirt, I obtained a big bunch of bananas. Then one of the natives tempted me with an offer of curios. These were coconut shells that had been cut in two, stripped of their copra and fibre, polished, and fitted with hinges, so that the top portion made the lid of a rounded receptacle. These fancy boxes had flowers painted on the outside, with the words "Souvenir de Pitcairn."

I asked the man who offered them what he wanted in exchange. "A timepiece!" he answered.

Sadly, I shook my head. "No timepiece." He tried again, "A Bible?"

"Yes," I told him. "I have a Bible!"

Hurrying into the half deck, I opened my sea chest and took from it the gold lettered Bible, bound in limp black Morocco leather, which my father had given to me inscribed, "To Gordon, on his first going to sea," two years and eight months previously. I regret to confess that the Bible was in excellent condition, having had very little use, partly because life under sail gave few opportunities to apprentices for religious studies. When I showed it, the islander's eyes glinted with the greed of acquisition.

"Yes, yes!" he said, eagerly, holding up one of his coconut boxes.

"Not enough!" I said.

He held up three boxes, and the deal was done. I gave him my Bible and put the souvenirs of Pitcairn in my sea chest with the bottle of sand and the ship in a bottle. Soon afterwards a breeze sprang up, we raised the anchor, and stood away to the south-eastward, headed for Cape Horn.

That afternoon, as we were sailing along sweetly in a fair following breeze, with everything drawing, I was on the poop with the Mate, in his watch, when he said to me "Jimmy, I saw you swap your Bible this morning for those knickknacks. It was a silly thing to do. An apprentice should read his Bible every day and never part with it!"

I looked at him in astonishment. I had not thought of him as being a religious man. He continued, "I learned that lesson many years ago, Jimmy, and this is how it happened. When I first went to sea as an apprentice — and that was before you were born — my aunt gave me a Bible and made me promise to read it every Sunday. 'If you are ever in need of help,' she said, 'be sure to turn to the Fifth Chapter of St. Matthew.'

"'Yes, aunt,' I said, 'I'll be sure to read it.'

"Well, that was a long voyage. We were away two years, and she was a hungry ship. Like all apprentices, I was hungry all the time and never had enough money in ports to buy cakes and fruit and suchlike. Being a young fool, I took no notice of my aunt's good advice. I left my Bible unread in the bottom of my sea chest. When we arrived home, my aunt said, 'And did you read your Bible on Sundays as you promised me?'

"'Yes, aunt,' I said very untruthfully. " 'Have you got it with you now?'

"'Yes, aunt,' I said, 'it's in my sea chest.' "'Well, show it to me,' she demanded.

"I went and got my Bible from my chest. 'And did you read my favourite chapter, the Fifth Chapter of St. Matthew?' my aunt asked.

" 'Of course, dear auntie,' I said.

"'Well, give me that Bible,' she says, and I handed it to her.

"She opened the good book, at the Fifth Chapter of St.

Matthew and showed me what was in it, between the leaves — a new five-pound note! — 'I put that there for you to find,' she says, sarcastic, 'but now I know that you are a wicked boy, and you never opened your Bible at all!' With this, 1he puts the five pounds in her purse, saying, 'Seemingly you didn't need this!'

"Well, Jimmy," the Mate continued, "how do you know that there wasn't a five-pound note in that Bible you swapped this morning for a mess of pottage?"

I was so taken aback at this suggestion that I worried about it for weeks, until I came to the conclusion that my father would not have played such a trick with Holy Writ; but I never had the nerve to ask him if he had.

Soon we worked up to the howling fifties and squared away to round the Horn in July, in midwinter weather, when the gales and blizzards are at their fiercest and the following seas tower fifty feet (15m) from trough to crest.

But this was my second rounding of the Horn, and I felt that I was a veteran. We drove on, in the usual discomforts and perils, but without mishap. After ten days of severe ordeals, with decks awash, wet clothes, frozen fingers, wrist boils, and long hours on deck, we rounded the Falkland Islands early in August and stood to the norrard in good heart, homeward bound, and yearning to be home.

14

*Northward in the Atlantic — More Marine Trophies — The
Albatross Relics — A Flying Fish — My Sennit Mat — Catching a
Shark — Gruesome Exhibits — The Sargasso Sea — Queenstown
For Orders — Nearly Drowned — The Pay off at Dublin — Home to
the Mersey at Last — A Long Voyage Ends — Travelers' Tales and
Souvenirs.*

HEADED off by unfavourable winds, we made slow progress
northward in the Atlantic, with the usual routine of furbishing ship
and holystoning the decks as we neared the doldrums. There we
were becalmed for nearly three weeks, except for short intervals of cat's paw
breezes, which enabled us to make laborious headway.

A strange incident had occurred while we were rounding the Horn, when
an albatross, which had been soaring around the barque for days, took it into
his head to fly athwartships, between the foremast and the mainmast. One of
his wings had struck the foretopmast stay, and in some unaccountable way
he was hurt in his struggles and fell dead to the deckhouse roof. This was bad
luck for him, but not for us, as we had not killed him — he had committed
suicide.

Before throwing the bird's body overboard, one of the sailors cut off his
head and feet and put them into a tin of brine, obtained from the cook. Now,
in fine weather, when seamen off watch had leisure for hobbies, the grisly
relics were taken out of the brine and skinned. I assisted in this process,
hoping to gain an addition to my collection of marine curiosities. The skins
of the big, webbed feet, bright yellow, were dried in the sun after having been
peeled off like a glove. The result was two tobacco pouches of doubtful
utility, too big to go into a man's pocket, and furnished with claws.

The old salt who performed the operation kept one of them and gave the other to me. I stuffed mine with rope yarn, to give the foot a realistic appearance and, although it was rather smelly, put it in my sea chest with my other treasures. The sailor then told me that I could have the head also. This was smellier than the feet, as particles of flesh adhered to the skin on which the beak, feathers and eyes were still intact. With care I mounted the head on a piece of wood. My efforts were far from successful, as the result was more gruesome than beautiful; but it too went into my sea chest to be presented, I hoped, to my mother as a rare marine curiosity.

After a few days the stink became unbearable, so I stowed my trophy in the bo'sun's locker. My zeal as a collector next impelled me to take home a flying fish also! We were in a stretch of the ocean where these were plentiful, and many came on board. They were more numerous at night than in the daytime. To trap them, we hung a hurricane lamp in front of a small canvas screen, rigged fore and aft, amidships. This acted as a lure, as the fish flew toward the light, hit the screen, and fell on deck — to go straight into the frying pan as a welcome addition to next morning's breakfast menu of tea and weevilly pantiles.

I secured one as a specimen and, after gutting him, put him into pickle in the harness cask, where the ready use salt horse was kept. A few weeks later I took him out and sun dried him, then spread out his transparent wings, gave him a couple of coats of varnish, and mounted him on a wooden stand. He was even more odoriferous than the albatross head, but he went into the bo'sun's locker with it. Another of my marine curiosities accumulated on this voyage was a sennit doormat, which I made myself. It was the spare time labour of many months. The material was manila rope yarns, plaited into sennit or what would be known ashore as braid. The sennit was then worked into a fancy flat design and sewn together. This job wore out my patience and made the ends of my fingers raw, but I kept on at it until the mat was completed, in a true labour of love.

Then came a chance for a splendid addition to my collection. One Saturday afternoon, when we were flat becalmed in the doldrums, the Captain decided to catch a large shark which was cruising tirelessly astern, waiting — as the sailors said — for a man to fall overboard. The shark, ten feet (3m) long, was accompanied by three "pilot fish," about fifteen inches long. These serve as guides for the shark, which has poor eyesight, and lead him to his prey. Their wages are scraps from whatever the shark kills.

A shark line could be set only by permission of the Captain or the Mate, chiefly because of the mess made on deck by blood and oil when a shark was caught; but the seamen were always eager to catch one, for four good reasons. First, a shark's tail nailed to the jib boom end would bring fair winds. Second, the death of a shark was an act of justice and revenge for the sailor men it had probably eaten. Third, to open a shark's belly was like a lottery, as old hands told of finding coins, gold rings, watches and chains, pocketknives, buttons, and other indigestible objects of value in sharks' stomachs — all that remained of sailors and passengers who had fallen overboard in bygone years. Fourth, catching a shark provided excitement and a change in the monotony of the doldrums.

The Captain ordered me to get the shark hook. I fetched it from the Mate's cabin, where it was kept with paint brushes and other light gear which might be pilfered in port if left lying around. The shark hook, of barbed steel, with a shank eight inches long, had a fathom[1] of chain attached to it, so that the shark, after swallowing the hook, could not bite it off.

The Captain rove a stout line to the chain, then baited the hook with a piece of fat salt pork from the harness cask. The fo'c'sle hands stood by expectantly on the main deck, as the Captain veered the baited hook astern. They watched the shark cruising on his tireless search for scraps from the galley or for living prey.

In the clear blue water we saw the pilot fish nosing at the bait, ten fathoms astern. They reported it to the shark, who decided to take it. There was a flash of white as the monster turned belly upwards and swallowed the pork. The Captain waited for a moment, then gave a strong heave at the line, and the hook struck home inside the shark's gullet.

"Hooked!" he sang out. The hands came running aft and laid on to the line in a tug o' war, as the monster of the deep thrashed the water to a flurry of foam in his wild attempts to get away. It was a contest of brute strength, as the men tailed on to the line had no aid of reel or ratchet to play the fish, using only their brawny muscles in a direct pull against his violent efforts.

Hauling on a line was what sailors could do best, through ample practice! The muscles of their arms and shoulders were wonderfully developed, to an extent which was noticeable by observant people on shore, so that a sailor could be picked out in a crowd of landsfolk by the peculiar manner in which he held his arms in a "bent-at-the-elbows" position as if hauling on a rope.

When the shark was fresh, it was all that the men could do to hold him, but they refused to concede him an inch of play and kept the line taut, knowing that it was so strong that all his efforts could not break it. The tussle went on for half an hour, until the shark tired before the men. He was drawn in toward the stern, then, still thrashing, though more feebly, maneuverer alongside amidships. Here another line with a loop on it was lowered down the hook line, allowed to settle around the shark's tail, and hauled taut. It would have been impossible to haul him on deck with the hook line, as he weighed some six hundred pounds.

The line that was made fast around his tail was passed through a block at the davit head. Then, with eight lusty sea dogs swaying on both lines, the brute was hauled up over the rail and dumped on deck, amidst great excitement as he continued to thrash around the planks. "Stand clear of his teeth!" the Captain sang out. "He can still bite a man's leg or arm off!"

The head and tail lines were made fast, and a capstan bar was rammed down the shark's throat. Then the cook, who had been sharpening his cleaver and butcher's knife in anticipation, approached, cleaver in hand, and began chopping off the shark's head, with sickening thuds of the heavy blade in the flesh and gristle, while blood and oil spurted on to the snow white holystoned deck planks and spattered the paintwork.

In a dozen strokes the deed was done, and the head, with eyes glazing and jaws still snapping convulsively, was thrust into the scuppers, so that the hook could be removed later from its gullet. The cook then turned his attention to severing the tail. The carpenter took this, to nail it to the jib boom end.

Next the cook, with his long knife, began flensing strips from the shark's back, to get out the vertebrae, which have some value as curios. As he did so, he threw strips of flesh overboard. "Anybody want a feed of shark meat?" he asked sarcastically, knowing that, as a rule, sailors are too squeamish to eat the flesh of a maneater, thinking this equivalent to cannibalism.

The Negro seaman who had been crimped on board at Portland had no such qualms. With a broad grin he took the knife from the cook and cut off two large, juicy steaks from near the shark's tail. Later, when these were grilled In the galley, the smell was very appetizing. The Negro consumed them with relish, but no other man would touch them.

Several of the seamen cut strips from the shark's hide, to be plaited into greenhide belts. Chunks of the flesh were cut off and thrown overboard, where other sharks soon appeared for a cannibal feast. Then the sailors, in a welter of gore and oil, ripped open the shark's stomach, searching for treasure. They found no gold or any other metal — from which it appeared that our shark had not eaten any sailor men or passengers, after all. His reeking remains were thrown overboard, with the exception of the head and tail and backbone. All hands then turned to with a will, to wash down the deck and paintwork and holystone the deck to get the blood and oil out of it. This gave the Mate some satisfaction, as the men were working in their own time. They were usually not required to do anything except the essentials of working the ship on Saturday afternoons and Sundays.

The Captain, who knew of my collection of marine curiosities, presented me with the shark's head. "Cut away the flesh," he said, "and mount the teeth on a board. They make a fine ornament on a parlour wall."

I suspected that no one else wanted the shark's head, but I accepted the gift with pleasure. I cut out the jawbones, complete with teeth, and spent my leisure hours for several days cleaning and picking them. The cook also presented me with a length of the shark's backbone, sufficient, as he said, to make a very nice walking stick when suitably reinforced. He had passed a wire through the vertebrae, to keep them in their correct position, though looped into a circle like a giant necklace. It was my task then to pick the flesh off the bones and clean them, as I was doing with the teeth and jawbones, hanging the relics up in the sun and wind, to bleach whenever I was not working on them.

The carpenter showed me how to mount the teeth, in a fearsome open position, on a board, the jawbones fixed with hidden pieces of wire. Then he put a thin steel rod through the backbone to stiffen it, to make a walking stick, which few men would want to be seen carrying, unless they wished to attract horrified public attention. Nevertheless, I proudly added these trophies to my collection, keeping them in a spare bunk in the half deck, as they were too big to go into my sea chest.

The shark's tail, which the carpenter had nailed to the jib boom, soon brought us the fair wind that the old hands, including the Captain, had confidently expected. I believe it was for this reason that the Captain had set the line to catch the shark, after he had tried whistling for a wind without success. The desperation of being becalmed in the doldrums was such that no well tried method of raising a wind could be neglected. The fact remains that a fair wind did spring up a few hours after the shark's tail was nailed to the jib boom end. Let sceptics mock as they may.

With this wind we soon arrived in the zone of the NE trades, and, dose hauled on the starboard tack, made good progress northward. Our course, which was to the west of the Azores Islands, brought us through the eastern fringe of the Sargasso Sea. Here one day we ran through a patch of light brown seaweed, which stretched to the horizon all around us.

My zeal as a collector impelled me to hook up several pieces of the weed, which was of pretty design, with small white nodules. I scrounged a glass jar from the cook. It was a large jar but never mind! Filling it to the brim with salt water, I inserted several pieces of Sargasso seaweed into it and hermetically sealed it with cork covered with cross pointing (plaited twine), then brightened up the bottle with thin bands of paint in five colours, leaving enough transparent glass for the seaweed to be viewed, like a fairy illusion, within.

This was my last opportunity of collecting marine curios on this voyage. We ran into autumn gales in the North Atlantic and made slow progress, arriving at Queenstown, where we were bound for orders, early in October, after a passage of 152 days from Portland, Oregon.

Safe in this home port, I nearly lost my life. On the morning after our arrival, I stripped and plunged overside at dawn for a swim.

As I dived in off the bulwark rail, the water gripped me in an icy clutch. It was very much colder than I had expected, and in a few minutes my limbs were seized with cramp. I sank and rose twice, powerless to swim, and called for help.

As I was going down for the third time, one of my shipmates saw my plight and raised the cry, "Man overboard!" Others came to the rail and, knowing that I was a good swimmer, did not think it necessary to do anything except throw me a line.

I failed to grasp this and went down for the third time, almost unconscious. They saw that the matter was serious and launched the Captain's gig, which fortunately was already slung out in the davits. Despite the legend that the third time is the last time of sinking, I rose again, and they secured me, though I was now more than half drowned and blue with cold.

They got me on board, squeezed the water out of my lungs, wrapped me in blankets, and revived me with a nip of brandy followed by hot coffee. In a short time, I was fully recovered, though well aware that I had been very near death. The only sympathy I got was a jawing from the Captain, who said that sailors should keep away from the water!

Remarkable though it may seem, very few sailors could swim. This was true at least of seamen from the colder countries of Northern Europe, including Britain, who were the world's best sailors, but perhaps had had few opportunities in their boyhood of learning to swim and never learned thereafter. The apprentices and some of the younger seamen had enjoyed a dip in the warm water at Carrizal, but the old hands preferred to wash themselves in buckets of water drawn up overside and mistrusted the briny deep.

After a few days at Queenstown, we were ordered to Dublin to discharge our cargo. I had written a letter home from Queenstown, announcing that I was safe and sound after a voyage that had lasted a little over two years. I did not think it necessary to mention what a narrow squeak I had from drowning at Queenstown. I was now over eighteen years old, having celebrated my eighteenth birthday in a howling gale off Cape Horn, and I was well grown, healthy, and strong. I had served three years of my term as an apprentice and had the confidence of a man who had twice circumnavigated the globe. I had a growth of downy beard and bought a razor from a Queenstown bumboatman to remove it.

The Captain gave me a day's leave to go to Cork, to visit some relatives there. On the way upriver in the ferry, I was surprised to see the *S.S. Mariposa* in a dry dock. The last time I had seen her was at Algoa Bay, seventeen months previously, a burnt out shell on the beach. She had been towed some 6,300 miles (10138 km) to Cork to be refitted and renovated; a fine feat of salvage and seamanship.

The *County of Pembroke* being ordered to Dublin to discharge, we were towed there. from Queenstown by the tug *Sarah Joliffe*, a distance of some 200 miles (321 km). Such movements of sailing vessels, under tow from port to port around the British coasts, were usual. It was scarcely more expensive to be towed all the way than to be towed out, make sail, and be towed in.

My brother David, two years older than I, came over on the Dublin packet from Liverpool to greet me and to see the sights of Ireland, as he was on holidays. The Captain allowed him to sleep in the spare bunk in the half deck. I showed him my collection of marine curiosities, but to my disappointment he only said, "Why didn't you bring back a parrot or a monkey?"

Our crew were paid off at Dublin. When the cargo was discharged and ballast taken in, we were towed across the Irish Sea to dock in the Mersey, in the first week in November 1901, after an absence from our home port of two years and seven weeks.

Having earned four pounds for my second year and five pounds for my third year at sea, less deductions for cash advances and purchases from the slop chest during that period, I now had a credit of something over three pounds in my account. The Captain paid me with three golden sovereigns and some silver, and I felt like a millionaire.

Hiring a four-wheeler cab, I put my sea chest and sea bag and all my marine curiosities into it and drove home in style. After the excitements of a family reunion and the expected exclamations of astonishment at my having grown into a full blown sailor man, I prepared to display my collection of curios.

The moment when I unpacked these wonders before my admiring parents, brothers and sisters, telling the story of each trophy in detail, stands out as one of the supreme moments of my seagoing career.

Everything was there to be admired — the bottle of sand, the bottle of seaweed, the ship in a bottle, the "Souvenirs de Pitcairn," the head and foot of the albatross, the stuffed flying fish, the sennit mat, the shark's teeth, the walking stick made of the shark's backbone, and my oil painting of the *County of Pembroke* with all sail set.

What a collection of hideous monstrosities they must have appeared to my mother, who was houseproud and fond of beautiful things! But she hid her feelings well, for I was so proud and happy and felt that I had enriched our home with priceless ornaments.

CHAPTER FOOTNOTES
(1)   Fathom: a unit of length equal to six feet (approximately 1.8 m), chiefly used in reference to the depth of water.

ON a bleak wintry day, 23rd November 1901, the *County of Pembroke* was towed out of the Mersey and set sail, bound for Wellington and Dunedin, New Zealand, with a cargo of general merchandise. This was my third voyage in her, and I had now entered on the fourth year of my apprenticeship.

The Master of the barque on this voyage was Captain John Hughes, a Welshman who had the nickname of "Wingy" because his left forearm, having been broken and badly set, was stiff and of little use to him. The Mate was Mr. Owen, and the Second Mate Mr. Slater, as on my previous voyages. Four of the fo'c'sle hands were Welsh and the other eight of various nationalities, as usual. As senior apprentice, I had two younger boys with me in the half deck. Jack O'Connor, now beginning his third year, had developed into a handy seaman. Archie Bucknell, a first voyager, was for the time being "green" but would learn. Chips and Sails bunked with us in the half deck, as formerly.

My father had impressed on me the necessity for studying the prescribed books on navigation, mathematics, and seamanship, so that I could sit for the Board of Trade examination for a Second Mate's certificate when I returned from this voyage, as by that time my apprenticeship would be completed. He had obtained the books for me and warned me to waste no time, at sea or in port, in foolish hobbies, idle pleasures, or lazy dreaming and sleeping, but to spend every spare moment that I could find in studying for the examination.

Good advice, but not so easy to follow on shipboard! As I looked through the books, I became sadly aware of my appalling ignorance of the theories of navigation and seamanship, despite my ever growing practical knowledge learned the hard way. For the first few weeks, as we battled with winter gales in the North Atlantic, I had no time or inclination to get my books out and study them, but, when we got into fine weather in the trade winds, I began to struggle with exercises in arithmetic and elementary plane and spherical trigonometry, helped a little — but not very much — by the First and Second Mates.

As I was in the First Mate's watch and Jack O'Connor in the Second Mate's watch, we were together with both the Mates on the poop at the change of the watch at noon, when they and the Captain took observations with their sextants of the sun's altitude — or "shot the sun" — to ascertain what parallel of latitude the barque was in. Seeing that we were fascinated by this procedure, the Second Mate sometimes allowed us to look through his sextant at the small image of the sun in the horizon glass, and showed us how to move the index arm to bring the lower edge or limb of the sun's image into exact contact with the horizon, and how to read off the angle of arc on the Vernier attachment through the microscope. He then patiently explained, and demonstrated, how to ascertain the latitude, after allowing for the declination of the sun at that season of the year, as stated in *The Nautical Almanac.*

All this, which at first seemed perfectly mystifying to me, at last became clearer with practice. Then, in the night watches, when there was very little else to do, the First Mate sometimes took the trouble to point out to me the stars useful in navigation, Polaris, or the North Star, and the Great Bear and Little Bear, Arcturus, Vega and Capella; then the Constellation of Orion, with Betelgeuse, Rigel, Sirius, Aldebaran, Castor and Pollux and the Pleiades. . . . So the unlimitable universe was opened to my imagination, and I was struck with wonder when the Mate informed me that the positions of these and other stars and of the sun, moon and planets, were all pinpointed by astronomers, and their positions set forth in *The Nautical Almanac* for the benefit of mariners, so that, by observing the altitude of these bodies, and calculating accordingly, in relation also to Greenwich Mean Time, we could ascertain our position on the surface of that little planet named The Earth.

Longitude was more difficult to fix than latitude, as the calculation depended on the accurate rating of our chronometer, of which only one was carried in the *County of Pembroke*, as in most sailing vessels, and it was not perfectly dependable. The whole theory of navigation at first seemed fantastic to me, but my interest was keenly aroused, and I began to study a book which my father had given to me, Lecky's *Wrinkles in Practical Navigation*, which was known as "The Sailors' Bible." Two other books he had given me were Reed's *Navigation* and Norie's *Epitome (Nautical Tables)*. I worried my way through their pages until I at least partly understood the rudiments of navigation. This groundwork stood to me well in later years, as we remember best what curiosity provides the impulse to know and understand anything, however difficult it may seem in the beginning.

One day the Mate gave me a lesson in taking sights and let me the task of working out our position. After covering several sheets of paper with calculations, I announced the result. The Mate scratched his head in pretended perplexity and showed my calculations to the Second Mate. "We've made history on this voyage," he remarked. "At the present moment, we are sailing down the main street of Timbuctoo, the first time any ship ever reached that port. Try again, Jimmy!"

On Christmas Day we were sweating in the doldrums, and on New Year's Day of 1902 we picked up the SE trades and bore away in a general SSW direction, braced sharp up on the port tack, in the South Atlantic. Ten days later we picked up the westerlies and began to run our easting down. As this was midsummer in the Southern Hemisphere, Captain Hughes worked into higher latitudes and ran the easting down between Lat. 45 deg. S and Lat. 50 deg. S, where the following winds were stronger. My mathematical studies were now put aside for the demands of practical seamanship during many weeks of hard work and bodily weariness.

An experienced and agile apprentice was simply an extra hand in working the ship, required to do all the work of an Able Seaman, but for much smaller wages than seamen earned. My pay for my fourth year would be eight pounds, equivalent to thirteen shillings and fourpence a month, compared with three pounds, ten shillings a month earned by the fo'c'sle hands. The system was fair enough, as it taught the future generation of officers what was possible and what was not possible in the handling of sail and in the general working of the ship. By laying out on the yards with the seamen in all weathers, an apprentice gained the knowledge which would stand him in good stead when the time eventually came for him as an officer of the watch, to send men aloft.

The ideal was that an officer should be able to do everything in a ship as well as, or better than, the average Able Seaman, thereby winning the respect of the men he would command. Four years' servitude as an apprentice was not an unduly long period in which to learn all that had to be learned of the practical aspects of working a sailing vessel; but navigation and some of the finer points of seamanship could be acquired only by book study combined with experience.

In mid-February we passed the meridian of the Southeast Cape of Tasmania, in Lat. 47 deg. S, far from sight of land, then drove on northeasterly across the Tasman Sea. We had seen no land for more than two months since sight-ing the Cape Verde Islands. Each day was like every other day in the ordeals and monotony of the wild waste of waters, whipped by the westerly gales to mountainous seas endlessly rolling up astern as we drove on, like the Flying Dutchman of the legend, seemingly destined never to arrive at a haven.

When one day is much like another, in a vast expanse of ocean, the individual may lose all reckoning of time and it may seem that a voyage will never end. Only the sounding of the bell marks the passing of the hours and of the watches; and the Captain in his log notes the passing of the days and the vessel's position. He knows where we are — we hope — even if nobody else does.

One day the Mate said to me, "Do you see that long white cloud on the eastern horizon? Keep your eye on it! If it does not change shape, it's the land!"

Sure enough, that long white cloud was immovable. It was the summit of the snowclad Alps of the South Island of New Zealand, which rise to 12,000 feet (3657m), visible far out at sea. That brave old Dutch navigator, Abel Jansen Tasman, who discovered and named New Zealand in 1642— sailing almost on the route which we were now following—described it as "a large land, uplifted high," a beautiful and exact description. The "Long White Cloud" (so named first by the Māoris) has been the landfall for many a navigator, by sea and by air, since Tasman's day and will remain forever one of the most enchanting first views of land to be seen from seaward anywhere in the world.

We altered course to the northward, and a few days later got a fix from the lighthouse on Cape Farewell, at the entrance to Cook Strait, between the North and South Islands of New Zealand. We hove to during the night, then sailed into the Strait next day in sunny weather, with a fair breeze. A pilot boarded us as we neared the entrance to Port Nicholson. We sailed in through the heads and dropped anchor. Next day, a tug berthed us, with our sails stowed, at the quayside in Wellington City, on the western side of the port. It was early in March 1902; the outward passage had lasted 100 days.

For three weeks we lay at Wellington, leisurely discharging part of our cargo of English ale and stout, Scotch whiskey, and similar colonial comforts, including Manchester cloth and Cheshire salt and soda. As the capital city of New Zealand, Wellington had a clean and thriving appearance, with many buildings, mainly of timber, which, to my English eyes, seemed brand new and temporary. The business part of the city, with good shops and some fine stone buildings, public offices, banks, and churches, extended along a narrow strip of land on the waterfront, with a steep hill behind, to which dwelling houses clung amid the trees, making a picturesque background scene.

There were some other sailing vessels in the port, including schooners trading to the South Seas Islands, but most of the trade was in steamers, both coastal and overseas. This was a very respectable city, in which there were few inducements to sailors to indulge in carousals or to desert at the enticement of crimps. As we were there in autumn, fruit was plentiful and cheap, and this was my chief form of indulgence when I was allowed ashore with half a crown in my pocket.

I wanted to see some Māoris, but there were none on view except a few who worked in civilized garb, driving carts or as labourers, looking little different from white people. Most of the inhabitants of Wellington were Eng-lish or Scots or seemed so in their respectability. It was different, I was told, at the timber ports of the North Island — such as Onehunga, Hokianga and Auckland — which were very lively, thronged with sailing vessels loading kauri (New Zealand pine) for Australia and Europe, but we did not go there, to my regret.

Toward the end of March 1902, we towed out of Port Nicholson into Cook Strait and set sail for a short run of 350 miles (563 km) southward, to Dunedin at the southern end of the South Island of New Zealand, to discharge the rest of our cargo. Our route was offshore, in variable winds, along the eastern coast, with glimpses of the snowy Alps in the far distance to the westward. After three or four days we were taken in tow and brought into Otago Harbor, a beautiful landlocked haven of still water, like a fjord, with Dunedin City at its head.

There we went alongside, discharged our cargo, took in 300 tons of stone ballast, and were towed out to an anchorage in the stream while the agents attempted to get a cargo for us. The climate in this latitude, 46 deg. S, was cold and rainy as winter closed in, but the Mate thought of a way to keep the crew warm. The barque had not been in dry dock for two and a half years. Her bottom was foul with grass and barnacles, accumulated in many a port, and she was sailing sluggishly. We had scraped these off as far as we could reach, whenever cargo was discharged, as she rose in the water; but we could not reach the underwater portions of the hull.

She could have been drydocked at Wellington or Dunedin, but this would have cost money. The Mate now dealt with this problem in his own way. All hands were ordered into the hold, to shovel the stone ballast toward the forward bulkhead. This was heavy and uncomfortable work, as the hold was soon filled with stone dust, but the exercise kept us warm on a cold day.

As the ballast was shovelled forward, the barque's stern rose out of the water until her rudder was almost fully exposed. The crew were then put overside, in stages and some in the dinghy, with scrapers and wire brushes, in drizzling cold rain and icy wind, to scrape as far under the stern as possible.

This task completed, we shovelled the ballast back to an even trim, and a few days later piled it all up toward the after bulkhead, to tip her bow up for scraping underneath the stem. That done, the ballast had to be spread again to an even trim. The operation was made feasible only by the perfectly calm water in the landlocked harbour in which we lay.

While we were discharging our cargo at the wharf and later, when manning the gig to take the Captain ashore from our anchorage, I had some opportunities of seeing the city of Dunedin, which was founded mainly by Scots Presbyterians, and was known as "the City of Churches." It had many fine buildings of grey stone, including the churches, and an imposing statue of Robert Burns, in a central "Octagon." The city had sprung to prosperity during the Otago gold rushes and had lively traditions also as a whaling port; but at the time of our visit its wealth came chiefly from the export of wool and the newly introduced trade in frozen mutton, which was exported under refrigeration in steamers to Britain.

There were only two or three sailing vessels in the port. This was the wrong season of the year to load wool for a run homeward around Cape Horn, since shearing did not begin in this cold district of New Zealand until the end of winter. Our agents were unable to obtain a cargo for us and, in consequence, after cables had been exchanged with the owners, we were ordered to proceed to Newcastle, New South Wales, in ballast, to load coal there for Callao in Peru. These arrangements had taken time to complete, and it was not until the end of May that we cleared out of Dunedin, after a stay of fifty-eight days in that port. As the barque was lightly ballasted and inclined to be "cranky," and as heavy westerly gales were raging, the Captain decided to sail around the north of the North Island of New Zealand, hoping to pick up the SE trades, in warmer latitudes, for our run to Newcastle. This decision was sound in the circumstances, though it added to the distance we would have to sail. We met with variable winds and were twenty days on the passage to Newcastle, arriving there on 13th June 1902.

Towed to Number 13 Berth, we found that another of the vessels of William Thomas & Co., had arrived a few days before us and was lying at Berth 18, waiting, like us, to load coal for Callao. She was the full rigged ship *County of Cardigan*, 1,323 tons, Captain Jones. I soon paid a visit to her to examine her rig, as she had the reputation of being a smart ship and this was the first time I had seen her. There were forty sailing vessels in port, but on this occasion our agents, R. B. Wallace & Co., were able to make arrangements for us to load fairly quickly. After taking in stiffening and discharging ballast, we had to wait only a fortnight before we were moved to Number 7 Crane and there loaded 1,637 tons of coal from Seaham Colliery. This put us down to the Plimsoll mark and was therefore the limit of weight that the *County of Pembroke* could carry.

As a matter of the agents' convenience, we were cleared out before the *County of Cardigan* and left Newcastle on 5th July 1902, after a remarkably short stay of only twenty- two days in that port.

The route from Newcastle to Callao, some 7,000 miles (11265 km) across the Pacific Ocean, passes among coral reefs to the north-eastward of New Zealand. Our Captain, being a prudent man, chose the open ocean route, passing to the southward of New Zealand, where we picked up the westerlies, and pursued a general east-northeasterly course until we picked up the SE trades and gave the coral reefs a wide berth. Being deeply laden, we ploughed along with decks awash, at a speed of seven knots, or 168 miles (270 km) a day, and often less than that after we entered the tropics.

Ten days out from Newcastle, I attained my nineteenth birthday. In the

An undated/uncredited photo of Capt. James Bisset displayed on the back cover of the first two books. (Bisset)

lethargic atmosphere of this leisurely voyage in the blue and balmy Pacific Ocean, I attempted without much success to apply my attention to mathematical studies in the dog watches and on my other watches below during daylight hours; but concentration was difficult, and more often than not I fell asleep, book and pencil in hand, or daydreamed until aroused from my reveries by the call to turn to.

The famous port of Callao, only twelve degrees south of the equator, port of entry for Lima, the capital of Peru, had a romantic history as a great haven of sailing vessels for over 300 years since the days of the Spanish conquests of Mexico and Peru. The wind dropped almost to a flat calm as we made our landfall twenty miles (32 km) south of the port and drifted northward, close inshore, with a current and very light airs and all sail set to the royals.

The Captain was anxious, as, if the wind dropped completely, the current might carry us helplessly past the entrance to the port, but fortune favoured us. A gentle, though fitful, north-westerly breeze sprang up as we neared the entrance, and we were able to sail in, in style, and come to anchor in the lee of La Punta ("the Point"), in seven fathoms, near the mole surrounding the docks. About twenty other sailing vessels were riding at anchor in the bay, waiting to discharge cargoes of coal from Australia, wheat from California, sugar from Hawaii, silks and fancy.

*A Sailors' Spree in Callao — Weekend Carousal — A Deal With a
Ship Chandler — A Torrid Tropical Port — Last Chance of a Fling
— Beachcombers and Harpies — A Tavern Brawl — Efficient
Gendarmes — The Calaboose — The Treadmill — Rolling Home*

AFTER the *County of Pembroke* had been at Callao for six weeks, sailing day drew nigh. The Mates kept the crew busy overhauling the standing gear and running gear, bending sail, chipping and painting overside in the ceaseless war against rust, and scraping off, as far underneath as we could reach, the copious grass and barnacles that grew on the barque's bottom as she lay inert in the warm tropical waters of the bay. These were never ending routines. I was surprising how rapidly the grass grew in warm water ports.

The Captain made a bargain with a crimp to deliver two seamen to him on sailing day. He decided to sail on a Sunday, which, though supposed to be a day of rest, was a day on which an ample supply of sozzled matelots readily procurable by the crimps, after the Saturday night sprees for which Callao was so renowned.

When we knocked off work on Saturday afternoon, day before we were due to sail, the Captain mustered the work weary crew and the two apprentices at the break of the poop. He handed each man one dollar and each boy half a dollar, for going ashore, as we were entitled to do, on this last opportunity that would occur for many a day. "Now, men," he said, "it's my duty to explain to you that when we leave this port it will be a long time before we get any more provisions. We are going to the Chincha Islands to load guano, and we will be there for several weeks. After that, we will be sailing home around Cape Horn.

"When you go ashore this afternoon," he continued, "don't spend your money on drink! Keep out of trouble, keep away from the crimps, and make no mistake about being on board before midnight. The two new hands will be coming aboard tonight, and we'll sail at dawn. Now, as I've told you that it will be a long passage home, I advise you to lay in some extra provisions for yourselves! You'll get your pound and pint at sea according to law, but at times you will be glad to have something extra, according to your own fancy. As you all have a good deal of pay due to you, I have decided to give you an opportunity of buying some groceries for yourselves, if you want to, from a ship chandler on the quay."

He told us the name of the chandler and explained that each man and boy would be allowed to run up a bill for three dollars for groceries. "Your purchases will be sent on board for you, in separate parcels with your names on each one, according to what you have bought. I will hold the parcels for you until after we put to sea. I will settle the bills and deduct the amounts from your wages at the pay off. That'll do you now. Get away forrard and consider yourselves lucky to have a captain who takes such an interest in your welfare."

After we had cleaned ourselves up to go ashore, the crew had a discussion in the fo'c'sle, on the meaning of the Captain's offer. The oldest seaman, Llewellyn Owens, was dubious. He had a wife and seven children to support at Liverpool, and he wanted to take home as much pay as possible for his dependents.

"Indeed to goodness," he said, after making sure that the Captain was well out of hearing, "and what makes Old Wingy suddenly generous? He's a hard man, and this is a hungry ship. 'Tis saving himself and the owners some expense if we buy groceries for ourselves, now isn't it? He's nothing but a hypocrite, and a blooming old skinflint!" "He keeps the Sabbath," remarked one of the other Welsh seamen, sarcastically.

"Yes, he keeps the Sabbath," said Lew, "and everything else he can lay hands on! It isn't right to ask us to buy groceries for ourselves. He should take in a proper supply of provisions at the owners' expense!"

Presently we hailed a passing boatman and were rowed ashore, for a few cents' fare. Despite the doubts of Lew Owens, we could not resist the attractions of the Captain's offer. We went in a body to the ship chandler's store and spent a long time selecting what we fancied. Packets of tea, sugar, cocoa, and tins of condensed milk, jam, and sardines were the most favoured items, with many careful calculations so as to get as much as possible within the limit of three dollars per man.

Our purchases were stacked in separate heaps on the counter, with a ticket bearing the name of the purchaser laid on each heap, ready to be parcelled and sent on board. Then some of the seamen had a bright idea. Desirous of having a last fling before midnight, they entered into private arrangements with the wily chandler to give them a dollar each in cash and to take the value out of their parcels, plus a liberal commission.

Lew Owens and I and the apprentices disdained this conspiracy, preferring to have our purchases intact. Their business being completed, the apprentices wandered off by themselves to buy fruit and keep away from taverns. I stayed with the sailors. This was my first time ashore as an AB., free to do as I liked, and I was determined to sample the "fleshpots."

The streets of Callao on Saturday afternoons and nights, in that heyday of the sailing ship era, were thronged with crowds of roistering matelots of many nationalities, eager to quench their thirst and, in every other way possible, to have a "good time" after a week's hard work in the vessels lying at anchor out in the bay. Some, from vessels newly arrived, were ashore for the first time after months at sea. Others were deserters, on the spree at the expense of crimps. Many in the throng were "beachcombers" — men who had deserted ships in previous years to earn a precarious living in Callao by casual labour on the waterfront, or as boatmen or riggers, or living from hand to mouth as vagrants, loafers, scouts for the crimps, or touts for the taverns. This cosmopolitan riffraff mingled with the residents of the town who included Spanish Peruvians, native Peruvians, Negroes, Chinese, Indians, Kanakas, and mixtures of all these and other races, together with merchants and agents from most of the countries of Europe, Asia, and North and South America. It was a colourful medley. The crowds included also adventuresses of many different races, shapes and ages — known to the sailors as "harpies" — attracted to this torrid tropical port to consort in carousals with the local grandees and the "floating" population.

Among the vessels in port was an American four masted barque with a crew of forty. She had put into Callao for repairs and provisions and medical aid, after a heavy buffeting by winter gales on her westward passage around Cape Horn. She was bound for China from Pensacola, Florida, and most of her crew were raw• hands who had been shipped in that port and made into handy seamen by the Bucko Mates on the passage. The medical aid was required for one of the Mates, who had been stabbed by a Negro seaman. Her crew came ashore now, after three months at sea, to join the roistering throng and savour the lurid pleasures for which Callao was so notorious.

Some of them intended to desert and enjoy the hospitality of the crimps, who scented big business supplying the master of the barque with new hands after enticing as many of his crew as possible away from him.

There was no "respectable" entertainment offered sailors ashore at Callao, which, from any "moral" point of view, was simply a red hot hellhole. The Peruvian police, well accustomed to dealing with jolly sailors, were a tough body of men, organized on military lines. They carried batons and revolvers and wore a uniform with much gold braid and cocked hats. Most of them had curled mustachios, and they looked extremely fierce and theatrical as they patrolled the streets in squads of eight or ten men, commanded by an officer with gilt epaulettes and a sword. Yet they knew their work.

As I had only rarely tasted strong drink in my life, I felt a little nervous when my shipmates suggested that we should go into a tavern for a drink and a feed, but Lew Owens reassured me. "Indeed to goodness," he said, "we'll just have a drink or two, and something to eat, then go back on board."

We entered the tavern. It was a large hall, furnished with tables, chairs, and palms in pots, with a stage at one end, on which an orchestra of guitarists was playing lively Spanish music. About two hundred sailors and beach combers were seated in groups at the tables, drinking and supping in company with "ladies of the town," with whom lonely strangers had no difficulty in striking up an acquaintance.

Food and drink were served by a gang of waiters — strongly built men — who frequently had to act as "chuckers-out" if brawls developed. Everything on offer was cheap, the prices adjusted to the basic fact that most of the customers were limited in spending power to one dollar unless they were financed further by the crimps, who worked in with the management.

We sat at a table and ordered chili con carne and a bottle of red wine. In quick time a dish of the savoury meat was set before us, with Lima beans, and a bottle of wine and glasses. At first taste of the chili con carne which was oversalted and seasoned with cayenne pepper, I felt my tongue burning, but this was nothing to the extraordinary sensations I felt when I took my first sip of the wine. Surely no worse wine than this Peruvian vintage had ever been made in the long history of toping! It looked and tasted like red ink fortified with nitro-glycerine and had a kick like a mule.

My shipmates gulped it down with relish, smacking their lips. "Don't sip it," they advised me. "Put it down the hatch at one go, and you'll get the feeling all of a sudden."

Unwilling to be scorned as a novice, I tossed the fiery fluid down my gullet and thought for a moment that my innards were on fire. "Have another," said Lew.

The price of a bottle of the wine was only ten cents, and of the chili con carne twenty cents. We ordered more wine, and after I had consumed a few glasses of it I began to feel decidedly dizzy. It was now nighttime, and the tavern was lit with kerosene lamps hung from the rafters. The air was blue with the smoke of two-cent cigars, and most of the customers were noisily drunk, singing and laughing uproariously with their girlfriends.

Most of my shipmates went off with harpies who ogled them. I was left with Lew Owens, who was keeping a fatherly eye on me. He kept on saying gloomily, "We must get back to the ship," but he made no move to go. Two harpies came to our table. "Go away," said Lew, firmly.

Presently a greasy-looking fellow came up to us, all smiles. He was a crimp's tout. "Want a good time?" he said.

"No!" bellowed Lew. "Go away, you dirty pimp. I'm a Chapel man; I'd like you to know!"

The pimp looked mystified and went away. "Let's get out o' here, Jimmy," said Lew. "Must get back to the ship. Think o' my wife and kids. Wine is a mocker, strong drink is raging, saith the Proverb."

We stood up. The room was going round and round, and my legs were made of rubber. By a great effort of will I got the scene in focus and made my wobbly legs obey my wishes.

At this moment there were frightened screams from the harpies at a table near us, where two seamen from the Yankee barque began fighting. One of the sailors fell to the floor, stabbed in the chest. I saw only dimly that waiters and others rushed to intervene, and a free-for-all brawl began, with bottles, chairs and glasses flying, men yelling and women screaming, in a regular pandemonium. "Let's get out o' here, quick!" mumbled Lew, taking my arm. "Don't get mixed up in it ... put up job ... get out quick!"

We lurched toward the door as a squad of police came charging in to arrest the brawlers. As we emerged into the street, I saw police coming from all directions on the run, converging on the tavern. Half a dozen of them grabbed Lew and me, evidently considering that we were brawlers trying to escape. We struggled violently. Then everything went black as I was thumped on the head from behind with a truncheon and fell to the ground.

When I came to, I was securely handcuffed and saw that Lew was in a similar plight. He was swearing volubly in Welsh, and the gendarmes were cursing him in Spanish as they knelt on him and rubbed his nose in the dirt. They pulled us to our feet and propelled us along the street for a few hundred yards to the calaboose, a large stone building near the waterfront. They thrust us into a large damp, dungeonlike stone cell, which was lit only by the rays from a lantern outside an iron barred grating high in the wall.

The only furniture in the dungeon was a wooden "night tub" in one corner. Presently the door opened, and two more handcuffed sailors were flung in, to keep us company. At intervals, more and more joined the rueful throng. Most of them were drunk — some gloomy and some singing or yelling defiance. After a while Lew and I were sobered. I had a splitting headache. "We'll miss our ship!" Lew kept on lamenting. "Oh, my poor wife and family!"

Sleep was impossible. At dawn the door opened, and we were ordered out into the yard. The warders were heavily- built, s owling men, who carried "niddies" — wooden batons. They were well accustomed to dealing with sailors in our position. In a corner of the high, stonewalled yard was a water tap, where we drank and doused our aching heads. At the end of the yard was a sinister looking machine — the treadmill!

Presently we were released from our handcuffs and given pannikins of coffee and a piece of bread. I felt better after the coffee, but utterly miserable as I reflected that, at that very moment, the *County of Pembroke* would be heaving up the anchor to sail out of the bay, homeward bound. What would my parents think when she arrived home without me? How could I explain that I had been wrongfully detained at Callao?

The warders now seized six of the prisoners, including Lew Owens, and bustled them to the treadmill, prodding them with their niddies. If any man resisted, he was given a smart blow on the back or arms. The treadmill was a wide wheel, with lateral wooden steps or treads and an iron rail overhead. The prisoners were shackled by their wrists to this rail.

"March!" the chief warder sang out.

There was nothing else for them to do. As they stepped onto the treadmill, it began to revolve with a loud clanking sound, and they had to keep on walking up the revolving steps. If any man stopped treading, the mill continued to revolve, and he hung by the wrists while his knees and shins were battered to pulp by the treads, so that he soon began treading again. In the meantime, the rest of the sick and sorry seamen, including myself, sat gloomily on the stone paving of the yard, waiting our turn.

The treadmill was geared to a pump which raised water from wells to high tanks for the town supply. A batch of weekend drunken sailors was therefore a municipal economy and necessity at Callao. The treadmill was kept going all day Sunday, each gang of six being obliged to tread for half an hour before being allowed to rest and replaced by another gang. This torture in the hot tropical sunlight was guaranteed to sober up the sozzled matelots, who were released on Monday morning to rejoin their ships, feeling that they were very unlucky to have been arrested, and their weekend spree spoiled.

Lew and I were the only two men in the yard from the *County of Pembroke*. I tried desperately to explain to one of the warders that our barque was sailing that morning, but he either could not or would not understand English. At this moment, an official entered the yard with a piece of paper in his hand and began calling out something which I could not understand. It appeared later that he was trying to pronounce "Llewellyn Owens" with a Spanish accent! Getting no response, he called out "Bisset! Bisset!"

"Here!" I said, with sudden hope, standing up, as my morose meditations on the prospect of being left on the beach at Callao, stoney broke, were agreeably interrupted.

He spoke to me in Spanish and showed me the paper. I saw on it my name and that of Lew Owens. By signs I indicated that Lew was on the treadmill. The machine was stopped, and Lew was unshackled. We were both led out of the yard into the front office of the calaboose.

Captain Hughes was standing there with the agent. He had come to bail us out. His face was red with rage. "You should be ashamed of yourselves," he said ferociously. "A fine pair of drunk and disorderly scallywags you are.

You've held up our sailing."

"We did nothing wrong, sir," I tried to explain.

"Only got drunk!" sneered the Captain. "Hold your tongue, or I'll log you for insolence as well."

The agent acted as interpreter in the proceedings with the officials, as the Captain paid our fines, and we were released. It was only a short walk to the quay, where we got into the agent's boat and were taken out to the *County of Pembroke*. "You've been fined five dollars each, for being drunk and disorderly on shore," said the Captain. "I've paid it, and it will be stopped from your pay, you worthless scoundrels. I'll also log you both, and fine you a pound for failing to be on board by midnight on sailing eve. It would have served you right if I had sailed without you and left you on the beach to find another ship. You can thank your lucky stars that you have a captain who thinks of his men's welfare. Let this be a lesson to you!"

Arrived on board, we were sent forrard immediately to the fo'c'slehead to trudge around the capstan, helping to heave up the anchor to the hoarse strains of "Rolling Home."

During the night, all the other seamen (from whom we had parted at the tavern) had returned safely on board, in various stages of drunkenness, and the crimps had delivered two new men, according to their contract. These had been delivered unconscious drunk and doped but were now partly recovered after being revived by having water thrown over them in the scuppers. The barque's complement of twelve seamen were all sick and sorry for themselves as we were ordered aloft to loosen sail.

Scarcely a breath of air stirred in the bay as we got under way, but at noon a gentle breeze came from offshore, and we moved sluggishly from our anchorage toward open water. By nightfall the lights of Callao — that port of fabulous renown — were dipping below the horizon astern.

The Mates had picked their watches, and we were rolling home.

THE Chincha Islands lie a few miles offshore, in the Bay of Pisco, 110 miles (177 km) southward of Callao. In the conditions prevailing in that region, with light and fitful airs and a current of two knots sweeping northward along the coast, sailing vessels were usually a week on the passage from Callao to the Chinchas. It was almost impossible to make headway due southward, close inshore, so they stood out to sea on long tacks, as there the current was not as strong as it was inshore, and the breezes were a little fresher.

The ballast we had taken in at Callao consisted of 300 tons of round pebbles, which would be very shifty and dangerous stuff in heavy weather but was considered good enough for the short run to the Chincha Islands. In that stretch of the ocean storms were almost unknown, and the conditions resembled those of the doldrums. There were occasional "line squalls" of short duration, but these were rarely encountered.

Before taking in the ballast, we had lashed a row of short planks along the midship stanchions in the hold, to divide it into two sides. These were known as "shifting boards" and, in ordinary circumstances, would prevent the ballast from moving bodily to one side or another when the vessel listed under sail. Further precautions, such as laying planks on top of the ballast and tamping them down with baulks of timber under the deckhead beams, were considered by Captain Hughes; but, as planks and baulks cost money, he took a justifiable risk and sailed without them.

We stood well out to sea and in a few days, with all sail set to the royals, sailing lazily in light airs, we were a hundred miles (160 km) offshore. The two new men obtained from the crimps at Callao were seamen who knew their work, but they were inveterate grumblers, who from the beginning complained of the poor quality of the provisions served out from the cook's galley. The complaints were reasonable, as the beef and pork were going high and the pantiles were weevilly, having been taken in at the beginning of the voyage, eleven months previously. The new men had served in Yankee Down Easters, in which provisions were good, even though discipline was tougher

A typical American "Down Easter" (Public Domain)

than in lime juicers. They grumbled also at being crimped on board a vessel that was going to load guano, knowing, either from hearsay or from their own experience, that this is an unpleasant cargo and that taking it in at the Chincha Islands adds many weeks to a homeward voyage.

But, having put themselves in the hands of the crimps, they had only their "bad luck" to blame when they found themselves at sea in a vessel which was not of their choosing, a "hungry ship," and facing the prospects of a long voyage around Cape Horn, parish rigged. Life was a lottery for crimped sailors, who never knew where they were bound until they were at sea, too late to exercise any choice in the matter. Their grumblings were of no use now, but their discontent simmered and affected the other members of the crew, creating disunity and forebodings of a miserable voyage.

After we had been a few days at sea, we decided to ask the Captain for our parcels of groceries which we had bought from the chandler at Callao.

"Muster at the break o' the poop at one bell in the first dog watch," said the Old Man.

He spoke to us there. "Now, men, I have your parcels, but I advise you not to open them yet. You would be wise to leave them in the lazarette until later in the voyage. If you open them now, you will gobble the contents in a few days, and then you won't have those extra provisions later, after we round the Horn. You will appreciate them far more than you will now, at the very beginning of this long voyage. I will give them to you now, if you haven't enough gumption to look ahead to the future. That'll do you now. Go forrard and think over what I've said. Then, if you want your parcels, the cook will hand them to you."

We trudged forrard to discuss the situation. All were agreed that we should have our parcels straight away. Food was all important to hungry men and boys. We were impatient to begin on some of the good things we had bought. It was more urgent to allay today's appetite than to plan for a remote future.

The Captain, being informed of our decision, ordered the cook to hand out the parcels. We carried them forrard and opened them with gluttonous haste.

After a few minutes of stunned and incredulous silence, groans and curses resounded in the fo'c'sle and half deck, as we compared notes and found that all the parcels were packed with rotten stores, and even those were short of the quantities we had ordered! The tins of milk, jam, and sardines were dented, rusty, and leaking, the cocoa full of weevils, the tea of such poor quality that it smelled and tasted like mouldy hay.

Hoping for the best, we opened some tins of jam. They were mildewed. "We've been robbed by a rascal!" lamented Lew Owens. "I knew there was a fraud in this scheme to swindle poor hard working sailors!"

Going aft in a body, we asked to see the Captain and showed him what we had been sold. He asked a few questions but showed us no sympathy. "You blithering fools!" he said. "It's your own fault, for not waiting to see the parcels packed up in the shop. I tried to help you, but you let yourselves be diddled. Have I to be a nursemaid for nitwit sailors? Lay forrard now and learn more sense next time."

Sullen, we held an indignation meeting which lasted all through the first dog watch, the two new seamen joining in the discussion to add fuel to the flames of our resentment. All were of the opinion that the Captain's scorn of our folly was unmerited. Even if we had waited in the shop until our groceries were parcelled, the rascally chandler, having decided to unload his condemned stock on us, could easily have substituted the contents of the parcels before delivering them on board. Unless the Captain took our part and eventually made some claim through the agents, the swindle would pass unheeded.

"In my opinion," said Lew Owens, bitterly, "this was a put-up job between the Old Man and that Dago chandler. I reckon they split the profit on the dirty deal!"

All agreed — with no proof except suspicion — that this explanation fitted the circumstances. "He's a hypocrite!" Lew added.

Agreed again, but what could we do? Nothing, except grumble! "I'll wring that Dago's neck if I ever go back to Callao," vowed Lew — a vain boast, as it might be years before he saw that hellhole again, and time heals worse wounds than we had suffered. Yet what a mean fraud it was.

While we were holding our meeting, the Captain was on the poop with the Mate, eyeing us and the weather. At 6 p.m., at the change of the dog watches, the barque was moving at three knots in a light NE breeze on the port quarter, with all sail set. While the watches were being changed, the Captain suddenly sang out to the Mate, "Hey, Mister, I don't like the look of that squall to windward! All hands on deck and get the royals and topgallants off her! If there is any wind in it, we may find ourselves in trouble with our shifty ballast!"

The Mates sprang to it, and so did the crew. Within a few seconds the royal and topgallant halyards were being lowered away, and we were hauling lustily on the clew lines and buntlines.

"Up aloft!" yelled the Mate. "Put a rough furl on them and get down on deck again quick and lively. We may have more to do, by the look of it."

While I was working on the main topgallant yard I looked to windward. A great black cloud was coming up in that direction — "Out of the Blue." Below the cloud, in the rays of the setting sun, was heavy slanting rain, and below that the sea seemed to be boiling. The squall was rapidly approaching us.

Urged on to our utmost efforts by the Mates' singing out on the deck, we hurriedly put rough furls on the royals and topgallants, then made our way quickly down the rigging to the deck.

The Captain was standing by the helmsman. "Lower away the topsail halyards," he sang out. "Let go the fore and main sheets!"

It was too late. The squall was upon us, with a howling gust of wind and rain. The barque heeled over and gathered way. Then came a terrifying rumble from below decks, and we realized with dismay that the ballast had shifted.

While the squall lasted, we were in imminent danger of capsizing or being demasted. With the deck at an angle of forty-five degrees, it was difficult to stand or move on it. We tried to lower the topsail yards, but, at that angle of heeling over, and in the strong wind, we could not get them lowered.

"Let go the sheets!" the Mate roared. With great difficulty we let go the foresail and mainsail sheets — a "sheet" being a manila or wire rope or chains secured to the lower corners of sails — thereby easing the strain on the canvas aloft, but in the violent gusts the flapping and slatting of the released sails threatened to pull the masts and yards down to crash on our heads, and the sheets flailed the decks like giant whiplashes, adding to the menace.

The only sails now set were the two lower topsails. If the wind suddenly shifted during the squall, these would be taken flat aback; but if they held, they would then have a righting tendency (to correct the angle of list to some extent).

The squall lasted for ten minutes of chaos and imminent danger, then, as suddenly as it had struck, it subsided.

Bewildered, the crew stood by while the Captain and the Mates hurriedly surveyed the damage and the list and decided what had to be done first. Darkness had set in, and there was no moon. The barque was on her beam ends, rolling about in a long northerly swell, and the lower yards were almost dipping into the water on the low side as she rolled.

The first thing to do was to secure everything aloft, in case another squall should strike during the night. "Lay aloft and furl the sails," the Mate sang out. It was a frightening task, but every man knew that another squall would be disastrous and that the lives of all were in danger. There was no hanging back when the order was given. All hands crawled aloft in the darkness, one watch on the fore and one on the main, feeling rather than seeing what we were doing, with "one hand for the ship and one for ourselves," as the Mates, peering from the deck, directed us with a volley of orders roared at the top• of their voices until they were hoarse.

We took each sail in hand and furled it. Some of the sails were split, but these could be sent down later for repairs. It was extremely difficult to balance on the foot. ropes, with the masts projecting far out over the water, but somehow, we held on and finished the job by midnight, after nearly six hours' work aloft.

On deck again, tired and hungry, we joyfully heeded the order to lay aft for a tot of rum. As he doled the grog out from a demijohn, the Old Man did the right thing. "Thanks, men," he said, "for doing a risky job so well!" In the meantime, the cook, working under difficulties, had got the fire going in the galley stove and made a brew of coffee. This, and the rum, put us in good heart for the next job — to get her upright.

Opening the fore part of the main hatch, all hands and the cook, with hurricane lamps and candles, clambered down the iron ladder, into the hold. As we stood on top of the ballast we could see, in the flickering light, that some of the shifting boards had carried away and were sticking out above the pebbles — snapped like matchsticks. The barque's list was to starboard, and the ballast had sagged over until it was almost touching the deckhead of the hold on that side.

The Captain and the Mates conferred briefly on the situation. I was sent up on deck with the two apprentices to fetch shovels, buckets, dishes, and any other receptables that would carry a few pounds of pebbles. There were only four shovels in the barque's equipment, but with these and whatever other utensils we could find we returned to the hold, and work began.

To men already wearied, 300tons of pebbles seemed a mighty big quantity to shift, by manual labour, with inadequate tools. The plan of action was to shovel and scoop the pebbles from the starboard to the port side in two operations, first forming a heap amidships, then later moving that heap over to the port side. It was gruelling work, made worse by the fact that the pebbles were loose underfoot, so that we sank to our ankles if we attempted to walk over them. To overcome this hindrance we formed two "human chains," and passed the receptacles from hand to hand.

After five hours of toil, we had a sizable heap of pebbles amidships, but all hands were dead beat. At 6 a.m. we were ordered to climb up on deck for a "spell-oh," a breath of fresh air, and a meal of coffee, pantiles, and tinned mutton. It was a beautiful, calm, tropical dawn, with not a cloud in the sky, scarcely a breath of wind stirring, the surface of the water unruffled, and only a gentle ocean swell in which the barque wallowed awkwardly with her ungainly list.

The crew, exhausted after twelve hours strenuous work and anxiety, sprawled on the deck or in their bunks, and most of us fell instantly asleep. At 8 a.m., we resumed four-hour watches and again attacked the pebbles in the hold.

I was in the gang sent down below — six of us, in the Mate's watch. Our task now was to shovel and scoop the pebbles from the heap amidships to the high side. To "contain" them, we first lashed a spare topsail fore and aft in the hold, with the corners of the sail tied up so that it formed a long canvas box. This prevented the pebbles from rolling back as we threw them over it.

Four hours later we wearily dragged ourselves up the ladder for the change of the watch at noon, and the Captain announced, "She's starting to right a bit!"

After a meal of pork and pantiles we fell into our bunks, lulled to sleep by the sound of pebbles being shovelled by the other watch. At 4 p.m., it was "All hands down below," to finish the job. By 8 p.m. she was on an even keel again.

We were then able to get some sail on her and, with a gentle breeze in our favour, resumed the voyage and stood in toward the coast of Peru, in light and variable airs until we sighted the Chincha Islands, ten days out from Callao.

The ordeal of being on our beam ends had caused the crew temporarily to forget their discontent at having been swindled by the chandler. When the lives of all were in danger, we were a united company of shipmates, with no time for growling, and each man's pride was to strive to his utmost, for the survival of all.

Captain Hughes had been to the Chincha Islands five years previously and knew the ground. On a sunny afternoon, the wind being fair, we sailed slowly into the narrow channel between the two biggest islands and dropped anchor in thirty fathoms of water, paying out seventy-five fathoms of cable. Our anchorage was two cables' length (400 yards) from a small landing stage on one of the islands. Some huts on another island housed the entire population, consisting of twenty-five convicts and their guards.

Millions, literally millions, of sea birds wheeled overhead, with a continual

**Sailmakers working on a sail in port while being watched by a Mate.
(Bisset)**

loud clamour of screeching cries, and dived into the sea to pounce on the surface swimming pilchards and other fish which teemed in the warm coastal current scouring Pisco Bay. The Chincha group consists of three rocky islands, like mountain peaks, entirely devoid of vegetation or surface water, and a large number of outlying rocky islets. These islands and rocks have been, from time immemorial, a resting place for the sea birds, and their mating and breeding place.

From the deck of the barque we could see the birds clustered on the rocks, peaks, and slopes of the islands which looked like snow — a strange illusion in that torrid and almost rainless region. Evidently the birds were resting there to enjoy the pleasures of digestion after catching fish or in weariness after hours of soaring. In the caves around the base of the islands, and basking on the rocks, were hundreds of sea lions, who at intervals emitted harsh roars.

The islands belonged to the Peruvian government, which made a profitable trade selling the guano, or dried bird droppings, collected by convict labour. There was a keen demand for this manure as a soil fertilizer in France, Belgium, and other European countries because it is especially rich in phosphates. When the guano deposits were first discovered, they were said to have been some hundreds of feet thick. In the course of time hundreds of thousands of tons were exported to Europe, in sailing vessels which found this a profitable cargo for the homeward run around Cape Horn, after delivering coal or general merchandise to ports in Peru or Chile.

When the original deposits were worked out, the government declared the islands closed to trade for several years, to allow the guano to accumulate again. They had been reopened a short while before our visit. The *County of Pembroke* was one of the first vessels to call after the "dormant" period.

The convicts who gathered the guano were long term prisoners from Callao, who earned some remission of their sentences by "doing their stretch" of hard and disagreeable labour at the Chincha Islands. They gathered the guano in handcarts and brought it to the top of the cliffs. Here it was tipped through canvas chutes into lighters holding about ten tons and lightered out to vessels at the anchorage. Provisions and water were brought out to the convicts and their guards in a small steamer from the port of Pisco, ten miles away (16 km). (This is the district where "Pisco" spirit is made.)

When we were at anchor and the sails stowed, Captain Hughes went ashore in the gig, rowed by the two apprentices, to make arrangements for the lightering. It happened that at this time a steamer came to the landing stage with provisions. Our Old Man bought a demijohn of Pisco, and some horse meat, pumpkins, and sweet potatoes — these being the only fresh provisions obtainable here. A few days later the loading of the guano began. In the meantime, we had been shovelling our accursed pebbly ballast into baskets from both ends of the ballast heap and had discharged about a hundred tons of it overside into the water. We would now be able to load guano into the forehatch and afterhatch until we had enough weight in her to discharge some more ballast. This process would go on alternately until the ballast was all discharged, and we would then be able to spread the guano evenly throughout the hold.

When the first lighter came alongside, we had an indication of the ordeals ahead of us. The guano, a brownish, sundried powder of the consistency of pepper, was mixed with feathers and bones of dead birds. It smelled strongly of ammonia and other stinks. It was not bagged, but loaded loose into the lighter, which was manned by six convicts of ferocious appearance, guarded by two warders armed with rifles, seated in the stern.

The convicts propelled the lighter out from the shore with sweeps and brought her alongside. We had rigged a dolly winch, with a block and tackle on a spar lashed out overside, and baskets to discharge the ballast. This gear was now used to haul the guano inboard and dump it into the hold. The convicts had the task of filling the baskets in the lighter. They were not allowed on board. We were sorry for them as they stood in the hot sun, up to their knees in the powdery guano.

But soon we were sorrier for ourselves. As we tipped the guano into the hatches from on deck, the air rising from the hold became acrid with ammonia fumes and our nostrils were choked with the stinking dust.

As the work proceeded, after several days all the ballast was discharged and we were then sent down below to shovel the guano into the far corners of the hold, and to rake, trim and tamp it down, to get in as big a cargo as possible. This meant that we had to plod around in the powdery stuff for hours on end, sinking in it up to our knees and breath-ing in the dust and fumes. The convicts in the lighter had an easy time compared with us, as at least they had their noses in the open air. The fumes made us gasp for breath and bleed at the nose. When this happened, we climbed up the ladder to the deck for a breath of fresh air.

Work went on until 6 p.m. daily, except on Saturday afternoons, Sundays, and Saints' Days. Fortunately for us, there were many Saints' Days in the Peruvian calendar, when the convicts were not expected to work and, in consequence there was no lightering or loading. On those days the crew could enjoy a breath of fresh air, painting overside or scraping grass and barnacles or blacking down the rigging, greasing down the masts, and overhauling gear. On days when we worked in the hold the Captain gave all hands a tot of Pisco at 5 p.m. to keep us going for the last hour of the day.

Loading proceeded very slowly. There were only two lighters, each holding ten tons of guano, and the convicts were never in a hurry — we could not blame them for that! What with the heat, poor food, shortage of drinking water (our whack being strictly limited, in view of the long voyage ahead of us), the all-pervading stink of the guano, and hard labour in the daytime and roaring of sea lions to keep us awake at night, we longed for the day when we would heave up the anchor and set sail from this place of torment.

One Sunday morning, in a mood of generosity, the Captain allowed me to go in the dinghy with the two apprentices to have a closer look at the sea lions basking on the rocks. This would be a treat for the boys. "Don't go near them," he warned. The dinghy was a light boat, which like the Captain's gig, was for handy use when we were in port. It was already overside in the water, secured with a painter under the stern, as we had used it for scraping barnacles and chipping rust on Saturday morning, and it had not been hauled inboard. I sat in the stern sheets, while the two strong boys took an oar each and bent their backs to the task with a will, pulling to the rocks, a quarter of a mile (1.6 km) from our anchorage, where we could see a big sea lion basking. As we neared him, he raised his head, with what seemed a supercilious smile, and lazily regarded us. We came in close and rowed around the rock on which he lay inert. "I'll liven him up, for the fun of it," said Jack O'Connor, the Irish lad from Drogheda. He stood up in the dinghy and poked the sea lion in the ribs with his oar.

The beast, who weighed about half a ton, immediately flopped off the rock and fell into the dinghy, tipping us all into the water! Then he dived and disappeared. We had only a few yards to swim to the rock. The boys held on to their oars. The dinghy was swamped, but I managed to grab the painter, and with this we hauled it up to the rock and then bailed it out.

Looking toward the barque, I saw that the Old Man was on the poop, his telescope trained on us, to see if we were hurt or the dinghy damaged. Most of the crew were also on deck, evidently ordered to stand by to launch the gig or one of the lifeboats if we needed rescue. As we had suffered no harm except a fright and a ducking, we soon got into the dinghy again and rowed back to the barque, feeling very foolish.

"What happened?" the Captain sang out, as we neared. "A sea lion jumped into the dinghy, sir," I answered.

All the seamen burst out laughing, considering that I was making a fantastic excuse for clumsiness on our part in capsizing the dinghy. The Captain was taken aback by my perfectly truthful reply. No one on board had been looking in our direction at the moment when the sea lion jumped on us; but a sailor had noticed us struggling in the water and had raised the alarm.

"Make the dinghy fast and come up here at once, all three of you," the Captain sang out menacingly from the poop.

When we stood before him, dripping wet, he said, "Now what's all this nonsense?"

"It's true, sir," I said. "A sea lion jumped off the rock into the dinghy and capsized us!"

"Tell that to the marines," the Captain growled.

"It's true, sir," said the two apprentices earnestly.

The Captain considered the matter for a while, then asked, "What made him jump?"

"I stuck an oar into his ribs," Jack O'Connor confessed.

At this the Captain roared, and looked like a sea lion himself, ready to jump on us.

"And what did you do that for?" he said.

"To wake him up, sir!"

"Well, don't do it again, and don't ask me to let you have the dinghy again! If you'd damaged that dinghy, who would have paid for it? Yourselves! I would have taken the cost of it out of your pay, as you were using it for pleasure. And next time you see a sea lion on a rock, let sleeping dogs lie. That'll do you now. Lay forrard and change your clothes."

On deck the seamen, who had nothing better to do, crowded around us and quizzed us about our misadventure. "Indeed to goodness," said Lew Owens, "and what was it like to have a sea lion sitting on your knee?"

"It was finished before it started," Jack from Drogheda grinned. "Just a smack in the face from a wet fish and thank ye!"

With this exception, our stay at the Chincha Islands was uneventful, monotonous, and disagreeable. We lay there at anchor six weeks before the hold was filled to the deckhead, with 1,000 tons of guano, rammed into every corner and packed tightly around the two iron freshwater tanks. These, as in all sailing vessels, were set amidships in the hold, abaft the mainmast, and water was drawn from them into buckets by a hand pump on deck, for our whack of three quarts per man per day.

It was a great day when we battened down the hatches and put the guano out of sight except for the thick layers of it which had settled on all the decks and superstructures and penetrated to every nook and cranny of our living quarters, bedding, clothes, and utensils.

No other vessel was loading while we were there. The authorities at Callao controlled matters so that one vessel at a time proceeded to the islands.

The little steamer came out from Pisco three of four times during our stay, and our Old Man purchased small additional supplies of scraggy meat, pumpkins, sweet potatoes and some dried beans. He had a chance here to obtain from the town provisions such as coffee, rice, flour, and other groceries, if he had chosen to do so, knowing that his supplies of food were running low. He had taken in very little at Callao. Perhaps this was on instructions from the owners; perhaps he was hoping to make a smart passage home; whatever the reason, the barque was seriously under provisioned.

The crew did not know this, but the Captain must have known. On 3rd December 1902, a scorching summer day, we manned the windlass and began to heave up and down on the long levers, to the song of "Rolling Home." This type of windlass was known as "the Armstrong Patent." Some idea of its efficiency may be gathered from the fact that it required more than two hours' hard heaving to get in the seventy-five fathoms of cable link by link and break the anchor out of the rocky bottom.

With a moderate breeze from the southeast, we got a press of sail on her and, farewelled by a few feeble cheers from a gang of convicts on top of the rock, sailed safely out of the passage and headed southward toward Cape Horn.

Two hours later the Chincha Islands, and the millions of birds wheeling around them, were out of sight, but not out of mind. For many a day we were scrubbing decks and cleaning the guano dust from every accessible place in which it had settled; but even though fresh breezes blew, the smell of ammonia, seeping from the hold ventilators was all-pervading and could not be got rid of.

Hungry Days — "No More Burgoo" — A Substitute for Coffee —
Rounding the Horn on Empty Bellies — A Captain's Worries —
Rations Reduced — Threat of Mutiny — Discipline Gone —
Polluted Drinking Water — The Last of the Pork — A Raid Under
the Poop — Eating Slush —Starvation and Despair — Standing On

STANDING to the southward in fresh southeasterly breezes, we made good progress and, in two weeks, picked up the roaring forties and ran into cold and dirty weather. It was usual in cold weather for the crew to be given "burgoo" (porridge) for breakfast. The cook had to be reminded of this. He grumbled and said that the weather was not cold; but next day we had our burgoo, and every morning thereafter for a week. In that time, we had squared away for the Horn and the decks were awash, with high running seas astern and gales of icy wind.

Then, the "burgoo" disappeared from the breakfast menu. "The oatmeal is finished," said the cook. This left us with only hard biscuits and coffee for breakfast. It was Christmas Day of 1902 — my fifth Christmas at sea — and if I wasn't a sailor by then I'd never be one.

This voyage had now lasted a little more than thirteen months, since our departure from Liverpool in November 1901. We were still living on provisions taken in at the beginning of the voyage.

The Captain had not thought it necessary in June at Newcastle to replenish the salt provisions and groceries. There, these would have been readily procurable. He knew then that we were bound for the west coast of South America, with the prospect of delays there and a long homeward voyage.

He had neglected also to take in provisions at Callao in October, even though he knew that we were bound for the Chincha Islands and homeward on the long haul around Cape Horn. Finally, he had neglected his last chance to take in provisions which could have been sent out to him in November, from the port of Pisco, in the supply steamer running to the Chincha Islands. Such carelessness, or meanness, may have been due to a failure on his part to examine the stores as the voyage proceeded; but more likely it was due to instructions given to him by the owners to avoid expense in ports. Such instructions, which were handed to shipmasters and marked "Strictly Secret," were drawn up in legal terminology designed to exonerate the owners and put the blame on the Master of a vessel for almost any mishap that might occur. They cast the utmost responsibility on the Master and at the same time restricted his freedom of action in a hundred different ways, especially in incurring expenditure.

A shipmaster had to know much more than navigation and seamanship. He was required to have a working knowledge of accountancy and business methods and of mercantile and maritime law, applicable at sea and in many a foreign port. As all blame was put on the Captain when anything went wrong, even when the mishaps were due to the avarice or business acumen of the owners, he was viewed as the symbol of tyranny, meanness or ineptitude in all adverse contingencies, even though he was himself intimidated by the tyranny of his secret orders.

At the end of a voyage his accounts would be scrutinized by the owners and every item of expense questioned. It was impossible or very difficult to economize on port dues, towage, purchase of ballast, and various other working expenses on a long voyage; but the owners — who in most instances had never been to sea themselves — were intensely suspicious of any purchases made by shipmasters in foreign ports if these included provisions and stores. They had reason to believe that some shipmasters would make a profit on the side from such deals. For this reason the owners preferred to supply all necessary provisions and stores in the home port, under their own supervision, at the outset of a voyage.

The *County of Pembroke* had been provisioned at Liverpool for a twelve-months voyage. This would have been sufficient if we had succeeded in picking up a cargo in New Zealand, for a direct home run without undue delays; but when we were ordered to Newcastle, Callao, and the Chincha Islands, the voyage was extended by many months. In these circumstances the Captain could have used his own discretion or could have cabled to the owners for permission to take in extra provisions and stores.

If the accounts of the voyage showed a loss, the Captain would be blamed, whether it was his fault or not; but this voyage was a profitable one. We had carried three cargoes. One of general merchandise to New Zealand, and then coal to Callao, with our final cargo of guano for the home run — with no undue waste of time as time was reckoned in cargo voyages under sail. It was therefore an act of excessive meanness to economize on the food required by law to be supplied to the crew, especially in such a comparatively trivial expense as that required to lay in enough oatmeal to line the bellies of the crew with burgoo for the few weeks that we would be in cold latitudes while rounding Cape Horn.

But worse was to come. On New Year's Day of 1903, we were off the pitch of the Horn, in summer weather but with a strong breeze on the port quarter, high following seas, flooded decks, and an overcast sky.

In the absence of burgoo, a breakfast of weevilly pantiles and hot coffee was something to look forward to after the vigils of the night. The cook doled out the coffee into our "hook pots," which were then taken to the half deck and the fo'c'sle as usual. The cook was a Cockney of a surly temper, who, in accordance with custom, was known as "the Doctor." He lived under the poop, combining the duties of cook and steward and, in this latter capacity, over- seeing the provisions and stores. "This is a new kind of coffee," he said, with a smirk. "You can like it or leave it."

Suspicions thus aroused, we sniffed at the coffee and tasted it. Though black and hot, the liquid had no other resemblance to coffee. It tasted like charcoal, or worse.

"What's this —?" "What the —?" Yells of consternation arose in the fo'c'sle. Presently some of the seamen emerged on deck, pannikins in hand, and went to the door of the caboose. "What's this, Doctor?" they demanded.

"We've run out of coffee," said the cook. "This is a substitute!"

"It's undrinkable!" Lew Owens growled. "What is it?" "Ask the Captain!"

"Damn you, tell us the truth!" "Blimey, don't you like it?" "No! What is it?"

"Find out!"

Some more seamen in an ugly mood came to the galley door. The cook decided to reveal his secret. "The Cap'n ordered me to make a substitute for coffee by burning biscuits black in the oven and grinding them to powder, just like coffee beans. What else can I do? We've run out of coffee!" he whined.

The seamen retired to the fo'c'sle and held an indignation meeting. All agreed that the brew of charred biscuit powder was undrinkable. Pannikins in hand, we went aft in a body to the break of the poop and asked to see the Captain.

Presently he emerged. Lew Owens was our spokesman.

He voiced our complaint in well-chosen words.

The Captain sniffed and tasted the brew. "It's very good," he declared. "Quite healthy. It's the best we can do, as the cook unfortunately neglected to notice that we didn't have enough coffee in our stores. Otherwise, I could have got some for you at Callao."

Scowling, the seamen murmured in the incoherent beginnings of mutinous resentment. It was a weakness for the Captain to put blame on a subordinate. Lew Owens began speaking rapidly in Welsh, and the Captain answered him in the same language. This too was disruptive of discipline, as it worried the majority of the crew who could not understand what was said; but it was a common practice in Thomas's ships, in which most of the officers and usually some of the seamen were Welsh.

Whatever Lew Owens said, the Captain appeared to be arguing with him and ultimately, he said, in English, "Very well, then, you will have tea instead of coffee, in future. That will do you now, men. Go forrard, and remember that this is a long voyage, and I am doing my best for your welfare."

For the next ten days, as we drove on around the Horn, encountering some adverse weather, we had tea to drink with our meals, but it was so weak that it was little more than boiled water tinctured with stewed tea leaves. Then, as we headed north, rounding the Falkland Islands, the Captain one morning called all hands aft to the break of the poop.

"The cook has reported to me, men," he began, "that we are unfortunately running short of salt provisions. There is no need for alarm, as we have sufficient in hand for some time; but, if we are delayed by headwinds on our northern passage, there may not be enough beef and pork to last us until we reach Falmouth. I have therefore decided, as the barque is sailing very sluggishly due to her foul bottom, that it will be in the best interests of all concerned to cut down the whack of beef and pork, as a wise precaution.

"I am sorry this is necessary, but you will realize that there is nothing else I can do, so you must put up with it without grumbling. Fortunately, we have a plentiful supply of biscuits, so you will not starve. From tomorrow, you will be on half rations of salt provisions, but you will get your full whack of biscuits. That'll do you now. Lay forrard, and don't make any complaints about what can't be helped." This serious news caused consternation in the fo'c'sle, as well it might. The beef and pork rations coming out of the ready use harness casks were so putrid that only very hungry men could stomach them, but to have even that supply cut to a half whack was a glum prospect. On making investigations, the crew became aware that only one tierce of beef and one cask of pork remained in reserve in the fore peak. This was a hopelessly inadequate supply for a barque's complement of twenty-one souls on the northward run in the Atlantic, which would require not less than two months!

Usually the reserves of beef and pork were stowed in the hold with the cargo; but, as we were carrying guano, the salt provisions had been transferred, at the Chincha Islands, from the hold to the fore peak, where they could be seen by the fo'c'sle hands. In this situation, Captain Hughes would have been justified in putting into Port Stanley in the Falkland Islands, or even into Montevideo, to obtain provisions; but the additional expense thus incurred would have got him into trouble with the owners, as his orders were to "keep the seas" except in dire emergencies.

He considered it would be less disagreeable to put the crew on half rations than to confront the owners with unauthorized expenses of putting into an intermediate port. A few days later the cook announced that he would be serving cocoa instead of tea, as the tea had run out. The cocoa was mildewed and in very short supply. Though the cook brewed it so weak that it scarcely coloured the water, the supply ran out in a few days more. We then had nothing but water and lime juice to drink with our meals; but, as we were working into warmer latitudes, perhaps we did not need the stimulants of hot drinks! "Water is good for you," said the Cockney cook, "especially wiv lime juice in it."

Unfortunately, the water was not "good for us." The two iron tanks in the hold had been filled at Callao, four months previously, with fresh water which was not of the purest quality. It was tainted with some vegetable or animal substance, which, under the influence of heat generated by the guano packed around the tanks, had fermented or decayed and gave the water a bad taste and smell. So considerable was the heat generated by the guano in the hold that, when we pumped water out of the tanks into a bucket, it was tepid and gave off steam on exposure to the outer air.

In the previous weeks, when the water had been boiled and tinctured, however slightly, with coffee, tea, or cocoa, we had been able to stomach it; but now, when we began drinking it un-boiled, to quench our thirst, we suffered from severe "guts ache" and vomiting. To prevent an outbreak of typhoid or dysentery, which seemed imminent, the Captain studied The Ship Captain's Medical Guide. With this inspiration, he searched in the medical chest and found a tin of permanganate of potash crystals. He gave orders for a few of these crystals to be stirred into each bucket of water drawn from the pump, "to kill the germs." The result was a purple fluid, which the sailors refused to drink. The Captain then ordered that all water should be. boiled before we drank it. This was done with good effect; although the boiled water tasted peculiar, we could drink it without vomiting or stomach pains.

In the meantime, the contents of the last tierce of beef and cask of pork had been transferred to the ready use harness casks lashed to the poop rail, and smelled there to high heaven, even in the strong brine. The stores of "Harriet Lane" tinned mutton had been finished while we were at the Chincha Islands. Even on the half ration of six ounces of salt beef, or four ounces of salt pork, per man per day, the contents of the harness casks could not last much longer. Soon after we entered the tropics the cook informed us that the beef was finished, and the pork nearly finished.

Other provisions specified in the Board of Trade scale, such as tinned butter, sugar, peas, beans, jam, molasses, and dried fruits, had been reduced in the whack and gradually gave out. One of the worst strokes of fate came, for most of the crew, when they tried to buy tobacco from the slop chest and were informed by the Captain that the tobacco was finished!

A mutinous situation now developed. The Captain and the Mates carried revolvers in their pockets and seldom ventured from the poop, being content to sing out their orders from there when handling of sail was necessary. The Mate made a few half-hearted attempts to get the men to holystone the decks, but, though no man actually refused orders, they worked so listlessly that he saw it was futile to continue.

Almost daily the men went aft to the break of the poop, with one request or another to the Captain. The bad food and water had caused most of us to break out in boils. It was pathetic to see how the instincts of discipline struggled with mutinous feelings, as most of the men stood dumbly and listlessly by, while their spokesman appealed to the Captain to make for the nearest port or to get them out of their plight somehow.

The grumblers in the fo'c'sle, especially the two new hands signed on at Callao, urged violent action. They wildly suggested that the Mate should be asked to put the Captain under arrest and to steer for Rio or the Cape Verde Islands or wherever the nearest port might be! Lew Owens was deputed to seek some opportunity to ask the Mate to do this. Accordingly, the next time Lew had a trick at the wheel he spoke to the Mate quietly on the poop and told him that the men would support any action he thought fit to take.

But the Mate had no stomach for any such drastic action and told Lew (who was a kinsman of his) that the men were not actually starving while there was an ample supply of biscuits, lime juice and water. Lew then argued that the water was undrinkable.

Next day, as we were then in the doldrums where there were often showers of rain, the Captain announced that he would obtain fresh water for us from the heavens. The Mate took charge of the operations. We emptied one of the tanks, by pumping its smelly contents into the other tank. Then we rigged up a flat sail amidships, with a canvas hose sewn into its centre, leading down into the tank supply pipe. Presently there was a heavy shower of rain, and a considerable quantity of pure water gurgled into the tank. We began drinking this at once, and, within a few days, with some more showers, the tank was filled.

Though this water was tainted by the scum which remained inside the tank, we could drink it without boiling it. This was a godsend, as the supply of coal for the galley was now nearly finished — not that this mattered much, since the pork was now finished and there was nothing to cook!

The shortage of food caused discipline to break down. The grumblers in the fo'c'sle spread a rumour that the Captain and the two Mates and the cook were living on tinned provisions, of which they supposedly had an ample supply. for themselves under the poop. Though this statement was not correct, starving men will believe anything.

The crew went aft in a body and sullenly demanded to be shown all the stores that remained on board. The Captain at once realized that any bluster or bluff on his part could provoke an act of mutinous violence, for which he would be held responsible even if it were quelled. He and the two Mates stood shoulder to shoulder, with their hands in their coat pockets. In any brawl they would be backed up, as they well knew, by the apprentices and possibly others who were in duty bound to uphold authority at all costs; but the Captain had no wish to put the matter to the test.

Even the Welsh seamen were against him now. He said, quietly, "Very well, men, I will allow you to search under the poop, to examine the stores for yourselves. Three of you will be enough. The others stand by." He beckoned to Lew Owens and the two malcontents from Callao. The Second Mate escorted these three, with the cook, into the saloon and the other compartments under the poop.

They came on deck again, after ten minutes, carrying a few tins of sardines and salmon and bottles of preserved fruit. Apart from these, they announced, there were no stores left except biscuits and lime juice. In these circumstances the Captain agreed that no man, whatever his rank, was entitled to more food than another, and that the tinned fish and bottled fruit should be carefully meted out in equal portions to all before and abaft the mast.

That matter settled, the men made their next request, which was that the Captain should steer for the nearest port to obtain supplies.

"That will be the Azores Islands," the Captain said. "I will show you our position on the chart." He got the chart and said ingratiatingly, "I have your welfare at heart, men. The nearest and easiest port to make for is the Azores, and I will set course for there. It is on our homeward track, and we should reach it in two or three weeks if the weather permits. In the meantime, you have fresh water, and plenty of lime juice, and I will increase the whack of biscuits from five to six, per man, per day, and double the ration of lime juice. That is the best I can do, and we will have the same under the poop as you have forrard. Further, if we sight a steamer, as we may do on this track, I will signal for assistance. That'll do you now. Lay forrard, and no more grumbling. Make the best of what can't be helped!"

Lew Owens handed one tin of fish and one bottle of fruit to the Captain, gave me one of each for the half deck, and took the rest into the fo'c'sle, where it was duly shared out in one luxurious repast.

The cook was now a nonentity, having nothing to cook. Once a day he handed out the whack of biscuits, and his work was finished.

It was then that someone suggested a raid on the slush. This was the fat and scum which the cook had skimmed off the pots in which salt beef and salt pork had been boiled in the previous months. It was stored in two casks, under the fo'c'slehead, and was carefully hoarded by the cook, being his perquisite, to be sold at the end of the voyage. However, the slush was accessible to the crew, because it was used for greasing down the masts and (when mixed with Stockholm tar) for splicing ropes.

When hunger overtook us, the slush assumed a new value. Though it was rancid and dirtied by many a tarry hand having been dipped into it, some genius in the fo'c'sle declared that it could help to keep life in starving men. His recipe was to soak pantiles in water until they were quite soft, then to fry them brown in slush.

This seemed feasible. A tin of slush was brought to the galley, but the cook rejected it with scorn. "It will poison you and give you scurvy!" he said. "It's full of salt, and you can't use it for frying!"

As most of the crew already had boils and ulcers from bad food and water and the insufficient diet, they thought they could get no worse. The cook took the tin of slush and showed it to the Captain. He returned to the galley, saying that the Captain had forbidden him to use it for cooking. At this, the seamen told the cook to clear out of his caboose, or he'd be thrown out. They said they would stand no interference from the Captain, the Mates, the Doctor, or anybody else. Discipline was gone and no work was being done except the trimming of yards and sails to keep the barque moving. The fire was lit in the galley stove, and some biscuits put to soak in water.

When the biscuits were softened, a dollop of slush was put into the biggest frying pan. Within a few moments, blue and acrid smoke filled the galley as the slush sizzled and scorched. The biscuits were thrown into the pan and left to fry until they were done brown. The choking smoke made it impossible for the amateur cooks to stay in the galley. They stood outside and made a quick dash in and out of the galley for the pan when the meal was considered done.

All hands before the mast sampled the delicacy, and most of them declared it very tasty and nourishing. After a few mouthfuls of it I felt deathly sick and vomited. Next day I tried it again, with a similar result, so I decided to subsist on biscuits, lime juice, and water. Several of the men, having stomachs of iron, continued eating the slush; but, after a week of it, they were nauseated as well as covered in boils. The experiment was gradually abandoned.

When would we reach the Azores? That was the question to which the Captain might know the answer, but the men did not. In the NE trades we were making good headway, braced sharp up, but this course was carrying us far to the westward of the Azores. Three weeks after the Old Man's tactful handling of the mutinous situation, no land was in sight. The crew were weak and emaciated, and some were scarcely able to turn to. We had sighted no steamers or other vessels.

The mutinous spirit had died down, and starvation had produced only apathy. The Captain and the Mates also looked thin and ill, but, having abstained from slush, they were in slightly better fettle than the men. One morning a fresh SE wind sprang up. The Captain called all hands aft and explained the situation. "This wind," he said, "is heading us off from the Azores, but it is a good leading wind for the English Channel. Braced fairly sharp on the starboard tack," he continued, "we should make Falmouth in ten days if the wind holds, and we'll be in the track of steamers. So I'll stand on for Falmouth and signal any steamer we sight. That'll do you now, men. Lay forrard, and work your watches, and do as you're told, and we'll soon be home."

So we gave up all idea of making for an intermediate port and stood on.

The Captain had his orders to keep to the seas. He had never had any intention of putting into the Azores . . . but now he was a very worried man. Anything could happen. The crew were like living skeletons. If we ran into a storm, they would be too weak to go aloft, and only the Mercy of Providence could help us then.

THAT day, at noon, only four hours after the Captain had decided to stand on for Falmouth, we sighted a smudge of smoke on the horizon to the north-eastward. "A steamer! A steamer!" the lookout man sang out, and the cry was taken up by enfeebled men on deck, bringing others tumbling and tottering out of their bunks below, haggard and gaunt, to line the rail and stare with burning, feverish gaze at the wavering black line that looked like a cloud low in the blue sky. That thin trail of smoke lay athwart our course. Yes, it was a steamer, but would she pass us by? In the SE breeze, her smoke trail would be blown to leeward of her course if she were headed westward across the Atlantic, as she evidently was, since we had first sighted her smoke well away on our starboard bow.

Her funnel was not yet visible, but it appeared from the movements of her plume of smoke that she was just below the horizon, about twenty miles (20 km) NE of our position, and heading due west. We had all sail set to the royals and were doing eight knots on the starboard tack headed northeast.

The probability was that the steamer was doing ten knots. If both vessels kept their courses and speeds, we would pass far astern of her and would not come within signalling distance. The Mate, whose burly frame had enabled him to survive the rigors of starvation better than anyone else in the barque, climbed to the fore-topsail yard, and got a bearing on the steamer. He reported this to the Old Man on the poop. They calculated that, if we altered course to due north, we would intercept the steamer in an hour and a half.

All hands tailed on, in good heart and high hopes, to haul around the yards, trim the sails and sheet them home with what remained of our vigour, as the barque answered the helm and veered to the north, with the fresh breeze on our starboard quarter instead of abeam.

Our course was now at right angles to the steamer's course. In half an hour we could see her funnel from our main deck, and the Mate estimated that she was thirteen miles (20 km) away NE.

The Captain now called me aft and sent me to the flag locker. On his orders, I hoisted to our gaff-peak the urgent two-flag signal, N-V, meaning, "We are short of provisions: starving."

Half an hour later we were within seven miles (11.2 km) of the steamer

N - November

(Blue Checkered)

V - Victor

(Red Crossbars)

and could see her superstructure, from which it appeared that she was a small, rusty old tramp. It would now be clear to the men on her bridge that we were headed across her bows. As they would probably be old sailing ship men, they would scan us with particular care. A few minutes later we saw to our great joy that she altered course to bear down upon us, and her answering pennant fluttered to her masthead, meaning, "I understand your signal."

"Back the main yards, Mister," said our Old Man, all smiles.

"All hands on deck!" the Mates roared in excitement, but unnecessarily, as all the living skeletons in the barque were already standing by, intently eyeing the steamer and ready to exert themselves, to the last ounce of their strength, in the hope of a good feed in the near future.

"Put your backs into it, my lads!" the Mate sang out as we tailed on to the heavy work of backing the main yards. This brought the barque to a standstill, or nearly so, with the wind and sea two points before the starboard beam.

After this exertion we were nearly dead beat, but excitement kept us going as the steamer, now fully in view, was coming up fast. She was flying the signal F-H, meaning "Send a boat," to which our Old Man hoisted the answering pennant. Then, as the Captain's gig and the dinghy were not available under davits, or suitable for such an occasion, he sang out, "Launch the port lifeboat, Mister. Get away in her yourself, with six good men, and lay alongside the old hooker there, and ask them for anything they can spare in the way of food. Careful, now, Mister, careful. Take a bucket with you for bailing!"

"Lower away the port boat!" bawled the Mate. In our eagerness, all hands tailed on to the falls like one man, to hoist the boat off its skids. Now each man, it seemed, had the strength of ten, summoned from the ultimate reserve

F - Foxtrot
(Red Diamond)

H - Hotel
(1/2 Red)

of human survival power; for, as we heaved, there was a horrible sound of splitting woodwork. Up came both ends of the boat, leaving the centre fast on the skids! "Holy mackerel!" groaned the Mate in despair. "Belay everything, you damned idiots. This blasted boat is caked with a hundred coats of paint, and she hasn't been out of her chocks for twenty years. By the seven holy ducks that sat on King Solomon's grave, I'll choke the gizzard out of any cockeyed son of a sea cook who paints underneath a lifeboat in future without easing her out of the chocks. Now look what you've done, you awkward galoots. You've gone and beggared up the boat!"

The Mate's annoyance was due in part to the fact that boats were always painted under the supervision of the Mates. Moreover, the mishap in launching the boat had occurred in full view of the officers and crew of the steamer, which had now come to a standstill three hundred yards on our lee side. The Mate wanted to put on a smart show of seamanship, worthy of the great traditions of sail, as he believed that men in steamers were ignorant of the finer points of the nautical art.

"Where's the carpenter?" the Mate asked.

"Here, sir," said Chips, who was standing by.

"Get your tools and chip away the paint under the starboard lifeboat," to free her from the chocks!"

"Aye, aye, sir," said Chips, moving on the run to get his tools.

The Captain sang out from the poop, "What's wrong, Mister?"

"Port lifeboat's holed, sir. Keel split and garboard strake buckled. She was secured to the skids with paint!"

The Captain considered the implications of this surprising statement, then sang out, loud enough for the men in the steamer to hear him, " 'Bout ship and launch the starboard boat!"

Then he added, much more quietly, "And see that she's free before you hoist her, Mister!"

It was nautically correct to put the barque about, to bring the starboard side to the lee, before launching the boat on that side in mid-ocean, the more so as the Captain now had doubts of the seaworthiness of the starboard boat, since neither of the boats had been put into the water for many a year. They had never been launched during the four years and five months that I had served in the *County of Pembroke* and perhaps had never been used since they were installed in 1881 — a serious breach of the Board of Trade regulations for the safety of lives at sea, which required the lifeboats to be used and the gear tested at intervals, to insure that they would be available in an emergency.

Now, under the eyes of critical spectators, the crew of the *County of Pembroke* had to tail on, haul around the heavy yards on the mainmast, get the barque under way, then put her about and bring her to again "in irons" with the main yards backed once again to windward of the steamer, as previously, but with our starboard side toward her. This manoeuvre required half an hour of hard work and skilled seamanship, which must surely have impressed the onlookers, since they knew that we were starving men, in the meantime the carpenter had freed the starboard boat from the layers of paint which secured it to the skids.

All hands stood by the falls, and the Mate gave the order, "Take it easy, now, gently, haul away! We want her up all in one piece this time!"

When the boat was free and hanging in the davits, we swung her cautiously over the side and lowered her level with the rail. The Mate looked around at the miserable, half-starved specimens of humanity standing by and picked out six of the least enfeebled looking — including myself — and ordered us to man the boat.

He instructed me to go forrard, to pull the bow oar and tend the painter. He took his seat at the stern and shipped the rudder. When all was ready he gave the order, "Lower away, gently now, gently. Keep her on an even keel."

Gradually we took the water, with only a slight splash and the Mate sang out, "Let go!" We unhooked the falls, I cast off the painter, and, as I shoved her off with the boat hook, the seamen shipped their oars and we got underway By this time, owing to years of exposure to tropical suns and sheer neglect, the planks began to open up at the seams, and she was leaking like a basket.

We bent our backs to the oars as smartly as possible in the circumstances, but this only opened her up more. By the time we were pulling around under the steamer's stern, she was completely waterlogged, and we were sitting in water lapping up to the thwarts.

When we got alongside and made fast, the Mate set us to bailing out with a bucket and an old tin can; but, after a few minutes of this, we realized that it was like trying to bail out the Atlantic Ocean with a teaspoon, so we gave up the hopeless task. In the meantime the Mate was carrying on a shouted conversation with the Master of the steamer on the bridge.

She was the *S.S. Lowlands*, 2,000 tons of West Hartlepool, bound from Palermo in Sicily to New York with a cargo of Sulphur. Her Captain, an old sailing ship man, sang out, "Who's your Master, Mister Mate, and where are you bound?"

"Captain Hughes, Falmouth for orders, with guano, 145 days out from Callao!"

"Who are your owners?"

"William Thomas & Co., Ltd., Liverpool."

"Welsh Thieves and Colonial Liars, eh? I've heard of their hungry ships. What provisions have you?"

"Only biscuits and lime juice. We are starving!" "What provisions do you need to make Falmouth? How many hands have you?"

"Any food you can spare, Captain. We have twenty-one souls all told."

"I'm fairly short of provisions myself, Mister Mate, but I'll let you have what I can spare. It's a damned disgrace. Your owners must be skinflints. They need showing up. I'll report you when I reach New York. My steward will put some provisions and stores overside to you. What's wrong with that leaky boat? Too long on the skids, eh?" While this conversation was going on, all hands in the steamer were hanging over the rail, watching us with commiseration as we resumed despondently bailing out the boat.

A seaman sang out, "Have you any 'baccy, mates?"

Lew Owens answered, "We have nothing except dog biscuits and slush! We've been eating slush."

"God's truth, slush!" said the seaman at the rail Another said, "Your owners ought to be hung."

Presently the steward of the steamer put his head over the bulwark rail, and said, 'I'm handing over forty pounds of salt beef, fifty-six pounds o' potatoes, twenty pounds of sugar, six tins o' condensed milk, ten pounds o' peas, and four plugs o' tobacco. Will that do ye? It's all we can spare."

"It's a godsend," the Mate answered, fervently.

From the bridge, the Captain of the steamer sang out.

"I'll send the bill to your mingy owners at Liverpool."

"Thank you, heartily, sir," said the Mate.

"Beef coming over," announced the steward, from the "Catch it!" From an altitude ten feet (3m) above us, he dropped sixteen pieces of corned beef, weighing about three pounds each. We caught them and put them in the bottom of our boat, which was now awash to the gunwales. Half a sack of potatoes was then lowered on a line. We put this in the stern sheets together with the tins of milk that followed.

"Here comes the sugar. Keep it dry," the steward out. This was lowered in a bag. The Mate took it and put it on his head, like a fantastic coif. Then the peas were lowered in a bag. I took the bag and balanced it on my head. Finally, the four plugs of tobacco were dropped into the boat. Lew Owens grabbed them and put them his pocket, to keep them dry.

Then, with a clang of engine room telegraphs, and many shouts of "Goodbye and good luck" from her crew, the Lowlands began moving slowly ahead, while we pushed off from her side, and bent to the oars, to get clear of propeller and wash. As she drew clear, we saw that the *County of Pembroke* had drifted down very near. Our shipmates, lining the rail, gave three hoarse cheers for steamer, to which the Captain of the Lowlands responded, with three blasts of his steam whistle.

We had to pull only twenty yards to reach the barque, and we were already in her lee. This was just as well, as the boat was threatening to sink under us. The lumps of beef were floating in the water about our knees and, as the boat wallowed in the swell, we had to grab at the beef to prevent it from washing out over the gunwales.

The Mate looked comical, sitting high on the sack of potatoes, with a sack of sugar on his head, but I had no time to see the funny side of things, as I needed all my powers of concentration to balance the bag of peas on my own head, pull an oar, and grab at pieces of floating beef while we ranged alongside the barque.

Willing hands took our precious freight inboard, but I had to rescue three pieces of floating beef out of the sea with the boat hook. Then we clambered on deck and all hands, except the cook, turned to, to hoist the boat. This proved no easy matter; she was filled to the gunwales with water and was kept afloat only by her buoyancy tanks and extremely dry timbers. We hooked the falls of the davits on to her and, on the Mate's orders, hoisted her up high at one end to spill some of the water out, then heaved on the other fall, got her even, swung her inboard and on to the skids, still spurting water from the seams.

"Brace up the main yards," the Old Man sang out.

We turned to, wearily, and got the barque on her original course, to the north-eastward, on the starboard tack, in the steady SE breeze. The smoke of the steamer was a smudge to the westward, and in half an hour she was hull down on the horizon.

In the meantime, the cook had some of the beef boiling merrily in the pot, with spuds and peas for garnishing, and put the rest of the beef into the harness cask. As soon as the cooking was done, about 3 p.m., a meal was served out to all hands; and never did salt beef, spuds, and peas taste better.

Only then did we realize that, in the excitement of the mid-ocean encounter, the Mate had forgotten to ask for tea or coffee! He blamed the men who had been with him in the boat for not having reminded him! "Have I to think of everything?" he growled. "Isn't there one of you with any brains?"

But the pangs of hunger were now partly assuaged, with much leeway still to be made up. The Captain reckoned that it would take us ten or twelve days to reach Falmouth, if the weather held. He therefore rationed the beef to three ounces per man per day, the potatoes to four ounces per man per day, the peas to one ounce per man per day, and the sugar to two ounces per man per day. The condensed milk was mixed with hot water and served as a drink, in lieu of tea or coffee, three times a day as long as the six tins lasted. With this, and our continuing whack of biscuits, lime juice and water, we could keep alive, but only just alive.

The allowance of three ounces of beef per man was only one-quarter of the Board of Trade scale ration of beef. The four plugs of tobacco were entrusted to Lew Owens, to be shared fairly among the smokers and chewers. He handed out one pipeful per man per day. Most of the men chewed the tobacco for hours. Some of them then carefully preserved the quid, dried it, and then smoked it!

As we stood on for Falmouth and into the Chops of the Channel, we sighted many more steamers and some windjammers, outward bound, but we flew no further signals for help. After ten days, our provisions were again exhausted, and we were subsisting on biscuits, water and lime juice. There can be no doubt that the vitamins in the lime juice saved our lives on this hungry voyage. God bless Captain James Cook, of the Royal Navy, who in 1776 discovered that lime juice is a preventative of scurvy — perhaps his greatest discovery.

At midnight on 17 March 1903, we sighted the Lizard Light and with reduced sail stood in toward Falmouth Bay. At dawn a tug ranged alongside us. By this time Captain "Wingy" Hughes was seriously worried at the possible consequences of the starvation his crew had endured under his command and was anxious to make some amends before the crew had a chance to go ashore and lay complaints against him with the seamen's societies or the Board of Trade.

The tugmaster wanted twenty pounds to tow us in.

Instead of arguing, our Old Man said curtly, "Very well! We are out of provisions. I will give you an extra ten pounds if you will run into port first and bring us some food, before you take our rope. That will be thirty pounds in all for your services!"

"Good!" the tugmaster replied. "I'll do it! Now, what do you want, Captain?"

Our mouths watered, as the Old Man sang out the list: "Twenty pounds of fresh beef, for frying steaks; five pounds of bacon; four dozen new laid eggs; three pounds of butter; a dozen loaves of new baked bread; two pounds of tea and two pounds of coffee; a dozen tins of jam; fourteen pounds of potatoes; six pounds of onions. Have you got all that written down?"

"Yes, Captain," said the tugmaster, who was scribbling on a piece of paper with a pencil. "Ten pounds of sugar," the Captain continued. "Now, let me see, what else? Oh yes, of course, five pounds of tobacco, in quarter-pound plugs! Don't forget that! And bring off a gallon of fresh milk, too, and a peck of apples!"

As these inspiring words resounded fore and aft, the emaciated crew could scarcely believe their ears. "Have you got that all down?" the Captain demanded.

"Yes, sir!"

"Well, make all speed, and we'll back the yards and lie here until you return. Can you spare us a pound of tea or coffee from your own caboose before you go? I'll make it good with you."

"With pleasure, Captain!" The tugmaster went to rummage in his cabin and presently passed across a coffee, a packet of sugar, and a tin of condensed mil'. this the cook hurried to the galley, while the Second got three men to the freshwater pump, to raise a few buckets of water for him.

The tug sheered off and the Captain ordered, "Back the main yards, Mister, while the coffee is being brewed!"

"All hands on deck!" the Mate sang out, but all were already there, in the waist. We hadn't missed a word of the Captain's colloquy with the tugmaster.

In good heart, we backed the yards while the marvellous smell of coffee was wafted out of the caboose.

"Come and get it!" the cook sang out. There nearly was a stampede. Grinning and talking excitedly, we sipped the wondrous brew, the best coffee we had ever tasted in our lives.

The sun rose, with a breath of spring in a light offshore breeze. "Start furling the sails, Mister," the Old Man ordered, "and get ready to take the towline when the tug returns, before we have our breakfast of ham and eggs!"

At these inspiring words, the crew willingly turned to and even gave a faint cheer and raised a shanty as we hauled. After an absence of two hours, the tug returned with the fresh provisions. In a few minutes we had them and his rope aboard and were towing into port. The cook was busy in the galley, and soon the bacon and eggs were sizzling in the pan while he sliced the bread and made tea.

That was the grandest feed of our lives. The Captain came along and urged us to eat sparingly, but he might as well have talked to the moon. Every man had a plug of tobacco as well. Just as the meal ended, we reached anchorage and dropped the killick in ten fathoms of water 157 days out from Callao.

After furling the sails, we had another feed at noon. Then all hands turned into their bunks, and most of us slept heavily for eighteen hours, until the next morning.

The barque lay at Falmouth for a week, and now the Captain was prodigal in his catering. We were supplied with plenty of fresh meat and green vegetables, and our boils began to disappear. The• steamer *Lowlands*, on arriving in New York had reported us as "starving in mid-Atlantic," and the newspapers in America and Britain had given prominence to the story, with many heart rending details of our plight.

The seamen's societies and various benevolent organizations took up the matter, bringing to light similar cases of starvation in other windjammers, and censuring the owners severely. About this time there was some political agitation against shipowners, led by a young Welsh solicitor, David Lloyd George, who was a Member of Parliament. He kicked up such a row that eventually the Board of Trade tightened up its regulations and decreed a new scale of rations, which was known among seamen as the "Lloyd George" scale. So our miseries had not been suffered entirely in vain.

Ordered to Antwerp to discharge the cargo, we cheerfully set sail, knowing that the payoff was nigh. Taken in tow off the mouth of the Schelde, we were towed upriver, putting the harbour stow on the sails, and berthed at the Antwerp Quay on 27th March 1903. This was the end of a voyage which had lasted sixteen months. The seamen who had been with us throughout the voyage were due to be paid between forty and fifty pounds each, which in those days of gold currency and cheap prices was a considerable sum for a man to take home, if he had a home to go to.

I was due to collect approximately twenty-two pounds. This was made up of eight pounds for the fourth year of my apprenticeship, and nearly twenty pounds for my pay as an Able Seaman since signing on at Callao: less cash advances at Wellington, Dunedin, Newcastle and Callao; some purchases from the slop chest; and fines at Callao for being "drunk and disorderly." (I hoped my father would not press me for details of the last item.) Despite the deductions, I was elated at the prospect of receiving such a lump sum in cash from my own earnings.

The good food we had eaten since arriving at Falmouth and the prospects of the impending pay off had restored the crew to bodily health and optimism. Most of them had forgotten their vows of vengeance against the Captain and now thought that he was not such a bad old fellow, after all.

The two "bad hats" we had shipped at Callao were not of this opinion. They were due to collect only six pounds each at Antwerp. From their pay there would be a deduction of ten pounds, eight shillings and fourpence (50 dollars) paid to the crimps, and a few pounds more for oil skins, dungarees, and tobacco they had got from the slop chest. They declared that they intended to lay in wait for the Old Man at Antwerp, if they could catch him in a dark lane, and stick a knife into him.

The payoff was on 30th March. The two bad hats went ashore and promptly got drunk. No doubt they woke up, a week or so later, at sea, with a big headache. Two of the other seamen elected to be paid off in cash at Antwerp and went ashore for a glorious spree that might last for several weeks, if the harpies didn't get all their money off them sooner.

The other eight seamen, including Lew Owens and myself, exercised or right to be sent home to Liverpool, on traveling warrants, at the owners' expense. We drew a pound each from our accounts, for out-of-pocket expenses on the journey, and were given orders to draw the balance at Liverpool.

So ended my service in the *County of Pembroke*. Though I had served my apprenticeship in her on three voyages around the world, and she had been my roving home for nearly four and a half years, I left her without regret. The hatches were open, and her cargo of guano was being discharged with shore labour. She looked dirty and dingy and was decidedly smelly.

Captain Hughes gave me a testimonial and wished me luck. I parted from him, too, without regret. The First Mate and the Second Mate and the two apprentices, who had to remain in the barque, gave me a little farewell party, and I was sorry to leave them. Perhaps I would meet them again someday — who knew? With the other seamen going to Liverpool, I took my luggage to be consigned by the *S.S. Colchester* — the steam packet in which we were to travel as passengers across the North Sea from Antwerp to Harwich. Then from Harwich we would go to Liverpool by train.

But, as I stepped ashore for the last time from the old *County of Pembroke* and took a last look at her, a low and aloft, I suddenly realized that she had taught me whatever I had learned of the ways of the sea and that, with all her faults, I loved her still.

*The Harwich Packet — Missing a Train — Home Again! — A
Pleasant Interlude Ashore — A Nautical School — The Noble Art —
Sampling Cain's Brew — Thirsty in the Morning — I Pass for
Second Mate — The Worries of a Youthful Officer — The "County
of Cardigan" — A Full Rigged Ship — Frigid Reception
— Signed On.*

I T was queer, being in a steamer. ...

The *S.S. Colchester* was the first steamer (apart from Mersey ferries) that I ever voyaged in, and on that voyage of 135 miles (217 km), from Antwerp to Harwich, I was a passenger in the steerage. The North Sea crossing took twelve hours, most of it through the night. I lay in. my bunk, listening to the throbbing of the engines, and disliking it intensely.

My seven shipmates from the *County of Pembroke* and I each had one pound in our pockets when we were paid off, and we were handed our tickets for the "packet-boat" passage to Harwich and third-class tickets for the rail journey from Harwich to Liverpool. These matters were arranged at Antwerp by the agents for the owners of the barque. Our luggage, labelled to Liverpool, was put in the hold of the steamer. Most of us had shore going suits of clothes, but some were in dungarees.

Before we left Antwerp, having a few hours to spare, we looked on the wine when it was red and thus arrived on board considerably exhilarated. As the steamer throbbed her way down the Scheide the exhilaration wore off somewhat, and we fell into our bunks to sleep off the hangover. It was Sunday morning when we arrived in Harwich. with a frightful thirst and no way of quenching it since the pubs were closed. We had two hours to wait before our train was due to depart and spent these in viewing the sights of Harwich, which seemed to be very few. Fortunately, or so we thought —

when we went to the railway station, in good time to catch our train, we found that the railway refreshment room bar served beer to bona fide travellers who held tickets. After putting our luggage into the train we went to the bar, to quench our raging thirst. This we did so effectively that, in our blissful disdain of the routine of railways, we took no notice of various urgent warnings to get aboard the train. When a whistle blew, we finished our beer in leisurely style, then strolled out to the platform, in time to see our train doing ten knots as it passed the forrard end of the platform, under a full head of steam.

On making inquiries, we found that there were no more trains going to Liverpool that day. The next train was at six o'clock on Monday morning. To make matters worse, the doors of the refreshment bar were now closed, as there were no trains due out of Harwich on Sunday afternoon. In this predicament, we counted our cash and found that we still had a few shillings each, enough for a feed in a waterfront hash house. That night we stretched out on the hard benches in the third-class waiting room at the railway station. In the morning, we managed to get a cup of tea for tuppence and to seat ourselves securely in a carriage on the train half an hour before starting time.

In all this we suffered much anxiety at the loss of our luggage, which had gone on in the train the day before. The stationmaster advised us to apply at the Lost Property Office when we reached Liverpool, but we could scarcely believe that we could find it there, for we were ignorant of the ways of land faring folk.

The cross country journey of some 200 miles (321 km) took most of the day. We went on the Great Eastern Railway through Ipswich to Cambridge, then changed to the London and North Western line for Bedford, Northampton, Rugby, Stafford and Crewe, bound for Liverpool. I mention these ports of call, as we termed them, because the trains stayed at them for ten minutes or more, for refreshments, which, in our parched condition meant beer at tuppence a pint.

After a few stops, and a few beers, I realized, with what remained of my fuddled wits, that it would be a very shameful thing if I arrived home tight. I therefore, by a superhuman effort of will the like of which I have seldom exercised either before or since that day, determined to drink only tea for the rest of the journey.

My shipmates laughed at me to scorn, but I held my ground. As the journey progressed I gradually sobered and, after a feed of sandwiches at Crewe, I was the only sober man in the party. As there were eight of us, we had a compartment to ourselves, which was just as well. The drunken songs that enlivened the journey were unfit for public performance.

At length we arrived at Liverpool, and, having some authority as a delegate while my mates went into the bar, I went to the Lost Property Office and found that all our luggage was there waiting for us! We sorted it out, and with much handshaking and black slapping we parted and went our various ways.

I had kept two bob in reserve for a cab and, with this spent, arrived home without a penny in my pocket, and twenty-four hours late, on April Fools' Day, 1903 — a man of the world, I hoped, three and a half months before my twentieth birthday.

My parents, brothers, and sisters were overjoyed to see that I looked fit and well. They had read in the newspapers that the crew of the *County of Pembroke* were starving in mid-Atlantic and that we were living skeletons when the steamer Lowlands succoured us. I had written a letter home from Falmouth mentioning the matter which obsessed me at the time, food. My father had ascertained, from the office of William Thomas & Co., Ltd., the date of the payoff at Antwerp and of my expected return home.

My mother wept with joy at seeing that I was not a bag of bones. She had laid in a fine larder to feed me up; and I was well able to do justice to it, for I was still below my normal weight and strength, though not as seriously as she had feared. Under this treatment I was fighting fit within a few days; but the occasion required a narrative, with all the gruesome descriptions possible, of the ordeals which had got our barque's name into the papers. These, after being tried out in the family circle, had to be repeated, with the utmost possible emphasis, for the benefit of admiring friends. I thereby gained not only much sympathy and admiration, but also some square feeds from the sympathizers, who considered that my constitution needed carefully building up.

After a few days I claimed my pay and put it in the savings bank. I also went with my father to see Mr. Thomas, who duly endorsed my indentures and repaid my father his "Twenty Poonds." The magnate graciously said that he was sorry we had run short of provisions on the homeward voyage from the Chincha Islands. "It was the Captain's fault," he added, with a fine show of virtuous indignation.

"And what are your plans now?" he asked me.

'I'm going to study for the Second Mate's examination, sir," I said.

"That's good! If you get through, you can apply to me, and I may be able to offer you an appointment in one of our vessels."

"There you are," said my father. "Study your hardest, and you'll soon be an officer!"

"We like officers we've trained ourselves," said the millionaire. "They know our ways." He shook my hand cordially and slapped me on the back. "You're young, but you'll shape all right, I believe," he said encouragingly. "I'll keep you in mind if we have any position to offer you."

A few days after this, I enrolled in the Navigation School of the Mercantile Marine Service Association, at Liverpool, to study for the Second Mate's examination, under the regulations laid down by the Board of Trade. About six other time-served apprentices were in the class. The school was conducted by Captain D'Arcy Morton, with the help of some other instructors. There were classes for older men studying for First Mate's, Master's and Extra Master's Certificates, the examinations in all these grades being conducted at frequent intervals throughout the year by officials of the Board of Trade at Liverpool and other ports in Britain.

The classes were held for six hours daily, in the forenoons and afternoons. The Second Mate's class studied elementary mathematics and theory of navigation, chart reading, and the theory and practice of seamanship, including splices, knots, the handling of sail and the rig of various kinds of vessels, demonstrated from diagrams and models. On Captain Morton's advice, the lads studying for Second Mate joined a "gymnasium" nearby, where a course of lessons was given, in the evenings, on boxing. Our instructor — an old professional pugilist with cauliflower ears and a crushed nose — called it "the noble art of self-defence." Though this was certainly not part of the Board of Trade syllabus, we were advised that a Second Mate ought to learn the scientific way of taking care of himself in case of need.

During my apprenticeship I had learned a little about fighting and wrestling in a few "goes" with other boys, but now the old pug taught me and the other lads of the class such basic principles of the noble art as the straight left, the right uppercut, the left uppercut, the right hook, the left hook, how to feint, duck and "block 'em," and the importance of footwork (which meant stance and balance). The practical instruction followed when we were paired for sparring and a few rounds of "all-out" boxing, which on the whole we enjoyed even if we sometimes got a bleeding nose or a black eye.

I also joined a football club, in the Junior Grade, and had a few games of soccer on Saturday afternoons. This helped to keep me in training, besides being one of the few opportunities which ever came my way of playing organized sport ashore.

On Saturday nights I was seldom home before midnight, as I went out with my cronies, new and old, on a "pub crawl," sampling Cain's beer. This usually meant that when the pubs closed at eleven, I was suffering slightly from Cain's Foot and Mouth Disease,[1] like tens of thousands of other men in Liverpool at that hour on Saturday night.

As I had a key and let myself in as quietly as possible, my mother did not know the cause of my intense desire, on Sunday mornings, to drink several cups of tea as soon as I got out of bed.

One Sunday afternoon two rather sanctimonious elderly ladies, who were old friends of the family, visited us, and my mother produced her sailor son for their inspection. They asked me many questions about my adventures in foreign lands. Then one of them, a member of the Band of Hope, said, "I hope you don't touch strong liquor!"

At this my dear and innocent mother hastily said, "Oh, no, Gordon is a good boy! I know he doesn't drink when he goes out at nights, because he's always so thirsty the next morning!"

After six weeks of this pleasurable sojourn ashore, I went up with the other lads of the class to sit for the Second Mate's examination at the Board of Trade office. The examination was both written and oral. After I had worked out some mathematical problems fairly correctly the two examiners, Captain Sargent and Captain Keating, put me through a tough questioning on seamanship and the rig of vessels; but, as our instructors had primed us well on the tricky questions likely to be asked, I knew most of the answers.

Then Captain Keating, with a twinkle in his eye, asked, "And what is the correct procedure if a vessel runs short of provisions at sea?"

Solemnly I answered, "Cut to half whack and stand on, if possible, into the track of steamers, then fly the signal N-V!"

"I see you know all about it," Captain Keating laughed. Then, after conferring, the examiners signed a temporary certificate, which Captain Sargent handed to me, saying, "Well, congratulations, Mister Bisset, you've passed! Here's your Blue Paper, and you'll get your Second Mate's Certificate in a few days. I wish you the best of luck!" Elated, and dazed at being addressed as "Mister" by a Captain for the first time in my life, I hurried home to show my proud parents my Blue Paper.

A few days later, I called at the Board of Trade office and was handed my certificate on parchment.

With this in hand I wasted no time, and, going to the office of William Thomas & Co., Ltd., I asked for an interview with Mr. Thomas.

The millionaire greeted me cordially and, after a glance at my certificate, said, "Now, Mister Bisset, what age are you?"

"I'll be twenty in less than two months from now, sir!" "Well," he commented, "that means you're only nineteen now! Do you feel capable of taking on a job as Second Mate of a large sailing ship?"

My heart stood still for a moment, but on a sound impulse I did not falter as I looked him straight in the eye and said, slowly and deliberately, "That was my intention, sir, when I went up for my examination!"

"Yes, yes," he said testily, "but you look so young! Do you think you will be able to control the men and make them obey your orders?"

My pride was nettled. "I served my full time in the *County of Pembroke*, and five months after that in her as an A.B.," I said. "I've been three times round Cape Horn, and I was in that barque when she took a purler over the stern, and when she was demasted, and when she went over on her beam ends, and...."

"Yes, yes!" he interrupted. "And you were in her on that last voyage when Captain Hughes neglected to provision her, which got him and us into so much trouble! Don't tell me what I already know, young man! I don't doubt your ability, especially as you have your ticket as Second Mate. I can see for myself that you are strong and healthy, stockily built, and as hard as nails, eh?"

"Yes, sir," I said firmly, "I'm fit! If you give me a job as Second Mate, I'll see that the men do as I tell them!" "Good! Good!" said Mr. Thomas. "Do you know our ship, *County of Cardigan*, now in the Salthouse Dock?"

"I've seen her there, and also at Newcastle in New South Wales, and at Callao!"

"Well, Mister Bisset, we'll give you a chance to go as Second Mate in her. She'll be going presently to Fremantle in Western Australia. Captain William Roberts is in command of her, and Mr. John Kinley is her First Mate. I'll give you a note to take down to the Captain. You can start work next week and help to get her ready for sea."

"What will be my pay, sir?"

"Ah, yes, your pay! Well, as· you are only nineteen, Mister Bisset, and this your first appointment, you should be well satisfied with four pounds a month, eh?"

I felt like telling the old skinflint to keep his job, as Second Mates were usually paid five pounds and upward a month, and I realized that he was taking advantage of my youth and inexperience to save expense; but, on the other hand, it was a big chance to go as Second Mate in a full rigged ship.

"Thank you, sir," I said. "I'll sign on at that."

The millionaire stood up and patted me on the back with a skinny hand, as I too rose and stood with my mind in a whirl. "Indeed to goodness," he said, "and I'm sure you'll do well, Mister Bisset!"

With a note from the manager of the company, Mr. Evans, I went straight down to the Salthouse Dock, entered the gates, rounded the wharf shed, then stood for several minutes carefully examining the *County of Cardigan* and quelling the tumult of my feelings. She lay on the other side of the dock and had been lying there for several weeks, after discharging a cargo of grain from San Francisco. She looked forlorn. Her sides were scarred with rust and the white paint on her masts and yards was grimed by the soot of the city. Aloft, she had been stripped to a gantline, and several frayed ends of gaskets and "Irish pennants" were whipping untidily in the breeze.

The *County of Cardigan* was a full rigged three masted ship, of 1,323 tons gross (1,245 tons net), built in Liverpool by R. & J. Evans, and launched in 1887. She had a steel hull, steel masts and yards, and planked decks. She was 229 feet long (70m), 37 feet (11m) beam, and 22 to 27 feet (6.7m – 8.2m) deep. She was therefore somewhat bigger than the *County of Pembroke* and could carry a cargo of 2,000 tons. Though not one of the most famous flyers of her day, she had made some remarkably smart passages to Australia and around the Horn. Her hull had trim lines, with a clipper bow and a low monkey poop, but to my eyes she seemed heavily sparred and clumsy aloft. This extra strength in the masts would enable her to carry a press of sail which might have demasted a more lightly sparred vessel; but I could see at a glance that she would be a heavy ship to work.

She had five yards crossed on each of her three masts. The yards of the "courses" — the foresail, mainsail and "Cro'jick" or mizzen sail — were fully sixty feet (18m) long and projected well out over the sides. They were of hollow steel, ten-inches thick in the middle, and tapering to seven inches at the yardarms. The lower and upper topsail yards were also of steel, slightly shorter and smaller than the yards of the courses, but heavy as compared with those in other ships of similar tonnage. The courses and topsails were crossed on the steel masts below the usual height, giving her a squat but very sturdy appearance aloft. Above the topmasts were wooden masts for the

County of Cardigan

State Library of South Australia The 'County of Cardigan' at Port Adelaide [PRG 1373/24/5]

topgallant sails and royals, with wooden yards crossed on them. The truck of the mainmast was one hundred and twenty feet (36.5m) above the deck, and the cap of the topmast ninety feet (27m).

The running rigging, to control fifteen square sails (as compared with ten square sails in a three-masted barque) was necessarily more complicated than I had been accustomed to in the *County of Pembroke*, but I knew that I would soon become familiar with it. Walking around the end of the dock, I had a nearer view and was disgusted at the dirty condition she had been allowed to fall into. The only sign of life was a sailmaker seated in the waist, sewing a staysail. I mounted the rickety gangway and jumped down onto her main deck. She had not been washed down for weeks. The remains of her grain cargo were strewn, damp and mouldy, around the hatches. I made a mental note that there would be much hard work to be done to get her ready for sea.

"Is the Captain aboard?" I asked the sailmaker.

He glanced at me and said, "He's in his cabin under the poop, if you know where that is."

"Look here, Sails," I said. "I'm to be Second Mate in this ship!"

Leaving him to ponder on that remark, I sprang up to the poop and called down the companionway to the cabin, "Is Captain Roberts there?"

A voice growled, "What do you want?" and a thin, wiry, tall, tough looking man, thirty years of age, emerged from the cabin. I sensed correctly that he was the First Mate, John Kinley. He was from the Isle of Man.

"To see the Captain," I said. "I have a letter for him, from Mr. Evans, of the owner's office."

"Come below," a gruff voice boomed from inside the saloon. I entered. Captain William Roberts, a Welshman, middle-aged, of burly build, with a leathery, wrinkled countenance and steely grey eyes, was seated at his table. He took the letter from me, opened it, read it in grim silence, looked at me with undisguised hostility, then handed the letter to the Mate, saying, "Shiver my timbers! Read that, Mister Mate!"

The Mate did so, then remarked, as though I were not there, "He looks rather young!"

"Young?" the Captain growled. "He looks like a boy, just out of his time!" Then he turned to me, and asked, "Ever been Second Mate before?"

I recited my history, in brief. It didn't please either of them. Ignoring my presence again, the Captain said complainingly to the Mate, "I asked the owners particularly to send me an experienced officer because this ship is a heavy ship to work, and they send me a beardless youth!" "Yes," the Mate agreed. "I should advise him to get a job in a smaller ship for a voyage or two, until he grows up and gains experience."

They both looked at me hopefully, expecting that I would back out; but I stood my ground and had the sense not to argue with them. I remained silent and listened while they discussed me for a few minutes more, in total disregard of my feelings. I was duly qualified and appointed to this ship, so why shouldn't I have the job? The thought of tramping the docks looking for a chance in a small ship did not appeal to me.

At last the Captain said, "I suppose we'll have to put up with him!" Then he turned to me and said, "Very well, Mister, start on Monday morning, and we'll soon see what you're made of. The riggers are coming then to bend sail, and we'll be taking in the cargo, too. Show the Second Mate his cabin, Mister Mate!"

The Mate led me to a cabin next to his, on the port side under the poop. It was a small compartment, with two bunks, one above the other. "That's yours," said the Mate, bitterly. "All on your own! I hope you're not frightened of work, for there's a hell of a lot to be done to get this grimy old hooker ready for sea. You'll have the four apprentices to clean her up, take in stores, and bend the staysails and jibs. I'll be busy keeping an eye on the riggers and stowing the cargo."

"I can handle the job, Mister Mate," I assured him. "Time will tell," he grunted.

Going ashore, feeling very discouraged by the hostile reception I had suffered, I had vague thoughts of growing a beard and moustache to hide my youthful appearance; but there would not be time to do that before Monday morning. However, I went and bought a peaked badge cap, of rakish design, with a patent leather strap over the top, and wore it well on the side of my head, in the approved fashion of smart young second mates of that period.

With my confidence thus enhanced, I was ready to begin work, come what may.

21

My Fourth Voyage in Sail — The "County of Cardigan" Puts to Sea — In Tow to Glasgow — Fog off Ailsa Craig — A Collision! — Lessons for a Young Officer — Docked in the Clyde — A Big Cargo of Whiskey — Jock the Cabin Boy — A New Hand Tries to go Ashore — Our Mixed Crew — Picking Watches — Making Sail — A Fight in the Fo'c'sle — Driving On.

O N that Monday morning, 26th May 1903, when I began work as Second Mate in the *County of Cardigan*, I was on deck at 6.30 a.m. — half an hour before the day's work was due to begin — making a survey, for my own information, of the ship and her rigging and gear. The apprentices came on board shortly before seven o'clock. Two of them were handy lads in their third year, and the other two were useless first voyagers, shy and nervous.

There were no seamen signed on as yet. I soon had the boys hard at work washing the decks. The scene suddenly became one of intense animation as a gang of ten riggers arrived with a foreman and, under the eyes of the Mate, swarmed aloft to examine and overhaul the running gear and standing gear before bending the sails. They were all old shellbacks who knew their work. In five days the appearance of the ship was transformed as the sails were bent and furled on all the yards.

In the meantime, a gang of stevedores had also arrived. They proceeded to load 1,000 tons of general merchandise, including several thousand bags of salt, which had been accumulating on the quay in the previous weeks. The Mate had the duty of supervising the loading, but he kept an eye on everything else as well. He couldn't bear to see the boys and myself idle for a moment.

After we had cleaned the decks, my job with the boys was to get the ship's stores in and stowed and to bend the jibs and staysails. The sailmaker was the busiest man in the ship; the riggers and I kept on pestering him to get more and more sails up on deck, ready to send aloft. It was his task to give each sail a final scrutiny before it was bent. The scene was lively as the riggers, boys, stevedores, and carters swarmed over the ship and the quay, as busy as ants and much noisier, while the Captain, the Mate, the Foreman Rigger, the Foreman Stevedore, and I kept an eye on what had to be done and saw that it was done well.

Sailing day was on Monday, 2nd June. I now learned that we were to be towed to Glasgow, with a crew of runners, to load more cargo there. On Sunday evening, after a last meal at home, I bade farewell to my family and went on board at 9 p.m. stowing my sea chest and sea bag in my cabin. During the evening the apprentices, a cook, a carpenter, and four Welsh seamen moved into their quarters quietly, since the pubs were closed. The Welsh seamen came from the same village as the Captain, and he could rely on them as personal acquaintances. We were to sign on another eight seamen at Glasgow.

Soon after dawn, all hands were roused out, and the stout tug Jane Joliffe came nosing to the river lock gate, ready to tow us from the Mersey to the Clyde, a distance of 200 miles (321 km). In these narrow and fairly sheltered waters there was little chance of breaking adrift from the tug and having to make sail to avoid running ashore, but the law required a sailing vessel to carry a full crew, in case of emergencies, when in tow.

The runners came on board, eight old shellbacks who had signed on at a contract price of one pound each, to work the ship to Glasgow. Their contract required them to do no work except that involved in handling the ship. As soon as we were safely through the river lock gates and towing downstream, they divided themselves into watches and stood by, smoking their pipes. This sight infuriated the Mate, but there was nothing he could do about it, as the men were within their rights.

The Mate and I picked watches — two Welshmen, two apprentices, and four runners each. In the circumstances, as there was no handling of sail, my first experience of watchkeeping consisted of walking up and down the poop and keeping an eye on the helmsman to see that he followed closely in the tug's wake.

The Captain and the Mate maintained an attitude of resentment to me and had no word of encouragement, even though they had not been able to find fault with my part of the work of getting the ship ready for sea. It was estimated that the tow to Glasgow would take two days.

On the first morning out, I was on watch from four to eight. At 6.30 a.m. a fog set in and thickened. It was unseasonable in the summer weather, but anything can happen in the Irish Sea and the North Channel. I called the Captain. He came on deck in a vile temper, looked around, and growled at me, "You must be the Jonah in this ship!"

Thinking that the remark was intended to be a joke, I replied, flippantly, "Jonah came out all right!"

The Captain's face darkened with rage as he snarled, "Keep a good look out there. If there's any more backchat from you, I'll log you for insolence and put you ashore at Glasgow as unsuitable!"

This taught me my first useful lesson as an officer: never adopt a familiar attitude with the Captain. I have never forgotten it. He held all the high cards in the game. Without a good reference from him at the end of the voyage, I would not be able to sit for my First Mate's examination. If he chose to treat me as a boy rather than an officer, I would have to knuckle under. Perhaps he thought he was giving me good training. I will admit that his methods taught me to control my feelings. When the fog set in, we were in the vicinity of Ailsa Craig Island, at the mouth of the Firth of Clyde, off the coast of Arran. "It's as thick as a hedge," the Captain growled. "Call all hands on deck, and make 'em stand by, to shorten in the towrope."

I hurried forrard, singing out, "All hands on deck!" and ordered them to the fo'c'slehead. The fog was now so thick that we had lost sight of the Jane Jolliffe and could barely hear her fog signal. I picked up our old fashioned hand foghorn, to make the signal to the tug to slacken the wire, so that we could shorten it.

At that moment I heard the foghorn of a steamer close on our starboard bow but could see nothing of her. I answered with the regulation signal on our squeaky foghorn — and a moment later my blood froze. Looming out of the fog was the dark shape of the high bows of a large steamer, standing directly across our bows, between us and the tug! "Hard-a-port!" I yelled toward the poop. The Captain and the helmsman heard me, but they could not see the steamer. Everything was happening at once. Our towrope sank down into the water, and a series of short blasts from the tug indicated that he had slipped the rope. We were adrift in the fog, with sails stowed, but we still had steerage way on.

The steamer stood on, and, as the *County of Cardigan* began to answer her helm, our jib boom struck the steamer a glancing blow near her stern and snapped off short. This carried away several wires and stays, which flailed around the fo'c'slehead, and several of the men there had to jump for their lives to avoid being whipped overboard.

In the next instant our port side passed under the stern of the steamer, clearing her rudder and propeller by inches, and our fore yardarm brushed over her taffrail. I looked up and took note of the name of the aggressor and her port of registry. Evidently the men on her bridge were not aware of the collision, or preferred not to notice it, as she stood on, and in half a minute was out of sight. The only visible sign of human life in her was a Chinese boy, whom I glimpsed staring impassively astern over the taffrail, with a vacant expression. Then he, too, vanished in the fog, like a creature of a dream.

Only our broken jib boom and gear, and the towrope slack over our bows remained as tangible proof that the incident was not an episode in a Second Mate's nightmare but had actually happened.

Captain Roberts and the 1st Mate came ramping and raging forrard, to inspect the damage. Expecting that they would blame me for the collision, I wasted no time in meditation, but got the crew tailed on to hauling in the towing wire, which was a drogue at our bows. Simultaneously, I kept our squeaky foghorn going, so that the tugmaster would be able to find us. Presently he ranged alongside. He and our Old Man held a bawled conversation and agreed indignantly that the whole blame for the damage would have to be sheeted home to the Captain and owners of the steamer.

This being so, Captain Roberts could not put any blame on me! I would be a valuable witness in the claim for insurance on repairing the damage. Having worked in an underwriter's office, I knew this quite well. "You did very well!" the Old Man said to me. "You did everything right. Not bad for a young fellow!"

That was a pleasant surprise. . ..

As soon as our rope was made fast again to the tug, the fog began to lift, and presently I could see a patch of blue sky overhead. "The sky's clearing, sir," I said to the Captain. "Damn it," he growled. "We're not going in that direction!" With this sarcastic thrust, I had my second lesson in the discipline of a young officer: never tell the Captain what he already knows.

Presently the fog cleared completely, and we proceeded in tow up the Firth of Clyde and into the river, in glorious sunshine. This grand and magnificent haven — which was to become a destination for me many a time in anxious days, forty years later — was thronged with shipping, mainly steamers, including a pleasure steamer going "doon the watter" to Arran. It was as well the fog had lifted, as otherwise our progress would have been hazardous, in such dense traffic.

We passed Ardrossan, Largs, Wemyss, Gourock, and Greenock, and then the shipyards of John Brown at Clydebank, where many a fine ship had been launched. Many more, including two well beloved "Queens," the biggest ships in the world, would someday be launched there, to go "doon the watter" to the wide oceans; but I could not even remotely have envisaged them then....

In midafternoon we berthed at King's Dock, in Glasgow.

This was my first port of call in my career as a ship's officer. I cannot fairly claim that my career began grandly — under tow in a rusty ship from the Mersey to the Clyde, with a collision for good measure — but such is life.

Next day the hatches were opened, and loading began. The purpose of our tow to Glasgow was to load bottled whiskey, packed in wooden cases, to assuage the cravings of the gold miners, pearlers, timber getters and other dry characters of Western Australia who appreciated a wee drappie o' Hielan' Dew. Evidently the intended customers had a great thirst, as we loaded 25,000 cases of Scotch whiskey; these were stowed on top of the Cheshire salt we had taken in at Liverpool, to fill our hold to the deckhead. I could scarcely have believed that there was so much whiskey — or so much thirst — in the world; but seeing is believing.

While the cargo was being taken in, the boys and the four Welsh seamen were put overside, in stages and in the dinghy, to chip rust and paint the sides, under my supervision. In a few days that job was finished; the ship sat deep in the water and was getting deeper every day. One day I had to go ashore with the Captain, to give evidence on oath at an inquiry into our collision with the steamer. I was able to swear to her name and port of register.

In the meantime, some riggers from ashore soon fitted a new jib boom, and the underwriters would see to it that the owners of the steamer had to pay the bill. The eight runners we had shipped at Liverpool were paid off and sent back to their homes by train, with traveling warrants.

The cargo was loaded speedily, and sailing day decided upon. On the day before sailing, Captain Roberts went to the Board of Trade office and picked up a tough looking crowd of eight additional seamen, consisting of an Irishman, a Scot, a Cockney, two Swedes, one Greek and two American Negroes. The four Welshmen went ashore for a last spree, and the whole crew came on board drunk and noisy at midnight, eyed carefully by the Mate and me as they staggered up the gangway and into the fo'c'sle.

The Captain also engaged a cabin boy at Glasgow. He was a wee bright lad of fourteen, named Jock, whose mother, a widow, brought him on board and tearfully asked me to keep an eye on him. His duties would be to wait at the Captain's table and in other ways to help the cook (who was also the steward) and make himself useful, but not in handling the ship except in dire emergencies.

Jock was allotted the spare bunk in my cabin. As he was a pleasant, well-mannered little fellow, I became reconciled to sharing my cramped living space with him.

At dawn on 11th June 1903, all hands were turned out to unmoor ship, in readiness for the tow downriver. The fo'c'sle hands had headaches and were in no mood for work. As we made the towrope fast, and began to move slowly away from the quayside, one of the crew decided to desert. He was a red haired Scot, Alec by name. He dashed into the fo'c'sle, grabbed his sea bag, emerged on deck, and threw the bag onto the quay.

The Captain sang out to me, "Stop that man!" I ran forrard, and, as Alec clambered onto the bulwark rail to jump after his bag, I mounted the rail and grappled with him. There was imminent danger that we would both fall between the ship's side and the stone quay, where we would almost certainly have been crushed and drowned. Then I managed to force him inboard, and we crashed together to the deck, in anything but a loving embrace. I succeeded in rolling on top of him. As I rose to a kneeling position, with one knee on his chest, one of the dock workers on the quay picked up Alec's bag and threw it back on board. The bag struck me on the back of the head and nearly knocked me out; but I managed to hold on to my man until we were clear of the lock.

This unrehearsed incident was a demonstration to the fo'c'sle hands that their youthful Second Mate knew something of the noble art of self-defence. Alec was roaring, "I willna go! Let me go!" This apparently contradictory utterance meant that he didn't want to go in the ship and wanted me to let him go, so that he could go ashore.

As we were now out in the river, the Mate came forrard and said to me, "Let him go!" I loosened my grip and Alec at once made for the rail, to jump overboard. The Mate collared him, with my assistance, and we dragged him aft, struggling, and locked him up in the sail locker. If this looked like a brutal kidnaping, the fact of the matter was that Alec had signed on for the voyage, in his sober senses, and had no right to change his mind at the last minute. If we had allowed him to desert, we should have had to work a heavy ship shorthanded.

The tug towed us forty miles (64 km) clear, into the Firth, in open water, then signalled to us to make sail. The crew were sent aloft, and we released Alec to work with them. He was a handy seaman, who now accepted his fate. He told me later that he had tried to go ashore because he thought that his "bonny lassie" might decide to marry some other laddie if our voyage lasted more than a year. He "didna ken" that Australia was so far away when he signed on.

Soon we had the foresail and topsails set and, with a fresh nor'west breeze on the starboard quarter, began to overrun the tug. She signalled to us to let go. I hurried forrard with some of the men and, as we threw the turns of wire off our bitts, it flew out with a shower of sparks, and so our last link with home was severed, for many a day.

The breeze being fair, all hands were kept on deck to set all sail to the royals, and soon we were driving on southward, past the Mull of Kintyre, at ten knots.

Then all hands were mustered aft, at the break of the poop, while the Mate and I picked the watches. We had both been observing the men closely while sail was being set and now picked them, turn and turn, according to our fancy. We had formerly picked two Welshmen and two apprentices each, on the run up from Liverpool, the Captain intimating that there must be two of his "townies" in each watch. These we now stood to the port and starboard sides, then picked the others. The Mate took one of the Swedes, and I took the other: these were big blond fellows and fine seamen. Then the Mate picked Greg, one of the Negroes, who was the biggest and strongest looking man in the ship, and I picked Murphy, an elderly but agile Irishman, who knew sailorizing from A to Z.

The Mate picked the Greek, a handy seaman, and I picked Alec the Scot This left only Walter Spragg, a runt of a Cockney, and the other Negro, Charley, a dirty shambling fellow. The Mate picked Walter, and I picked Charley, having no choice.

Now, watchkeeping began — four hours on and four hours off — as we drove on into the Irish Sea. My watch was from 8 p.m. to midnight, and I faced it with some trepidation, as the wind was freshening, and I was not fully used to handling the ship or the men in my watch, and we were in narrow waters, in one of the most frequented of the world's seaways. The Captain ordered me to take in the royals and topgallants, a piece of tricky sailorizing in the circumstances, which might better have been done in the second dog watch, under the Mate's eye, before darkness fell.

The Old Man remained on the poop and made things no easier for me by frequently interfering, countermanding and correcting my orders. When the work was finished and I went to the poop, he gave me three pieces of advice, in the hearing of the helmsman, Morris, one of his Welsh townies. "Never be familiar with the men," he began. "Never call a man out of his name. When you give an order, see that it is carried out to the letter."

This was all good advice, but the Captain did not act on the first part of it himself, as he was constantly "yarning" and joking in Welsh with his four townies. Neither he nor the Mate yarned or joked with me. The Captain was a fine seaman who had served his time, some twenty years previously, in smart clipper ships on the passenger run to Australia. He resented being in command of an old cargo hooker, for such the *County of Cardigan* was, but that was no reason why he should take his resentment out on me.

The Mate had served his time and had been Second Mate in small coasting vessels. His mentality and ideas had been warped and stunted in the process. He now held a Master's ticket but could not obtain a command. This, and a domestic worry, had soured him. Both he and the Captain had hoped that the owners would sign on a Second Mate of mature years, with whom they could have had much more in common than they would ever have with me. For the first three weeks of the voyage, they "knocked me into shape" in their own way and scarcely spoke a civil word to me; but though I resented their harsh tuition, it was effective, and I soon became proficient in sailing the ship to the best advantage.

When they saw that I was capable of doing things on my own, they became more tolerant of me. This enabled me to assert myself with more confidence, and I had little trouble in obtaining obedience from the men, who quickly sensed then that the Old Man and the Mate would support my authority.

In the fo'c'sle, Greg the Negro, who was as vain as a peacock, bullied and intimidated the other hands, until one day Morris, a Welshman in my watch, challenged him to fight. Though Greg was a heavyweight and Morris a middleweight, Morris knocked seven bells out of him, to everybody's pleasant surprise. After that Greg gave no more trouble.

Morris later confided to me that he had been in the prize ring, but "couldn't keep off the booze."

As we cleared the Chops of the Channel, and drove on to the south-westward in the NE trades, with all sail set, often logging twelve knots, I had many a moment of anxiety, thinking that the Old Man was carrying too much sail aloft and that he would "rip the sticks out of her."

As long as that didn't happen in my watch on deck! But Cap'n Roberts knew better than I what press of sail that stout ship could carry. If I ventured diffidently to ask him whether I should reduce sail, he only scowled and growled, "Carry on!"

My Twentieth Birthday — Excitement in the Doldrums — The
Cargo Broached — A Raid on the Fo'c'sle — Rough and Tumble —
The Black Jacks — Crime and Detection — The Mystery Solved —
No "Beg Pardons" — Cracking on to Make a Passage — We Arrive
at Fremantle — Time Saved is Not Always Time Gained — Our
Crew Deserts to go Pearling — Hung up for Seven Weeks
— Runners Engaged.

THE *County of Cardigan* was a smart sailor with the wind abaft the
beam, but a poor sailor to windward — as I dis-covered when we
arrived in the doldrums. My twentieth birthday came on 15th July
1903, when we were on the equator, and flat becalmed. It was one of the
most irritating days in my life. I went on watch at midnight, when there was
not a breath of a breeze to ease the oppression of the stifling, sultry
atmosphere. The sails were all set to the royals, but hanging listless and
lifeless, with only an occasional banging and thudding of the yards against the
masts and creaking of blocks, as the ship rolled slowly in the long scend of
the ocean.

At one bell (3:45 a.m.), heralding the change of the watch, a light westerly
breeze came without warning, in cat's paw puffs rippling the surface of the
water. I roused the men of my watch to begin hauling around the yards —
no easy work, this, for five seamen (one seaman being at the wheel) and two
boys (one a first voyager), as there were fifteen yards to haul around, and the
sails to be trimmed.

Very soon the ship gathered a little way. At the change of the watch, the
Captain came up with the Mate on the poop and ordered "All hands on deck"
until all the sails were trimmed.

As soon as this work was finished, the wind dropped to a flat calm, and the ship came to a standstill. Then, without warning, as my watch went below, a breeze sprang up from the eastward, and it was "All hands on deck" to haul around the yards again.

As before, the breeze died as soon as the sails were trimmed. Presently a breeze came from astern, and, when the yards were squared, it died. While we were wondering what would happen next, a breeze came from dead ahead and took us flat aback — so the cry was "All hands on deck" again.

These baffling conditions continued throughout the day, as the sun poured his burning heat down upon the sweating, cursing crew while they toiled without respite. The Old Man was determined to make every mile (1.6 km) of southing possible, to get out of the doldrums' grip. He had only one idea in his mind, to gain headway and make a smart passage to Australia. What would be done, after we arrived in port, with the days, hours and minutes we had saved by strenuous endeavour and risk on the passage was another matter entirely. For weeks we would be tied up in port, waiting for cargoes, or ballast, or orders, at the leisurely convenience of the owners, or their agents, or port authorities; but every moment while we were at sea was precious.

Throughout that day I and the men of my watch, and the Mate, and the men of his watch, had no proper intervals of rest below, as the Old Man had all hands turned out whenever a breeze stirred; yet, despite these efforts, we gained not more than twenty miles (32 km) of southing by nightfall, and every man was then dead beat.

At 8 p.m., darkness having fallen, the Mate's watch went below. We were again flat becalmed, and it was my watch on deck, after twenty hours of almost continuous hard work. I was on the poop with the two apprentices and the helmsman, Alec the Scot — all half asleep — while the five other fo'c'sle hands of my watch sprawled on the forehatch; all others were below.

Presently I became aware that there was much laughing and talking forrard. This was a little surprising, as the six men of the Mate's watch had turned into their bunks and, being greatly wearied by the exertions of the day, ought to have fallen asleep immediately; but the laughing and talking continued and became louder, with snatches of song, and the glim was not dowsed in the fo'c'sle.

At 10 p.m. I sent the senior apprentice forrard to see what was going on. In a few minutes he came back with the surprising report that the seamen were all drunk.

"You must be mistaken," I said. "They are only dead tired." Hurrying forrard, I saw that three of the men of my watch were sprawled, snoring, on the hatch. Then I put my head inside the fo'c'sle door. The six men of the Mate's watch and the two Welshmen of my watch were in the throes of a glorious spree! Three men, including little Wally Spragg, the Cockney, were stretched on the floor, unconscious drunk. The four Welshmen were seated at the table, merrily singing hymns in Welsh, with pannikins of whiskey in their hands.

Greg was prone in his bunk, in the act of drinking whiskey from a bottle. There were two full bottles of whiskey on the table, one half full, and several empties lying about. The lamp swinging from the deckhead beam was flaring and smoking, unheeded. I stepped into the fo'c'sle quickly, grabbed the half bottle of whiskey from the table, and retired aft, to report the situation to the Captain. On emerging, I peered at the three men lying out on the hatch — Niels the Swede, Murphy the Irishman, and Charley the Negro. They were all drunk.

Entering the Captain's cabin, I sang out to him, without any preliminary, "The men have broached the cargo, sir! All hands forrard are drunk!"

Snoozing on his settee, the Old Man sprang to his feet, instantly alert. "What's that?" he demanded.

"Cargo broached and all hands in the fo'c'sle drunk!" I repeated and placed my exhibit of whiskey on the table.

He glared at me in an intensity of rage. "You damned careless young fool!" he roared. "Have you let them broach the cargo under your very eyes?"

"l don't understand how they could have done that, sir!" "No backchat from you! Call the Mate."

It was not necessary to call the Mate, as he came out of his cabin sleepily, saying, "What's wrong?"

"Cargo broached in the Second Mate's watch," the Captain growled. "Hands all drunk forrard. Mister Bisset stood by on the poop while they opened the forehatch, I suppose. Dreaming, were you, Mister Bisset? Gazing astern, looking at the jellyfish, eh? By heavens, you'll rue this!" I was thunderstruck at the enormity of my neglect, yet puzzled to know how the seamen could possibly have opened the forehatch, even by loosening one hatch board, without my noticing them. Had I indeed been dreaming on watch?

"How many of them are drunk?" the Mate asked.

"All except the helmsman," I answered. "Six of them are stretched out dead drunk, and the others are more than half-seas over."

"I'll deal with the [sanguinary] beasts! How many bottles did you see?"

"Half a dozen, or more," I said.

"Search the fo'c'sle, Mister, and commandeer any grog there," the Captain ordered. "I'll inquire into this, and deal with the offenders."

He glared at me balefully as he said this. Obviously, he considered me the principal culprit.

The Mate went into his cabin and fetched two "black jacks" — short leather thongs, leaded at the ends. He handed one to me. "We'll go forrard and search the fo'c'sle," he announced, grimly. "If any man shows fight, knock him out!"

As we stepped on deck, Jock the cabin boy, who had overheard our palaver, plucked at my sleeve. "Gie us one o' they black jocks, Mister," he pleaded, "an' I'll lend ye a haund."

"Stand by with the apprentices, boy," the Mate said. "We'll pass the bottles out to you."

Followed by the two apprentices of my watch and Jock, the Mate and I went to the fo'c'sle door and looked in. The situation was as I had reported it a few minutes previously.

The Mate, who was as strong as an ox, stepped into the fo'c'sle, grasped the end of the two benches on which the cajoling Welshmen were seated, and tumbled the four of them under the table before they even realized what was happening. "If any man moves," he roared, "I'll brain him!"

Grabbing the two full bottles of whiskey which were on the table, I passed them out to the apprentices. As I turned around, Greg, struggling to a sitting posture in his bunk, hurled his now empty bottle at my head. I dodged. It shattered against the bulkhead.

With a roar like a tiger, the Mate leaped at Greg and gave him a crack on the forehead that knocked him senseless. Two of the Welshmen now crawled out from under the table and attempted to capsize the Mate by pulling his legs away from under him.

Crack! Crack! The Mate dropped them both senseless, and the fight was over. "If any. man moves," he announced, to the others recumbent on the deck, 'I'll drop him!"

We searched the fo'c'sle thoroughly, passed out the empty bottles to the boys, and discovered two more full bottles hidden in a pair of sea boots.

Emerging, we roused the three drunks lying out on the hatch and bundled them into the fo'c'sle. Then the Mate dowsed the light and locked the two doors, making the men prisoners.

"They'll sleep it off," he said, "but what a mess we'll be in if a squall blows up!"

The flat calm weather continued throughout the night, and the Mate and I, with the apprentices, Sails, Chips, and the Doctor, and the only sober seaman, Alec, trimmed the yards and sails and worked the ship in the occasional light puffs and capricious breezes, snatching a few minutes of sleep at intervals when opportunity offered.

So ended my twentieth birthday! The Mate was the hero of the occasion, and I was presumably the villain, in his and the Captain's eyes, for allowing the cargo to be broached.

After the crew were locked in, the Captain and the Mate and I, equipped· with lanterns, carefully examined the hatches, looking for some signs that the tarpaulin covers had been disturbed; but we found no clues there. This was mystifying, as there was no door into the hold. Then, casting around like bloodhounds, we found some wisps of straw near the midships ventilator. "A very small man might be able to crawl down there," the Captain said, "if others on deck hauled him up again with a line."

To test this theory, as daybreak came in, we lowered the smallest apprentice down the ventilator, with a candle lantern in his hand. He sang out almost immediately that he could see a whiskey case with the lid prized off and containing only straw — no bottles!

"Haul him up," the Captain ordered. Then he put his face close to mine and muttered, "In your watch, Mister, in full view of the poop, a man was lowered down that ventilator, broached the cargo, passed up a dozen bottles of whiskey to the deck, and was hauled up again — and you didn't see anything, eh? Were you asleep on watch?"

"No, sir!"

"Very well, I'll inquire further after breakfast, and I'll sift this to the bottom!"

At 6 a.m. the Mate unlocked the fo'c'sle doors, singing out threateningly, "Wake up, you sleepers!"

Revived with coffee and pantiles, all hands were mustered aft, most of them looking very sick and sorry.

"A fine lot of rogues you are," the Captain began, "broaching the cargo in the Second Mate's watch, because he happens to be young and inexperienced! Well, let me tell you that you have me to deal with now. You're a crowd of useless lubbers and drunken sots, putting your own lives in danger, as well as the lives of everyone else in the ship. If a squall had come up and hit her with all sail set, while you drunken swabs lay boozed and dead to the world, she would have gone over on her beam ends and drowned the lot of you, or else she might have been demasted by being taken aback, through not having enough hands to work her! Now, who broached the cargo?"

The seamen stood silent, shuffling their feet, and looking in every direction except at the Captain. "Well," he continued. "You needn't tell me, because I know! Able Seaman Spragg was the man who went down the midships ventilator and broached the cargo, stealing twelve bottles of whiskey!"

The crew gasped involuntarily at this proof of the Captain's omniscience. "Somebody's informed on me," wailed the Cockney. "I didn't do it by myself!"

"I know you didn't," the Captain roared. "The whole lot of you are equally guilty, but Spragg is the only miserable little runt small enough to crawl down that ventilator. Now, Spragg, when did you do it?"

"In the second dog watch, sir," Spragg confessed. "What? In the second dog watch?"

"Yes, Captain. It was while you and the Mate was on the poop, gazing astern, and yarning to Jones, the helmsman. We wouldn't do it in Mister Bisset's watch, sir, because 'e keeps 'is eyes peeled!"

This was a shattering blow to the Captain's complacency. The crime had been committed not only when he was on the poop, but while one of his townies attracted his attention, so that the dirty work could be carried on behind his back!

"The men have broached the cargo, sir! All hands forrard are drunk!"
(AI Image)

"Spragg fined one pound," the Captain barked. "Jones fined ten shillings. All other hands in the fo'c'sle who were drunk fined five shillings! I've a good mind to give you all in charge when we reach Fremantle. Anybody got anything to say?"

"Yaas, sir, I 'ave," complained Greg, "I'se got a lump on my haid like an egg!"

"If you broach any more cargo or attempt to assault an officer by throwing a bottle or anything else at him, you'll get worse than a lump on your head. I'll put you in irons, on bread and water for a week! Any other complaints?"

The crew stood silent and sullen. "Very well, then, that'll do you now. Lay forrard, and let's have no more o' this!"

After the crew had retired, I stood by for a minute or two, expecting that the Captain and the Mate might say some word of apology to me, for having wrongly blamed me. No chance of that! They only scowled at me. The Captain said gruffly, "Well, that's done with. The matter's settled. Let's hear no more of it! Have the ventilator properly secured, so that this can't happen again."

A few days after this excitement, we got out of the doldrums and picked up the SE trades, standing away to the south-south-westward, braced up on the port tack. In these conditions the *County of Cardigan* sailed poorly, as compared with the *County of Pembroke*; but she made up for all delays when we picked up the westerlies on 14th August and began running our easting down.

The winter gales of the high south had not yet expended their fury. We squared away before a howling gale that whipped spume from the crests of seas rolling precipitously ahead of us and astern, beneath a murky sky heavy with icy rain and sleet. A few days before entering the forties, we had changed the suit of sails and bent our storm canvas. Now for the first time I fully appreciated the heavy sparring and strength of the gear aloft in this ship, as, on the Captain's orders, we furled only the royals and topgallants and drove on with a quarterly wind, under six topsails, foresail and jib.

It was an unnerving experience, but exhilarating, as we logged from twelve to fourteen knots, with decks awash, for day after day, while the wind hummed in the rigging and the ship plunged on into the troughs and over the crests of the giant combers, with violent movements that made it seem that at any moment she would take a header into the depths or, alternately, that something would give way under the terrific strain and that her top hamper would crash to our ruin.

Grim visaged, the Captain came on to the poop at frequent intervals and refused to shorten sail, or even to consider heaving to, as he curtly ordered us to "Carry on" — until at times it seemed that he had gone off his head and was determined to drive us all to perdition.

In these conditions we covered approximately 6,000 miles (9656 km) in three weeks, averaging twelve knots, and every man on board was driven to the point of utter exhaustion by heavy work and long exposure to the bitter cold weather; for, though the Captain would not shorten sail, he frequently called all hands on deck to stand by, or for one watch to help the other in trimming the yards when the wind shifted a few points.

As we neared the coast of Western Australia, the gales increased in intensity and the Old Man was at last compelled to shorten sail. Perhaps, too, he was not perfectly sure of his position, as he ordered an extra lookout to be posted on the fore-topsail yard during the hours of darkness. Having no sight of the sun or stars for three weeks, he was navigating by compass and dead reckoning, with the aid of the hand log; but, by good luck or splendid sea-manship, he made an exact landfall, as the lookout man sang out, at 4 a.m. on 2nd September, "A flashing light on the starboard bow!"

"Land ahead! All hands on deck!" the Captain ordered. He identified the light as Rottnest Island, off the entrance to Fremantle. We hove to for several hours. Then as the wind dropped in the afternoon, we sailed in and dropped anchor in Gage Roads at sunset.

Next day we were towed to Victoria Quay and began discharging our cargo. The Port of Fremantle, sea gate for the city of Perth, capital of Western Australia, was frequented chiefly by steamers using the Suez Canal route to Australia from Europe. It was never a famous haven of sail, and there were only two or three other sailing vessels in the port at the time of our arrival.

We read in the Perth Morning Herald of 4th September: The British ship *County of Cardigan*, 1,323 tons, Captain William Roberts, arrived on Wednesday night, after a smart passage of 83 days from Glasgow. She left Glasgow on 11th June. She had an uneventful passage, marked at times by bad weather, especially when nearing Fremantle. She has a full general cargo, including a large quantity of whiskey.

While the whiskey and other merchandise were being unloaded by wharf labourers, some of our seamen quietly put their bags overside and vamoosed. The Captain did not worry about them, as he supposed that we could easily pick up others when required. The matter became more serious at the weekend, when all the fo'c'sle hands vanished except two — Murphy the Irishman and Charley.

The Old Man was puzzled to account for the disappearance of his four Welsh townies and made the usual inquiries of the police to see if they had been locked up for drunkenness. Then he was enlightened, as the police told him that our ten missing seamen had probably been persuaded to go in some pearling luggers which had cleared out on Monday morning, bound for the pearling grounds at Broome, 1,300 miles (2032 km) to the northward of Fremantle.

We had noticed some of these luggers moored in the harbour. They were schooner rigged vessels of from thirty to sixty tons, bearing romantic names such as *Queen of the Seas*, *Viking*, *Mars*, and *Bubbles*. Now we learned that good seamen were very scarce at Fremantle because the owners of the pearling luggers enticed them from overseas ships, offering them ten pounds a month and a "lay" (share) of the pearls and pearl shell.

Small wonder then that our crew had deserted! Murphy explained to me that he was "too old for that kind of work" and that the pearlers did not like the look of Charley. So these two stayed in the ship.

When our cargo was discharged and a little ballast taken in for stiffening, our agents tried to get a cargo or charter for us, but none was offering. Fremantle was too well served by steamers. There was a trade in jarrah timber, especially cargoes of railway sleepers, carried in sailing vessels from Fremantle to South Africa, European ports, and India, but the route to windward from Australia around the Cape of Good Hope was unfavourable for sailing vessels. While cables were being exchanged with our owners at Liverpool, we were hung up for weeks at Victoria Quay, in tedium. I took the opportunity of studying for my First Mate's examination and also went ashore and bought an assortment of light and heavy reading matter, including some volumes of poetry. I was very lonely and had no companionship in this port, so I took refuge in my books. We lay at that quay for two months. Early in November, orders came from the owners that we were to proceed in ballast to Newcastle, to load coal. The Captain now bestirred himself to find a crew, but this proved no easy matter.

With the assistance of the agents, he succeeded in signing on eight scallywags as "runners." They were a bunch of ne'er-do-wells who hung about the waterfront at Fremantle, taking occasional jobs as riggers or as runners on coasters in Western Australia, but they refused flatly to sign on for any voyage beyond Australian waters. The run from Fremantle to Newcastle, 2,250 miles (3621 km), hugged the coast of the continent of Australia and therefore could be described, in strict legality, as a "coastal" run; but to work a ship for that considerable distance was certainly not comparable with coastal runs around the shores of Britain and the North Sea ports.

The port authorities and water police agreed that there would be no chance of obtaining ten competent seamen at Fremantle, except as runners, in the conditions prevailing. Captain Roberts had the choice of signing on the men offering as runners or of being hung up in Fremantle indefinitely. He therefore signed a contract with the eight scallywags to work the ship to Newcastle for ten pounds each. This expense nearly broke his heart, but the runners were men of independence, who stated their own terms.

Even with these eight rascals, we were two men short in the fo'c'sle, but the authorities cleared us out, knowing the circumstances. On 5th November 1903, having hastily taken in more ballast, to a total of 500 tons, and tamped down, we towed out into the Roads and set sail, after a stay in Fremantle of sixty-four days.

What then had been gained by our "smart passage" out from Glasgow, attained with so much effort? Probably nothing except that the whiskey drinkers of Western Australia had their grog smartly delivered to them!

And that is the duty of the merchant marine to deliver the goods, safe and sound, without delay....

Rounding Cape Leeuwin — Our "Runners" and Their Legal Rights — Working the Ship — A Battle of Tactics — The Mystery of the Missing Deck Gear — Police Action — Christmas at Newcastle — A New Crew — Meditations on Sail and Steam — A Slow Haul Across the Pacific — Cook Smoked Out of His Caboose — A Seaman Runs Amok — We Arrive at Eten in Peru.

WITH the courses, topsails, jibs, and staysails set and a strong south-westerly breeze heading us off, we stood to the westward, to claw off the land, and to gain ample sea room to round Cape Leeuwin, 150 miles (241 km) to the southward of Fremantle.

The Mate and I picked watches. As Murphy and Charley were already in my watch, I had to pick only three of the runners; while the Mate, having lost the whole of his foc's'le hands at Fremantle, picked five. Each watch was one man short.

The Mate then set the watches. He took the first watch, beginning at noon. With one man at the wheel and one on lookout, he had only three runners and two boys to handle sail. As some of the runners were decrepit specimens and "beer soaks," there was not enough beef and brawn to haul around the heavy yards of the courses and topsails in a strong breeze, and it was evident that all hands would have to be called out frequently on our voyage to Newcastle, especially if the Old Man decided to "make a passage."

While the breeze held steady from the SW, and we con-tinued to run to the westward, braced up sharp on the port tack, there was no further handling of sail to be done for the time being. The Mate therefore decided that this would be a good opportunity to wash down the decks, to get rid of grime accumulated in port and the grit spilled around the hatches when ballast was being taken in.

He ordered the boys of his watch and the three men on deck to get the buckets, tubs, and brooms ready to scrub decks. At this, the three runners sauntered to the fo'c'sle head, stood under it, and lit their pipes.

"What the hell do you think you're doing there?" asked the Mate, irately.

"Standing by to work the ship, Mister!" "I told you to scrub the decks!"

"We ain't scrubbing no decks, Mister. We're 'ere to work the ship, and keep our quarters clean, and nothing else. Scrubbing decks ain't working the ship."

"We'll see about that!" The Mate went aft and informed the Captain of the situation. All hands were mustered at the break of the poop, where the Captain severely lectured the runners on the meaning of the words "to work the ship" which appeared in the contract they had signed.

The runners, unmoved by his eloquence, argued the point obstinately, in a manner which riled the Captain and the Mate.

"Very well, then," the Captain said, "I'll see that you work the ship! That'll do you now."

Thereafter, for several days, a good deal of unnecessary pully-hauly was ordered, as the Captain made frequent tacks, reduced sail during dark hours and resettled them at daylight, and in other ways acted like a nervous shipmaster navigating in unfamiliar waters, keeping the crew constantly on the jump.

In this fashion we rounded Cape Leeuwin and stood on across the Great Australian Bight, in heavy weather, with flooded decks. The runners dared not question any orders given them to handle sail, but their demeanour made it plain that they had a bellyful of being turned out in every watch below.

One day some of them overheard the Captain remark to the Mate, "I'll make the perishers work for their pay!"

Next day they got up a deputation to the Captain and complained that the biscuits were weevilly.

"Take them or leave them," said the Old Man. "You are getting the whack according to the Board of Trade scale, and if you can't work the ship on that, why the hell didn't you stay ashore?"

Ten days later we were standing into Bass Strait, having made an average of eight knots since rounding Cape Leeuwin, despite the passive resistance of the runners and their deliberate clumsiness in handling sail.

The westerly winds still favoured us as we drove on through the Strait, but when we rounded Wilson's Promontory, and stood to the northward, we were headed off almost immediately by a strong northeasterly breeze and had the shore on our lee.

The Captain ordered all hands on deck to haul around the yards as he altered course, and we stood well out to the eastward in the Tasman Sea. He hoped to get a clear run to Newcastle on the starboard tack if the weather held. But luck was against him. When we were 200 miles (321 km) out to sea and ready to tack ship, the breeze dropped, then sprang up again as a north-westerly, heading us off.

For several days we were beating about in these baffling conditions, with variable winds, all adverse to us, necessitating much handling of sail. The runners were now in a mutinous mood, as they considered, in their stupidity, that the Captain was deliberately getting the ship into difficult positions to annoy them by calling them out of their watches below at frequent intervals during the day and night.

A few among them may have realized that the adverse weather conditions were as annoying to the Captain as to themselves; but most of them, like shirkers in all trades, considered that they had a grievance when they were called upon to make extra efforts.

Lacking the manliness to defy authority openly, or the greater manliness required to obey authority cheerfully, they planned a sly revenge on their "persecutor." As we eventually stood in toward Newcastle, with a leading wind, various articles of the ship's gear disappeared from the decks. The first things to go were two washtubs. The Captain had ordered the carpenter to cut these from an empty beef cask and enjoyed himself one afternoon painting them a beautiful green, with black bands. They were left on the main hatch to dry. The next morning they were gone.

During the next few days holystones, brooms, belaying pins, winch handles, buckets, scrapers, marlinspikes, loose ropes and the grindstone vanished. No one had seen them go. The Captain called all hands aft and said menacingly that a charge would be laid against the culprits when we arrived at Newcastle. The runners all indignantly denied that they were the culprits.

On 3rd December 1903 — four weeks out from Fremantle — we made port and were towed in, to drop anchor in the stream while waiting for a berth. The Captain flew the signal for police assistance, and presently a water police launch ranged alongside. Another launch came out with the agents' representatives and port officials, and a conference was held in the Captain's cabin on the mystery of the missing gear.

The sub-inspector of police, on ascertaining that the Captain could produce no eyewitnesses of the alleged wilful destruction of property, told him that a prosecution could not succeed on mere suspicion and advised him not to lay charges against the eight suspected culprits, of whom perhaps only one or two may have been guilty. "But we'll deal with them in our own way," he added.

The police took all the runners off in their launch and questioned them individually at the police station, trying to get one or more of them to "split." But the runners showed solidarity and stoutly denied all knowledge of the alleged offence, while at the same time threatening wildly to "expose" the Captain for starving the crew.

The charge was therefore dropped, for lack of evidence, but we heard later that all the runners, after drawing their pay from the agent's office, went on the booze and were all "run in" by the "Johns" (police) for being drunk and disorderly, and given a week in jug for that offence!

So justice triumphed. In the meantime, after the runners had been taken ashore, a few new hands were engaged temporarily from the labour office, to help work the ship, in tow, to her berth. On going to heave up the anchor, we discovered that the two long iron levers from the windlass had gone the way of the washtubs and other deck gear. The tugmaster borrowed a pair of levers for us from another ship, and we were towed to Berth 3. There we lay next to a fine four-masted ship, the *Queen Eleanor*, 3,574 tons.

After discharging our ballast and taking in a stiffening of coal, we lay at our berth over Christmas — my sixth Christmas away from home. I went with our apprentices and younger officers and apprentices from many other ships to a Christmas Eve party at the Seamen's Mission. This was thoroughly enjoyable — even though strictly "teetotal" — with a concert and some nice, well-intentioned ladies for good company.

On 27th December, we were towed to the crane berths and in two days loaded 1,950 tons of coal from the Ducken-field Colliery, for Eten, a port 300 miles (482 km) northward of Callao, in Peru. From the crane berths we were towed to the Farewell Buoys, near Nobby's Lighthouse, at the mouth of the harbour.

The Captain went ashore and engaged ten fo'c'sle hands, who came off in a crimp's boat, looking decidedly bleary after their Christmas festivities. As soon as they were aboard, we cast off our moorings, on New Year's Eve — after twenty-seven days in port — and were towed out past the Nobby's, and well clear of the land.

As New Year's Day of 1904 came in, we cast off the tug and made sail, bound eastward across the wide Pacific, in subtropical summer weather, on a route of some 7,000 miles (11265 km), sailing to windward almost all the way to Peru in the SE trade winds.

Though voyages such as this were described, in the shipping columns of newspapers, as "uneventful" unless deaths or serious damage occurred, they were eventful enough for the men before and abaft the mast, who had to work the ships from port to port, encountering ever-changing circumstances, afloat and ashore.

In this narrative I have told of the daily events in a sea-farer's life under sail, as accurately as I can recall them after more than fifty years; but I am reminded that such great changes have occurred, at sea and on land, in that period, that the way of life here described may seem to modern readers to have been crude and callous.

It was not considered so at the time but was perfectly normal. Perhaps, in the year 2,000 A.D., the customs of the mid-twentieth century may seem crude to the people of that time, because everything that is "modern" must eventually become out of date.

Sailing ship days and ways were "on the way out" in 1904, and this fact was being borne in upon my comprehension in this, my first and last voyage as an officer in sail.

I had made up my mind to go into steam, if possible, for I could foresee that the glorious days of sail were drawing rapidly to a close, and that the mentality of sailing ship men was adversely affected by the depressing thought that all their skill and science, so laboriously acquired, was of little avail against the competition of mechanical power.

Inventive mechanical skill was never applied to the handling of sail, but only to abolishing sail as a means of propulsion. The power of the winds would no longer be captured and tamed for men's ocean transits. It would be disregarded; yet possibly a time may again come when wind driven craft of handy size may be seen on ocean routes, with mechanical devices for handling sail (such as motor winches for all hauling), auxiliary screws to work through the doldrums and into and out of ports, a higher freeboard to avoid flooded decks, water ballast that can be mechanically pumped in and out, electric light and refrigeration, and possibly nylon sails and cordage, aluminium or other light metal yards, "push-button" control, and radio and RADAR, and many other devices which would enable the power of the winds to be harnessed with the aid of machinery and the labour of only a few men in the crews.

If such a time should come, the lore of the old sailing ships, which were worked entirely by manual labour, will have been worth preserving. The introduction of steam propulsion made manually handled sailing ships obsolete, after it was found initially that crude combinations of steam and sail, such as those in the *Great Eastern*, presented some practical difficulties; yet it should not be forgotten that the world's first mammoth ship used her engines as an auxiliary to her sails, or vice versa. If engineers and inventors had studied the actual problems of handling sail, they could possibly have devised some method of continuing to use the power of the winds; but it was not to be, and sail went into the discard.

Men who obstinately clung to a way of life that was rapidly becoming obsolete were creatures of habit, either in the fo'c'sle or under the poop. Conditions of employment for the fo'c'sle hands were such that only "drifters," who could find nothing better to do, were available to be picked up as required, in ports far and wide. Many of them were signed on drunk; yet, when they found themselves at sea, they turned to manfully and cheerfully, in the great traditions of their calling.

The masters and officers of sailing vessels sensed, even more than the men before the mast, that their profession now offered little or no scope for advancement. The Captain and Mate in the *County of Cardigan* were morose from the continual worries and frustrations imposed upon them by the nature of their occupation. The Captain's pay was twelve pounds a month, and the Mate's seven pounds a month: no great reward, this, for the responsibilities put upon them and the ordeals and worries they endured. Their surly behaviour was no inspiration to me as an example to be emulated. If, by remaining in sail, I could look forward only to becoming as soured as they, the prospects were not enticing. It was for reasons such as these that, as I studied for my First Mate's examination while the *County of Cardigan* ploughed eastward across the Pacific Ocean, I decided that this would be my last voyage in sail, and that, on returning home, I would look for a billet in a steamer.

The ten fo'c'sle hands we had shipped at Newcastle were malcontents, who soon began making trouble. Though fed strictly in accordance with the Board of Trade scale, they complained of the rations — and who could blame them?

The cook was an old man who did his best, but the men "slanged" him at every meal and eventually got him worked up to such a pitch that one evening he threw a bowl of hot pea soup over half a dozen of his tormentors, giving them minor scalds. At this they declared their intention of throwing the cook overboard.

He barricaded himself in his galley, but one of the crowd climbed on top of the galley and dropped a handful of slush through the skylight onto the hot stove. This filled the galley with acrid smoke, forcing the cook to come out, but not before his yells for help brought the Mate and me to relieve the situation.

The rebels retired; but the cook began to cough so violently that he broke a blood vessel and was laid up for a week. In the meantime one of the loudest grumblers was put in the galley, but he made such a mess of things that everyone was glad to see the cook turn to again.

Next the crew began to torment Charley the Negro, who was a fellow of rather weak intellect and not much use. They teased him unmercifully, beyond his endurance, ignoring his threats that he would "do them in."

On a sweltering day, as we neared the coast of Peru, the five men in the watch with Charley amused themselves by tormenting him to such an extent that Charley picked up a marlinspike and stabbed one of them in the shoulder. At this the other four heroes, instead of downing the Negro there and then, ran out on deck, howling, "The Negro's run amok!"

Charley ran after them, his eyes rolling wildly, and frothing at the mouth, waving his marlinspike in the air. It appeared then that, having drawn blood, he had a thirst for more and had actually gone crazy. The fo'c'sle hands sprang aloft into the rigging, and Charley lost sight of them. He continued his raving career along the deck, coming aft to the poop, where the Mate and I stood considering the situation. As Charley sprang up the companionway, we picked up the coil of the main brace which lay at our feet and dropped it neatly over his head and shoulders.

That stopped his wild rush, and he fell backwards onto the deck; but as he fell he emitted a blood-curdling yell, and hurled his marlinspike at us. The point of it caught me below the knee, with such a stab of pain that I thought my leg must be broken. There being no time to look into this aspect of things, the Mate and I sprang down the companionway and, with the aid of the apprentices and Jock the cabin boy, secured the maniac and trussed him up like a fowl.

The Captain, who had come up on the poop on hearing the yells of combat, ordered Charley to be locked in the sail locker. This was done speedily. The wound below my knee was spurting blood but the bone was not broken. The Captain bandaged the cut, and I bear the scar to this day. Charley made the days and nights hideous under the poop, by howling in his prison like an animal. We gave him food and water, but kept him locked up for a few days, until we sailed into the bay of Eten and dropped anchor, ten weeks out from Newcastle.

As Charley had quietened down, the Captain paid him off and put him ashore. So ended another little event in our uneventful voyage.

*A Long Stay at Eten — Primitive Peruvian Port — Working Out
Coal — Six Deserters — The British Consul — A Train trip Inland
— The Copper Mines — Recruits from Callao — Charley "On the
Beach" — We Sail on to Talcahuano — A Harbor Chase —
Homeward Bound at Last — A Half-witted Cook.*

THE little town of Eten, port for the copper mines of Cajamarca (sixty miles (96 km) inland), was on the beach of an open bay, with very few facilities. No other ocean going vessel was in the port when we arrived, and no other came in during the many weeks that we lay there except a small coastal steamer from Callao, with mails and passengers. The coal we brought was required for locomotives on the railway that ran inland to the copper mines and for the engines at the mines.

The weather was excessively hot, as Eten is only six and a half degrees south of the equator. Our anchorage was a mile (1.6 km) offshore, this precaution being advisable in case the ship should drag her anchor if a "norther" or a strong westerly breeze blew into the unprotected bay. The only resemblance to a wharf was a short iron jetty for loading or discharging lighters and boats. Half a dozen lighters and a few boats were anchored near the jetty or moored to it. The town consisted of a few sheds and a few dozen huts straggled along the foreshore, near the beach.

The Captain went ashore in his gig, to make arrangements for discharging the cargo. On his return he in- formed the Mate and me that the consignees would provide bags, into which we would have to fill the coal, with the labour of the crew, no shore labour being available for this work. Assuming that each bag held one hundredweight of coal, we faced the task of filling 40,000 bags to clear our hold of coal — a dismaying prospect in that torrid climate.

On the morning after our arrival, a lighter came out from the shore, laden with empty bags. It was propelled by a crew of six Peruvians, with sweeps. We hauled the bundles of bags inboard with a hand-worked dolly winch and stacked them handy on deck. In the meantime the main hatch had been opened, and a gang of our seamen now began shovelling the coal into the bags, which were roughly sewn up, and hove out of the hold, one bag at a time, with the dolly winch, and lowered into the lighter. The capacity of the lighter was 400 bags of coal.

At our best working speed, handling one bag at a time, we could lift forty bags an hour. A little simple arithmetic indicated that it would take us a hundred working-days to discharge the cargo at that rate. With allowances for Saturday afternoons and Sundays off, and Saints' Days and "surf days" (when lightering was impossible) this rate made it evident that we would be at Eten a very long time. On the Captain's orders, we therefore opened the forehatch, rigged a second dolly winch there, and arranged for two lighters to come alongside simultaneously, dividing the crew into two working gangs, in accordance with their watches at sea — one under the eye of the Mate and one under my eye.

Never before or since have I felt such a slave driver! The fo'c'sle hands we had engaged at Newcastle declared that discharging cargo in this way was not the proper work of seamen and should be done by shore labour. There was a good deal to be said for their point of view, but apparently the consignees had stipulated this method of delivery when placing their order for the coal, and the Captain decided to save William Thomas & Co., Ltd., the expense of engaging shore labour to fill the bags, even if such shore labour had been obtainable in this benighted port.

Work went on from 6 A.M to 5 p.m. daily, with half an hour for breakfast, and three quarters of an hour for midday dinner. With four men and a boy in the hold, filling and sewing the bags, and two men and a boy on deck in each gang working the dolly winches, and the Mates pushing the bags over the side as the bags came up, all were soon black, and the decks were smothered in coal dust. The whack of fresh water remained at one quart per man per day. There were no facilities for taking in water at Eten, and the Captain was obliged to hoard our reserves.

The only fresh provisions obtainable from on shore were pumpkins, sweet potatoes and scraggy and gristly meat, as cattle did not thrive in that tropical region. After a few days, when the crew began to grumble seriously, the Captain brought off a supply of the local grog, a fiery spirit named anisou (Anisette) and served out a tot to each man at 11 a.m. and 4 p.m. daily, to keep them going.

Choked by coal dust down below; roasted by the blazing sun on deck; with no means of going ashore on Saturdays or Sundays, and nothing to do ashore even if a boat were available; thirsty, hungry and tired; the men quarrelled and fought among themselves and resented every order that was given to them. On Saints' Days and surf days we kept them at work down below, filling and sewing bags and stacking them on deck ready for discharge.

After three weeks, when less than one third of the cargo had been discharged, six of the men demanded to be taken ashore to see the British Consul. They declared that they would rather go to jail than continue working out the coal. Their request to see the Consul being one which the Captain could not properly refuse, he went ashore with them in a boat sent out by the agents, taking me with him, pos-sibly as a witness or bodyguard, and leaving the Mate to continue discharging the cargo.

The discontented seamen put their sea bags into the boat, thereby indicating that they had no intention of returning to the ship. On reaching the shore the Captain discovered that the Consul resided in the mountains at Cajamarca, and that a train was going there, departing within half an hour.

We embarked on the train and, after a crawling journey of four hours on the ramshackle railway, arrived at Cajamarca at noon. There we found that the Consul was out of town for the day but would return on the morrow.

The men demanded money to enable them to get lodgings for the night. The Captain gave them one dollar each, after arranging with them to be at the Consul's office next morning. He took me with him to a hotel, an inn in Spanish style, where we obtained quarters for the night.

Next morning, we presented ourselves at the Consul's office, but there was no sign of the complainants. The Consul made inquiries of the local gendarmes and learned that they had all got drunk and were believed to have gone to the copper mines to look for work.

"They'll find that harder than shovelling coal," the Consul remarked. "I'll have them on my hands later, when they'll come to me asking to be sent home, if they don't die of drinking anisou (Anisette) in the meantime."

As there was nothing more to be done, the Captain and I returned to Eten on the afternoon train. We learned at Cajamarca that Charley, our crazy Negro, had gone to the copper mines and was working there, but not enjoying the experience.

Being now seven men short of a full crew, the Captain sent a telegram to Callao, asking that this number of seamen should be sent up to him on the next steamer. As he had received orders to proceed from Eten to Talcahuano in Chile, to load grain, and then to Queenstown for orders, we were homeward bound. This fact made it easier to obtain good seamen who were stranded at Callao and on the lookout for a homeward bound ship.

With these reinforcements, which arrived ten days later, we completed discharging the coal. When 300 tons remained in the hold, it was shovelled into a heap amidships, and we began taking in ballast through the fore and after hatches. This was procured from a heap of stone on shore, discharged from vessels previously visiting the port. The Captain complained that he had "to pay through the nose" for it.

Knowing of the experience of the *County of Pembroke* with leaky lifeboats, the Captain ordered the carpenter to overhaul our two lifeboats • thoroughly, and to caulk the seams. One Saint's Day, when no lighters were alongside, we put the boats overside and tested them — the Mate and his watch in one, and I with my watch in the other — pulling around the bay for half an hour.

The men begged me to steer for the shore, as they wanted to see what the town was like. But I had to refuse, assuring them that there was nothing to see there and reminding them that if they were stranded at Eten, there were no crimps there, no chance of a glorious spree, and nothing to do except work in the copper mines, with little hope of coming out alive, or of getting another ship.

At last our ballast was all taken in and tamped down. The Captain went ashore with the apprentices in the gig, for clearance papers. On the jetty he found our former shipmate, Charley the Negro, in destitution and looking like a bag of bones. Having been paid off when we arrived, Charley had spent his money on anisou (Anisette) and then gone to work in the copper mines. After a few weeks of this, he could stand the hard work underground no longer and made his way to the beach, hoping to be signed on in the ship again.

He grovelled to the Captain to take him on, but the Old Man brushed him aside, saying curtly, "We have a full crew!" When the Captain returned with the clearance papers, to embark in the gig, Charley began weeping and wailing, declaring that he wanted to go to Glasgow, and begging the Captain not to leave him on the beach to starve to death.

"I've told you I can't take you," said the Captain firmly. "You stabbed a man, and you injured the Second Mate, so you can't come in the ship again."

As the Captain stepped into the gig, Charley did likewise, seating himself in the bows. "Put him ashore," the Captain ordered. This was no easy matter, as Charley picked up the boat hook to defend himself, but the apprentices gamely tackled him and tipped him into the water. The Negro scrambled up the nearby steps onto the jetty. As the boat pushed off, he picked up a piece of coal and flung it at the Captain's head, narrowly missing him. The boys bent their backs to the oars. As the gig drew away, Charley continued bombarding it with coal, screaming savage curses, until the target was out of range.

Such was our farewell to the primitive port of Eten. Next morning we hove up the anchor, to the strains of "Rolling Home," and set sail, after a stay of ten weeks' unmitigated misery.

Our next destination, Talcahuano, lay nearly 2,000 miles (3218 km) to the southward. We stood out to sea in the very light airs, but then we were headed off by the SE trades, and had to sail to windward, with frequent tacks. The ship sailed sluggishly; her bottom fouled with the long streamers of grass which had grown lushly in the warm equatorial waters as she lay for so long inert in Eten Bay.

On the passage we cleaned the decks and the hold of coal dust, in readiness for receiving our intended homeward cargo of grain. After a fortnight at sea, we sailed on past Valparaiso, and two days later dropped anchor in the busy, well- sheltered harbour of Talcahuano, half a mile (800m) from shore.

This port in Southern Chile, in Lat. 37 deg. S, has a pleasant climate and a hinterland of fertile farming country. The town, of some 13,000 inhabitants, was prosperous and seemed well civilized. Our crew were in good heart in the cooler climate, and with fresh provisions, including good meat and mutton that the Captain promptly obtained from chandlers ashore. There were two other "sailing vessels" in the port and a steamer once a week from Valparaiso, beside some larger steamers which put in here on the route to and from Europe via the Strait of Magellan. Above all, we were in good heart because we were homeward bound. Our voyage had now lasted a year, and the Captain and the Mate had more confidence in me than they had displayed at the outset of the voyage. The Old Man condescended to say that I was "a fairly useful Second Mate, even though too young."

Without delay, we began discharging our ballast into lighters and taking in our cargo of 2,000 tons of bagged grain, which was loaded by the crew with the aid of the dolly winch, hoisting one bag at a time.

No shore leave was granted to the crew, as the Captain feared that he might lose some of them and would be unable to obtain replacements. This caused discontent, especially among the men who had joined the ship at Newcastle nearly six months previously. One Saint's Day, three of these were put overside in the dinghy to scrape grass under the stern. They decided to pull for the shore. The Mate noticed them before they had gone very far.

It happened that a Chilean boy in a very small dinghy was near the ship, salvaging driftwood. The Mate beckoned him alongside, jumped into the little dinghy, took the oars from the boy, and set out in pursuit of the deserters.

Seeing the situation, the Captain ordered me to launch the gig, with the four apprentices, and to take part in the chase.

In the meantime, the Mate, with a mighty effort, overtook the fugitives a hundred yards from the beach. As he lay alongside them, they pushed him off with their oars, over-turned the little dinghy, and spilled the Mate and the boy into the water.

Then the rascals rowed for the shore, beached the ship's dinghy, and fled to the town, while I came up in the gig and rescued the Mate and Chilean boy. We righted the boy's dinghy and towed it to the jetty. Then we took the ship's dinghy in tow and returned to the ship, thinking it not worthwhile to attempt to capture the deserters.

Next day the Captain made inquiries of the police, but the missing men could not be found. As it was to be surmised that they had found some employment or hiding place on shore, the Captain looked around for men to replace them and by good fortune found three good seamen "on the beach," who had been discharged from hospital. He signed them on, and they turned to with a will, as they were seeking a homeward bound ship. We now had a good crowd of men, with no malcontents; the thought uppermost in everyone's mind was to get the ship loaded and home.

A few days later our old cook, who had been with us since the beginning of the voyage at Liverpool, collapsed in his galley with a heart attack. He was taken ashore to the hospital and paid the forty pounds due to him.

As we were sailing next day, the Captain hurriedly engaged another cook, who was "on the beach." He was a tall, raw-boned Liverpool Irishman. He said he was a cook, but we discovered later that he was a coal trimmer who had deserted from a steamer. Besides being a bad cook, he turned out to be half-witted. He couldn't boil hot water for a barber's shop, and his only reply to all complaints was a vacant grin. Unfortunately, we didn't discover all his bad points before getting to sea, so we had to make the best of him.

25

*Rolling Home — My Last Voyage in Sail — Squaring Away to
Round the Horn — Hurricanes and Blizzards — Those Wild Waters
— Northward in the Atlantic — "Man Overboard!" — Tragedy and
the Spirit of Adventure — The Voyage Ends — Paid Off on the
Tyne-Home for Christmas — I Pass for First Mate and go into Steam*

O N 2nd July 1904, with our storm canvas bent, our tanks filled
with fresh water, and a good store of fresh provisions, we heaved
up the anchor at Talcahuano, after a stay of only four weeks in
that port. The Captain of another ship, at anchor nearby, came off in his gig
with his four apprentices, and they helped us to heave up the anchor and set
sail, then gave us three cheers and left us as we got under way.

Cape Horn was 1,000 miles (1609 km) away to the southward. We stood
to the south-westward in the roaring forties for ten days, then squared away
the yards in a howling nor'westerly gale, to round the Horn. On 15th July, we
were off the pitch of the Horn, driving on in a blizzard. It was my twenty-
first birthday. All things considered, I would not care to have celebrated it
more suitably than as officer of the watch in a full-rigged ship loaded to the
Plimsoll mark, driving on, off Cape Horn, homeward bound!

This was my fourth rounding of the Horn and fourth circumnavigation
of the globe under sail, and I could feel that, in nearly six years since signing
my indentures as an apprentice, I had learned something of seamanship —
the hard way.

But I felt then that this would probably be my last voyage round the Horn,
and so it proved; for my youth had gone from me, in those six years, and I
had matured to manhood's responsibilities and the burden of care. Only the

memories of those wild days would remain, when Cape Horn was a symbol of seafaring ordeals at their worst and of the oceans in their grandest, most awe inspiring moods of raging fury.

Few seamen ever saw Cape Horn, and it was best not to, but to give it a wide berth and round it well to the south-ward; yet, as the extremity of the great American land mass and the most southerly point of all the continents, it was the supreme landmark in the days of sail: and to round it from the westward meant for sailors whose home ports were in Europe or on the eastern shores of North America, that they were homeward bound.

The blusterous Cape Horn passage, after the tedium and toil of long sojourns in torrid, remote ports, was endurable and even exhilarating — if it did not last too long.

On this, my last voyage in these wild waters, we were carried far to the south, in bitter winter weather, up to the fringe of the Antarctic ice, in unceasing storms which whipped the seas to mountainous heights — or so sailors named the angry seas towering from fifty to sixty feet (15m - 18m) from trough to crest, though scientists term them "precipitous." After ten days of hurricanes and frostbite, with snow and ice on the deckhouses and in the rigging, we squared away in a south-westerly gale and rounded the Falkland Islands a few days later, to stand to the norrard in moderating seas and weather, in the South Atlantic.

Our homeward passage from that point on was, as the saying goes, "uneventful" — with the usual tasks of furbishing ship, holystoning decks painting the masts and yards and deckhouses, sand-and-canvasing the teak rails, polishing the brasswork, and much pully-hauly in the doldrums. The ship was sailing sluggishly, being so deeply loaded and with her bottom foul, but every day was bringing us nearer home.

One fine day in the North Atlantic, after we had picked up the NE trades, I was in my cabin in my watch below, when I heard the dread cry resound, "Man overboard! All hands on deck!"

I sprang up to the poop, where the Captain, gazing anxiously astern, sang out to me, "Swing out the port lifeboat, Mister, and stand by to lower away when the Mate gets the main yards backed."

Already the Mate had his watch hauling the yards around, while I got my watch to lower away the lifeboat and man her, as I took the tiller. "Who's gone?" I asked, hurriedly.

"It's Jock, the cabin boy!" said old Murphy, sadly shaking his head, as he pulled vigorously on the stroke oar. "He climbed into the rigging and fell from the foreyard when she rolled."

Shocked, I urged the men on — though they needed no urging — as I steered the boat astern of the ship, scanning the seas for life belts, spars, and other flotsam which had been thrown overboard at the first cry of warning.

"A life belt was thrown very near him from the poop," said the senior apprentice who was with me in the boat, "but he seemed to be unconscious."

The ship had been doing eight knots, and had made a mile (1.6 km) of way before the yards could be backed and the life-boat launched. Presently we saw floating spars and life belts, which proved that we were near the scene of the accident. I steered the boat on the course they indicated, until we came upon the life belt that had been thrown from the poop. There was no sign of Wee Jock. It was hard to realize that he had gone so suddenly from life. For an hour we searched but found no trace of him. The ship had now been put about. She came up to us and again the main yards were backed to bring her to a standstill. At last the Captain recalled the boat, and with heavy hearts we proceeded on our former course.

The Captain held an inquiry, which established that the cabin boy had gone aloft without permission, and contrary to orders which had been given to him to keep out of the rigging. There was no one to blame — not even the boy himself — whom the spirit of adventure had lured aloft. If adventure consists only of sudden death, my experiences in sail were not adventurous, except in this one incident and the only fatality I have to record in these pages. I was lucky, as many others in sail had far greater misfortunes to narrate than any I encountered. We stood on, meeting with winter gales in the North Atlantic, and arrived at Queenstown on 18th November 1904, 139 days out from Talcahuano — a slow passage. At the Captain's request, I undertook the sad duty of writing to Jock's mother and sending her his diary and other personal effects, with a description of the circumstances of his death. In his boyishly written diary were several references to "my friend the Second Mate,"

I received a brave letter of thanks from his mother, in which she wrote, "The wee laddie always wanted to be a sailor, and he had his wish before the Good Lord took him. "For ten days we lay at Queenstown, then received orders to proceed to North Shields, in the Tyne River, to discharge, We sailed around and, with a few days of anxiety in a thick fog in the North Sea, arrived off Tynemouth and towed in on 2nd December 1904, after a voyage which had lasted exactly eighteen months.

The crew were paid off, and I also took my discharge here, as I had now served as Second Mate the required time to enable me to sit for the First Mate's examination.

Captain Roberts gave me a good written reference and surprised me a little by saying cordially, when he handed it to me, "Well, my lad, you stuck it out, and I'm just beginning to like you! Goodbye, and I wish you the best of luck!" Paid off with seventy-two pounds, I swaggered home, feeling that life at sea was as good a way as any, and better than most, of earning a living. That Christmas I spent at home, and a happy Christmas it was, "after you've been so long away," as my mother said.

My father added, "Ye're a man, noo. Ye've done well, and don't ever lose sight o' the fact that it was y'r home influence that helped ye to steer a straight course — and I hope ye always will!"

In the New Year, I enrolled again in the M.M.S.A. Navigation School, and, at the end of February 1905, passed for First Mate. Then I went looking for a job, and, as old salts say, "I knocked off going to sea and went into steamers." And in steamers of various kinds and tonnages, in peace and war, I served for forty-three years; but that's a different story, though it begins with this one: and many a time, from comfortable quarters in great liners, I looked back wistfully to the hungry, hardworking, but on the whole carefree days of my adventures in sail.